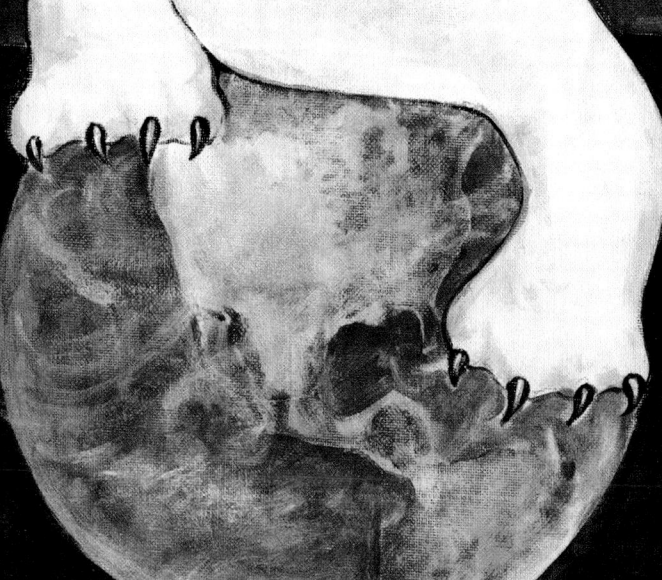

MICHAEL DAVIS

**CLEOPATRA BOOKS
LOS ANGELES**

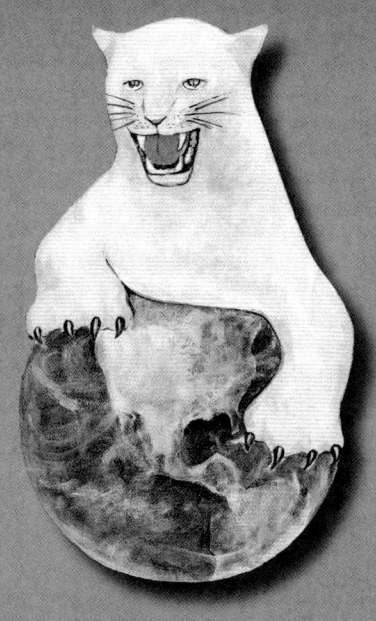

"There are many, many people who were such an important part of Mike's life (and still are a big part of my life and our boys' lives) who are not mentioned in this book. When Mike was writing, he found that he was much more comfortable with himself as a storyteller when he wrote about things that were most definitely in his past. That said, please know that if you don't see yourself mentioned in this book, it is most likely because you are forever included in the "and he lived happily ever after" part of Mike's story. You know who you are!"

Love,
Angela Davis

Copyright © 2018 Cleopatra Records, Inc

All rights reserved
No part of this book may be reproduced in any form by electronic or mechanical means, without permission in writing from the publisher, except by a reviewer who may quote brief passages in a review.

Cleopatra Press
11041 Santa Monica Blvd. #703 Los Angeles, CA 90025
ISBN: 978-0-9972056-1-9
Executive Producer: Brian Perera
Edited by Dave Thompson
Cover Painting and Back Cover Lettering by Michael Davis
Layout and Design by Nathalie Gardner
Printed in Hong Kong

Content

Intro
- Sandals and Needles...11
- The Apple Bites Back...37
- Like a Rolling Stone...49
- Everybody Must Get Stoned...65
- I Can Only Give You Everything...83
- Getting Down...99
- The New York Minute...117
- The Promise Is Broken...135
- Atlantic Crossing...153
- Out of the Frying Pan...165
- ...Into the Fire...189
- The Bridge To Nowhere...205
- Delirious Alcoholic Megalosaurus...225
- Play With Fire...251
- The Oven...271
- The Mind Shifts...287
- The Road With No Name...313
- My Time After Awhile...331

Epilogue

Introduction

Every story has "what ifs," its second-guessing, its inaccurate recall, its outright falsifying and, of course, its arbitrary embellishing. We are, after all, products of our own egos, and promoters of our personal will.

We remember what has passed with the kind of reverence that enshrines our triumphs in almost biblical glory, and casts our failures (should we even admit to them) into near-irrelevance.

In any moment, an event takes place, and is described by witnesses in any terms they can produce in an attempt to relay what was seen or heard. This is the method by which truth is determined in court, and the basis for all history. Because we are human, should there be discrepancies with the information, our perceptions color our memories of events.

Or, as the Rolling Stones's legendary manager, Andrew Loog Oldham, once put it, there are three kind of truth: There is *your* truth, there is *my* truth, and there is *the* truth. To which I would add a fourth; the *legendary* truth, the truth that builds though hearsay and rumor, until whatever once passed as reality is so clouded in myth that even the participants are sometimes no longer certain whether an event actually happened, or if that's simply what "history" insists took place.

I have been privileged to be a part of just such a scenario. While it has certainly been well documented, the story of the MC5 remains shrouded in legend and myth, a fog that is all the more impenetrable because it has never been told firsthand.

My intention here is to give you that firsthand testimonial, one that will inspire objection, rebuff, and debate. If I take the blame for the problems that befell the MC5, I expect that demands for my head will ensue.

But before you vilify me, remember: It's just a story, the tale of how a band of youngsters from the suburbs of industrial Detroit could mount the national stage at the apex of the late '60s, brandishing the banners of the youth underground counterculture in all its ideological splendor, before plunging back to earth like a meteorite, utterly burned to a cinder. And this book is the epitaph for our fall from grace.

It is a confession of sorts, for it was in the heart of the MC5 that the seeds of our destruction sprouted, not in external circumstances. Read it and learn that all roads do not necessarily lead to the place you had in mind; that, even after you have crashed and burned, it is still possible to realize maximum success in spite of yourself. Clear?

Right, then let's get started.

Sandals and Needles

The day I met Sandy was the end...and the beginning.

What ended was twenty-one years of being a straight, upstanding middle class kid with a wobbly *entree* to my peer society and educational institutions; a kid on the road to a mediocre-but-normal life in the tattered old city of Detroit, Michigan.

A kid raised with traditional values of fair play and American pride. A kid who didn't have a clue as to what was in store, nor any sense of purpose beyond immediate gratification. Oh, I had vague thoughts of marrying and being a family guy with children of my own, a career and a home. But the method of going about such a lifestyle was far from anything in my head at the time. All I could see were lots of dreams and fantasies.

My parents were good people. They worked hard their entire lives to have a home on the outskirts of Detroit, a decent neighborhood in those days, very proper and humble by today's standards, a good place to raise a family. Dad was a Ford Motor Company employee with a secure position having to do with numbers and shipping of parts to various factory locations around the country; Mom had worked somewhere when I was very young. But all the while I was growing up, she stayed home: a housewife. Sometimes she took in typing, and would sit at her typewriter in the evenings after supper, addressing letterheads and such… hundreds; no, thousands, of the things.

We had no particular religious leanings or social preferences. We were a family who practiced racial openness. We were Democrats as far as our national politics were concerned, without a doubt. My dad had been through all the union-busting action of the years before the Second World War, and he was also savvy on socio-political issues, having emigrated to the U.S. as a child refuge from anti-Semitic Eastern Europe. He was very sensitive to these kinds of issues, in fact. So I grew up in a comfortable, unassuming middle class family, with one sibling and a few pets along the way.

My family was something less than open, though. We just didn't communicate that well. Talking was not our forte; silence was our preferred state, each of us away in our own private world of thoughts.

To talk about anything led to a condescending jumble of words. Many years later, after my parents passed away, my sister remarked to me rhetorically, "Who were they?"

In truth, the mystery surrounding the details of my parents' lives was probably not as dramatic as I imagine. But always, when nothing is revealed, it is likely to cause suspicion. I always had the feeling that there were things they didn't want to talk about, that some things were better left under the rug.

On the street where I grew up, I was "Little Mikey Davis," and I grew up thinking everybody was basically good. When we start out, we're all on the same field, little kids with lots of enthusiasm and no concept of evil. We only learn that stuff later, when we have trouble getting what we want. I never wanted to hurt anybody, it just happened sometimes if a kid didn't like you and thought they could boss you around.

A couple of times I got pushed over my limit, and I stood toe to toe with some kid swinging madly until the other kid quit swinging and ran home after getting socked in the face a few times. Having a sense of fair play was kind of my golden rule, so I tried to stick to that as I grew up.

Then, when puberty hit, things got funny. I wanted to have a gang and wear black jackets with "Aces" written across the back. I wanted to grow my hair long enough to have "waterfalls" and a "DA" in the back. I wanted to wear my jeans low on my hips and roll the cuffs just a half inch. I wanted to wear the collar up on my shirt. I wanted to be a hood.

My parents were steadfastly against it. They forbade me the slightest pretensions. I guess I was a typical teen in many ways. I was even forbidden to listen to radio stations that played rock and roll music. But of course, I managed to slip around that without much trouble. My parents were pretty oblivious to anything unless it was right under their noses.

We were a musical family, though, and I've been listening to music of all kinds since I can remember. It has always had a presence in my life. Starting with records like *Peter and the Wolf* and *The Nutcracker Suite*, my dad's 78 rpm discs of Spanish guitar by Vicente Gomez, classical music on the radio on Sundays, and my old man playing his Latin collection on the record player. My dad had a great love of music as a matter of fact. It was probably from him that I got hooked. He loved bebop. He loved something called Jazz At the Philharmonic. I think it was a record series that featured people with names like Illinois Jacquet, Philly Joe Jones, and Zoot Sims.

He also had a pretty sizable collection of Latin stuff, although the only name I remember was Noro Morales. When he heard those rhythms he would snap his fingers and try to get my mom to dance with him. They were swing dancers, and I could tell they had really hit it off on the dance floor when they first met. He was entranced when he heard this stuff. When he got her to let her inhibitions go and step into the music, they had a real beat going, something from a previous era. It was "their music." So, music was ever-present in my childhood.

But when Elvis, the Platters and other vocal groups singing doo-wop got started in around 1956, my dad suddenly became intolerant. The first time I heard "Don't Be Cruel" in a hamburger joint on the way home from the lake, I was riveted by the intensity of it. The advent of rock and roll was upon us, and my old man just couldn't bear it. It was a frightening new culture that, to his sensibility, was nothing but jive. It happens to every generation. It's amazing that each generation forgets that it happened to them when they were young and immortal.

The mystique of rock and roll, hot rods and custom cars, and juvenile delinquency presented an incredible development in everyone's lives. The old stereotypes of the war era, the 40's and early 50's, were on the way out. Lucky Strike and Camel gave way to Marlboro and Kent, Lark and Winston.

Television, stereo, plastics replacing metal, color everything, jet propulsion, and all the stigmatic attitudes of the older generation being exposed as ludicrous, making our new world a fascinating discovery zone. Art, music, poetry, theater, film, literature, and pop culture were smacking us in the face. The whole world was Danish Modern. I couldn't wait to dive into it.

I grew up during those teenage years feeling repressed. I didn't feel satisfied at home in my parents' house. My sister had largely taken over as the main child in the house, and I stumbled my way through high school inching closer to the day I could make a break away from the sedate conformity of my parents, who were considered very liberal. Under the assumptive, strangely uncommunicative atmosphere of my parents, I seethed with discontent. I stubbornly ignored the many things that disturbed me. Like a martyr, I hung onto small sufferings and waited for the day I was free to go.

Sometime between high school and college, a couple of perilous years with a series of enticing pitfalls, I managed to join a fraternity (something expressly forbidden by my father), get a girl pregnant (she left town for parts unknown), become a male fashion model, spend two summers as a lifeguard, and journey from community college to a major university as a budding art student.

My head was filled with fantasy and foolishness. Bob Dylan was having a huge impact on me. I'd used my Gibson acoustic to learn some folk songs: Kingston Trio, Harry Belafonte, Jesse Fuller, Joan Baez, etc. But then things got edgy with the lyrics and all, talking about social issues and love issues with a completely different attitude than anything I'd ever heard before. I felt compelled to follow the rowdier road than stay on a familiar path. I went out looking for it, convinced that one day, it all would come to me.

I was a below-average student, and the only area in which

I excelled was art. In fact, I attracted the attention of an art teacher in grammar school, who recommended that I go to Cass Technical High School, a place that accepted students from all over Detroit, if they had an aptitude for specific studies.

After much squabbling with my father over the matter of going to a high school where I knew no one, I attended Cass Tech for the next four years, riding the Grand River bus to downtown Detroit for 45 minutes each way, every day from September 1957 to June 1961.

It made me tough in some ways, but it was also damaging. It depends on how you look at it, but it certainly set me apart from anyone else I knew in my neighborhood, and isolated me from any friends I might have had, as well. It left me seeking out characters like myself. It left me with the oddballs.

I didn't perform particularly well at Cass. I quickly discovered that, at best, I was average compared with those other kids that had genuine "art talent." Academically, somewhere between C and D was my domain. But graduate I did—barely. And, after a brief stop at a junior college to pull up my grade average and complete some of the tedious undergraduate transitional courses, I transferred to Wayne State University. This is where things went horribly awry.

For my parents, it must have been a nightmare to watch as all their efforts to raise a decent human evaporated at my first taste of independence. For me, it was like being released from prison. Without the watchdog presence of my father—who really wasn't a tyrant, but never seemed to approve of anything I relished—I felt I had control of my own fate for the first time in my life. At last, I didn't need his approval to do what I wanted.

In short order, I found myself an apartment near campus,

where I took up residence with a fellow artist named Doug James. We played our records and shared our discoveries, strummed our guitars and went off in separate directions to search for inspiring local inner city campus offerings, plays and pubs and music venues, anything that looked bright. We straddled the gap from being at home with the folks to being on our own in our own world, and we didn't even care that it was a dangerous place. We also knew that it would shape the rest of our lives.

Yet, despite these new liberties, nothing filled the urge I felt to tavel beyond the mundane emotions that went with being the person I was and not knowing how to rise above it.

I was an artist, or so I hoped to be, with an eye on developing and mastering a style that was consistent with classical art. I worshipped the old masters, Leonardo, Michelangelo, Caravaggio, Degas. Those were my people, my heroes, and my idols.

In a time of abstract expressionism and emerging pop art, however, I was a dinosaur, out of step with the current crop of artists, and that left me wholly out in the cold, feeling stubborn and snobbish.

I didn't respect modern abstraction because it didn't represent real skill. It was a quick step around true beauty to create a distorted picture that had no basis in reality. My drawing was gaining in quality and I knew I had a good shot at being a leading figure in the department. But all this was new and tenuous. It was the very beginning, and I was impatient, and it ended when I met Sandy.

Sandy was a real ballbreaker. Sandy was a hooker. Sandy was a beatnik and a whole lot of things that you wouldn't, and shouldn't, bring home to meet your mother. She lived down the hall with a guy who looked like he might be a bomb throwing revolutionary, or a deeply disturbed writer. They had a German shepherd dog named Dog, and a small child named Robin in tow, looking more like a package than anything else. The couple dressed in dark clothing that seemed to be an assortment of rags and leather. The man was bearded, short and wiry, intensely intellectual.

Sandy, *a.k.a.* Sam, used make-up and costume to give herself the most intriguing appearance. She was a gypsy and a harlot, and always barefoot. Her hair changed back and forth from black to red, sometimes piled atop her head in a *faux* beehive; other times hanging indiscriminately around her face to give her a frame of auburn importance.

Her eyes were completely enveloped in black eyeliner that pointed upward at the corners for a distinctly evil effect. A mole enhanced by eyebrow pencil completed the baroque courtesan in rags. Topping off the vision, a sneer at the corners of a pair of bee-stung lips invited the fly types like me into the spider's cotton candy web. A cigarette dangled perpetually from her fingers.

After a week or two, the man left, and Sandy was frequently knocking at the door across the hall from our apartment where a couple of girls lived. (One of the girls was named Becky, the future wife of one of the MC5.) I didn't really want to get to know her, though. It just happened.

One time when I was entering or leaving my apartment, she happened to be in the hall. We spoke. It should have been all too obvious, but I followed the pleasantry all the way into the den and started my initiation into the dark world of which I had only heard.

My life, my experiences, my attitudes, my values, would all be changed into something I only vaguely imagined previously. The new me, without will or power or limitations or caution or discrimination or resolve, was standing at the starting line. This adventure without end or meaning or honor or profit was an odyssey of idiocy. I was throwing the life I knew away to gain…what?

Sandy wasted no time in laying down her credentials. At the top of the list: ex-*Playboy* bunny. Number two: resident of the Village, Lower East Side of Manhattan, who had met everybody who's anybody. Number three: high-dollar downriver Birmingham-raised rich bitch, accustomed to affluence and doesn't need it. Knows men, what they want, how they think, how to use them, when to dump them. Don't even *think* for a moment you can outsmart this one; the man hasn't been born that can handle her. And last but not least: drug user extraordinaire, proud of it, condones all forms, ready for anything, open to suggestions.

In addition, she claimed to be well-read and well aware of every single hip author there was, who in turn were the only writers that matter.

I was in the presence of a truly avant-garde mind. The "square" world stopped where her's began, and I entered her domain fully aware that I was on thin ice. *This* was seduction. And, even though she challenged the male ego to keep pace, sex was the bottom line. The game was on, and she was in full control.

Her apartment was a quaint combination of castoff furniture arranged at floor level, surrounded by tapestries as wall covering. Mortar blocks held a small wooden board that served as a "coffee table." Colors and moody lighting bathed the room in opium-den coziness. My head was swimming, but I was relatively nonchalant. Being a sensitive artist, I believed, I could easily be fascinated without being overwhelmed by this wayward creature. She was subject matter; I was doing research. Whatever I called it, it was tempting disaster, but I didn't see it that way for some reason. In fact, I welcomed the chance to glimpse the unknown. It was exactly what I sought.

The first time I went there, a female friend of Sandy's was visiting. She looked to be a student. She was of medium build, early 20s, short blondish hair, wearing glasses, talkative, conservatively dressed.

She was no student. In fact, she was a prostitute. Judy was her name. She jabbered in hipster jargon as she rolled joints from a small pile of weed that was on the table. She was the girlfriend of a pimp named Tom, a black dude whom I was told was the hippest cat around, a very heavy dude.

"Do you want to get high? Oh, come on, you don't want to be a square for the rest of your life, do you, man?"

"What the hell, I'll try it," I said.

I had to imagine I felt anything at all. The women told me I was higher than shit. I didn't know what I was supposed to feel like. So I went along. They taught me how to roll a joint. I gripped the two ends of the rolling paper and twisted it into a small cigarette. Laughing, they told me it was a "stinger," a penitentiary joint. Trying another, I made what appeared to be a properly proportioned marijuana cigarette. I was congratulated for my quick learning ability. I sensed I was welcomed into the fold.

After Judy picked up her things and left, Sandy and I had sex in her tiny bedroom, with her child sleeping in a makeshift bed in the corner. I was ridiculed for wearing underwear, apparently a giveaway that I was a square. I felt ridiculous about it. I wondered if I should stop wearing underwear. I "scored," but I wasn't the winner here. I was clearly the one who had been had. Sam was a crafty seductress. She knew how to give enough slack so that the target would not become too frightened and try to escape. I was still free to think I had gotten away with something.

Some days passed, and I went about my business as a university student, going to classes and seeing my little sweetheart that I had been seducing on my own. Sharon was a girl that I had only casually known at Cass Tech. She was blond, pretty, a former cheerleader, someone with whom I would never have thought I stood a chance in high school. But after running into her at Wayne State, things seemed to be at a different level. I made conversation with her easily and found success, becoming more than friends in a short span of time. We had a completely typical boyfriend/girlfriend relationship, with thoughts of getting married at some point and doing the typical American family thing. I was flattered that she was into me, and she was intrigued by my artist's charisma.

I was always going over to the public library to listen to records. I was just beginning to discover early music, Bach, and Baroque music in general, and every time I ran across a new cantata or what have you, I would get Sharon to come to the library with me to check it out. I was not an ordinary guy. I had interests that put me ahead of anyone else that she knew. I was turning her onto things she would have passed by, and so that put me in a good light, even though I had shaky prospects. She just had no idea how desperate I was to break out of the normalcy I was surrounded by.

One of the more frustrating things was that we didn't have sex, other than heavy petting and some close calls. Sharon still lived at home with her parents. She was, in general, much closer to her family than I was with mine. And, as much as I liked her, things were suddenly moving too slowly for me.

I was on a fast track to get hip, and nothing was going to

stand in my way. I couldn't play the charade forever. Finally, I decided to pull the plug on our relationship. I went for the kill on an October evening, as I was getting out of her car at my apartment. I told her we were ending, and it would be best if we ditched our plans for marriage. She protested at first. Then, when she realized how serious I was, she exploded, giving me a wallop and burning out down the street, never to be seen again.

I suppose it wouldn't have been a successful match in the long run anyway. I lacked self-confidence, and a realistic view of life and my future. I was fumbling in the dark. So, it was best that things ended when they did. I hope she had a beautiful life thereafter. I hope she got all the things she wanted. I hope she is well today. But I will never know what happened to her or how things turned out. Maybe she'll read this book, and be damn glad that I was asshole enough to crash and burn our relationship and not put her through what surely would have been a nightmare down the road.

I really didn't know what a basket case I was until I got with Sandy. Right after the split with Sharon, Sandy ran out of rent money. There I was, like Sir Galahad to the rescue, and there was nothing to prevent me from taking the next irrational step. It didn't take much persuading to get Doug to agree to have Sam and her kid move in with us until she could get her own crib.

Anyone could plainly see the handwriting on the wall, but I refused to think I was being had. In a couple of weeks, Doug would find somewhere else to call home, leaving me with an instant family and a murky future. Then it was like living in a perpetual fun-house-spookhouse, with strange new behavior patterns and uncharted emotional ups and downs.

Sam told me that she had been called "the only true hedonist around" by one of the key people in her clique, a horn player named Charles Moore. It seemed like this was a desirable thing to be, and I immediately became a fan of hedonism. After all, I assumed, being a hedonist meant I was a free spirit. I could do as I pleased in the name of hedonism, that gallant unreason that needs no reason. To characterize my mental state as confused would be an understatement.

I started meeting Sam's friends. Naturally, they were the hipsters of the area. Several of them were actually doing avant-garde work in different media; a poet here, a jazz musician there, a painter or two, a writer, an actor. The aura of the beat world was dark, but thriving with wit and laid back intellectualism, and that was exactly what I was looking for: Gauloise cigarettes, cheap chianti, late night Chinese restaurants, reefer, much talking, and artists, artists, artists. It fulfilled my dream ambition.

Of course, it wasn't quite as glamorous as that. A few of Sam's circle were merely local residents who had drug or alcohol problems, lonely people who thought of he as a wandering angel of mercy.

I met an alcoholic friend of hers; who, aside from being a physical and mental wreck, was an intelligent talker and maybe a Detroit version of Bukowski. His barren room contained a bed, a table, a chair, and a refrigerator. The refrigerator itself contained two quarts of vodka and a half-gallon of milk. The milk was his stomach coater. There was no other food to be found. Meeting a character like that only enhanced the aura of morbid fascination surrounding Sam.

Also among Sam's associates was a character named John Sinclair, although he was someone with status in the local community. He was an organizer of sorts, providing the area with a rented house, the Artist's Workshop, where poets and musicians met to give recitals and perform improvised jam sessions, or show avant-garde films. On Sundays, people would crowd into the downstairs area to find a spot to stand and be entertained by the collective. And it was all vaguely relevant in the strange puzzle I saw and wished to be a part of, especially as Sam considered herself to be at least as important a figure in the mix as anyone, and maybe more so, given that she believed she had control over any man in existence. Where I lacked self-confidence, Sam exceeded all limits.

Sam had pushed me into breaking up with Sharon, because, as she put it, I was holding onto Sharon for safety. She claimed that I was afraid to let go of the sure thing, that I didn't trust my feelings. I recall getting into a weird argument with her one night about romantics vs. romanticists. She told me I was a jerk for being a romantic, and I defended myself by saying I was a romanticist, a romanticist being a stylish artist, not a lovesick bozo.

She must have been impressed by my argument, because I recall her telling me that I was going to be rich and famous someday. It must have been then that she decided that she was going to have to marry me. She claimed that if I really loved her, we should get married. Hard as it is to process, I didn't think it was a bad idea, and we started talking about how and when to do it.

So, did I really love her? The answer is "not at all." It was just fun doing whatever I pleased. I didn't care about the consequences, and I didn't give a damn about her really. Quite simply, it was all a big game. Early in the month of January, 1964, we were married at the courthouse in downtown Detroit.

One of Sam's friends, a single lonely guy named George that lived down the street from us, came along to witness the event. We went out for Chinese afterwards to celebrate. It was a very subdued event. The cost of the wedding without the Chinese was $5. George drove and picked up the tab at the Chinese restaurant as a wedding gift.

From then on, we went out less and less, withdrawing into our little apartment space. I went to class less and less. I drew less and less, and our time started being occupied almost entirely with pursuing drugs.

Sam's friends were horrified by our marriage. Jim Semark, a poet of some notoriety in the group, called our marriage "the mismatch of the century." My parents, on the other hand, were always gracious, even if they were torn and shattered by the events behind the grin-and-bear-it expressions on their faces. Still, they accepted the folly without flinching. They even came to our humble under-the-sidewalk basement apartment to pay a visit to their new family and daughter in law. At this point, they must have accepted that their son was demented beyond reason, and it wouldn't serve any purpose to be hostile. I was pulling out all the stops. It was natural that school would be ending for me as well.

Sandy got pregnant. I had no job or plans to get anything together that had real purpose. I was like an idiot who had been released on an alien planet. Not one shred of common sense lurked in my head, only my emotions and fantasies. Sandy, however, had no intention of having another baby. One baby might have been a cute accessory, but two would be an impossible situation and a death knell for our marriage.

I listened as she explained the process for executing an at-home abortion. I was horrified. Was she expecting me to perform this murder? Most absolutely, she was indeed. In fact, she was insisting on it.

Very simply, one takes a knitting needle and inserts it into the vagina, locates the tip of the cervix, where a clot has formed to prevent the menstruating cycle from taking place. Gently but firmly piercing the clot at the tip of the cervix releases the embryo from its protective environment. If all goes as planned, the pregnancy is terminated without complications.

We sterilized the needle, and with great reluctance, I tried my best to do as she had instructed me. I was truly scared but, after a lot of painful pushing, she told me that we had done it. Somehow, it worked. But it may also have been the most utterly heinous thing I have ever done in my life. I don't even want to think about the ramifications of it. What had I become in just a few months on my own? I'd rather not think about that either.

What kind of fire was I playing with? I wasn't thinking about anyone's feelings, including my own, as I trampled over everything in my path on my way to chaos. I liken this adventure to placing a blind person behind the wheel of a tractor-trailer and setting them loose on a freeway. And what can be said for my partner in this, for that matter? Was she just as loony as I was? Such disregard for the feelings of anyone who might care what happened to her or her two-and-a-half-year-old daughter had to be suspicious.

Were we both crazy? Our friends must have looked askance at our decisions and lifestyle. Then again, experimentation and rejection of conventional social wisdom were in vogue in those days. That which appears as lunacy now, may have looked very much like a brave sortie into the changing political climate of the early '60s. No one else knew about the "do-it-yourself" abortion. So, barring any psycho behavioral issues, we appeared to be a cliché couple of the radical non-conformist left.

As winter settled in on the Detroit inner city campus neighborhood, feelings of discontent rose up in the tiny sub-street level apartment.

Florida beckoned. It could have been something as simple as talking about how nice it was to go to Fort Lauderdale on spring break when I was with a different crowd a couple of years back; or, simply discussing how cold it was outside. But in those days, when a subject came up in conversation, there was a good chance that it would spur us to some action. All at once, we decided that we needed to get the fuck out of cold ass Detroit and go where it was sunny and warm. We had no money, no car, no job skills, no plan, no idea of what to do or how to do it. In other words, we were ready.

I began devising a scheme to accomplish the impossible/improbable task of moving everything to Florida. Sam said that it was easy. All you needed to do was get a "drive-away" going to wherever you want to relocate. If you could pass the security requirements for the transport agency, they would give you a car that needed to be driven to a specified location. I had a clean record and was bondable at that time, so I was able to get a car going to where we were headed without any trouble.

We left Michigan for Fort Lauderdale in early February 1964 in a 1963 Chevrolet Impala hardtop, packing every cherished item we could fit in or on top of the car. From under the seat, a terrified calico kitten that I named Kitone mewed every so often to remind us that this wasn't right. It was snowing when we pulled away from the basement apartment on East Forest, my wooden easel strapped to the roof, since it was too long to fit anywhere else. A cute little bed was created in the back seat area for the little girl. It was a picture of self-reliant ingenuity done beatnik style.

We were on the road and excited. I had dropped all of my

classes and gotten a refund on my tuition (which my father had paid); withdrawn whatever funds I had in the bank, filled the tank with money given me by the transport agency for that purpose, and now, in the darkness and falling snow, we headed out for the interstate highway bound south for Florida. I was 21, she was 22.

I had a fascination with the music of Bob Dylan at the time. His songwriting and lyrical messages meant more to me than anything. It was my reality. With Sandy, I saw myself attaining the character I was fascinated by in Dylan. As we began our present adventure of hedonism, it felt just like the cover of *Freewheelin'*, Dylan's second album. The dingy streets of Manhattan in winter, the raggedy looking characters with scarves wrapped around, arm in arm, plodding through slush and cold, it was a brave picture. Like the picture on the album, undaunted by all that we lacked, we pushed ahead toward our goal.

It sounds like a movie about a naïve couple hell bent on their own destruction. We had no possibility of success. And yet, something pulled me like a magnet into that unknown, as if it were the only destiny that mattered. What I felt for Sandy was more than infatuation with her persona, her sex, her unrestricted attitude, her insight, and her sense of adventure. Maybe we were more alike than it appeared on the surface. Maybe the two of us were both as insecure as we were reckless, and with that drawing us together, each one looking to the other for the strength they lacked is what made the attraction so powerful.

The road trip itself was wonderful: the Blue Ridge Mountains of West Virginia silhouetted against the moonlit sky, with curling smoke rising from distant shacks dotting the sides of the hills. We snaked our way along the winding concrete darkness in the red Impala, the radio fading in and out with strange music. Descending into Mount Airy, North Carolina, along the flat highways through farmland, the 10,000-watt signal of WLAC out of Nashville broadcasting the unforgettable sounds of Garnet Mimms and Solomon Burke.

I drove and drove, through Georgia and across the Florida panhandle, down the middle of the state. Darkness fell once again. The fragrance of oranges filled the air, coming in the now slightly opened windows of the car as we sliced through the orchard highway. Bonfires appeared in the distance of fields. In the darkness, the Impala hummed along at a steady pitch.

A song played while Sandy and the girl slept. "I saw you once before, when I got to your door…no reply. I know that you saw me, cause I looked up to see…your face. No reply…no reply." I perked at the end of that one. Who was that? Hmm…the Beatles. I'd seen them on the *Ed Sullivan Show*. I'd heard their record "I Want To Hold You Hand" as well, but this was different than that sound. This one had something else besides frenzied teenage silliness. This was about a fucked-up relationship and deceit. I wanted to hear more.

We got to Lauderdale the next morning. Exhausted and disheveled, we peered out the windows at the beachfront and the people walking the streets. It was much how I remembered it from the spring break trips. Lots of sand everywhere, bright sun, glitzy looking shops, palm trees, motels, bathing suits, a seriously relaxed atmosphere. I spotted a little house at the edge of the main street, a run down shack with shutters and things falling off the roof. A sign in the doorway said it was for rent, for $250 a week, which was just about what I had in my pocket.

We drove around looking for the crummy neighborhoods.

Finally we parked and tried to think of what to do next. We were in the wrong place. This was strictly for vacationers or rich people. It certainly wasn't for us. In those days, you could find crappy places to live in Detroit for 50 or 60 bucks a month. I was paying $65 in my first apartment for a one bedroom with a kitchen. But this wasn't Detroit and these weren't crappy places. It was clear we had to go to Miami.

Miami was a major metropolitan area with slums and strange neighborhoods, a place where the possibilities were wide open. We found a little apartment just off Biscayne Boulevard, where I could pay just enough to get us through the month. It was one block from the Bay, and being close to the water was what was important to me.

It wasn't too bad for a dive apartment, except for the Florida cockroaches that were about five times the size of a normal cockroach. Called palmetto bugs, they weren't worse in any other way, just a lot bigger. I set up my easel to start painting, set up the stereo for music—we never did anything without music—and put art around the walls, so we could feel like we were at home.

I went fishing down the street at the foot of the bay. A little pier provided a place to stand and cast into the water. Across the water, the high rises of Miami Beach stood in the sunlight. It was cool, and I stood there with my line in the water of Biscayne Bay thinking about how smart I was, and how all the poor suckers back in Detroit were freezing their asses off and plowing through the dirty snow that filled the streets. We did it, we were here, and now I had to figure out how to make it last.

I felt something bump on my fishing line.

Bang, there it went again.

I pulled up hard when I felt the next bump, and felt the weight of the fish that had just had my hook pierce his lip. I pulled him out of the water and gaped at his beautiful red and silver scales. It was a red snapper of about eight inches in length—dinner!

I went home to the apartment to show off my catch. Sandy was laughing at me like I was a little kid with a prize from the county fair with that red snapper. I felt like such a man, a real provider. We were like a couple of children escaped from the real world of our parents, playing at being grownups. Robin, the little girl, was like the dolly, and we were out of our minds acting like everything would be fine.

I had to take the Impala to the agency drop-off point. Once that was done, I took a bus back to our 32nd Street apartment. I knew I had to find transportation, so I did the next logical thing; I bought a motor scooter.

It was a Lambretta 175, an Italian motor scooter that I paid $100 for. It even had a little buddy pad so Sandy could ride with me. Actually, Robin was small enough so she could fit between Sandy and me as well, so we could all go on the Lambretta, which we did. And what does one do when one is in Florida and unemployed? You go to the beach, of course.

Just south of Miami, beyond the city proper and several miles down the highway leading to the Florida Keys, empty beach ribbons its way along for miles and miles. There, we found paradise by the side of the road. No people, no fences, no stores, no lifeguards, nothing but sea, sand, and blue crabs—what more could you ask for? I guess this is what we traveled all those miles to get to. And, for one afternoon, we had the very best of it.

I attempted to make a painting. I had Sam pose nude seated on a stool. She could hold a pose for about five minutes. It was enough to get a very general layout of what I wanted to paint. So I threw some color on the canvas just to get something started. I'd never even taken a painting class. I had no idea what to do. It was all play acting, really.

I heard a radio ad for a show happening somewhere near Miami that featured a singer I'd become familiar with some time before in Detroit. His name was Otis Redding. He was one of those black artists that you'd never hear on white radio stations, but being tuned in to all kinds of music, I'd discovered him. In fact, he was my favorite singer at the time. I'd heard "These Arms Of Mine" a year before on black radio stations in Detroit, and "I've Been Loving You Too Long," with which Sam was also familiar. His new record, "Mr. Pitiful," was on the radio in Florida, and this was a show that couldn't be missed.

We pawned Robin off on a neighbor and, after a lot of map research, climbed on the Lambretta and set out to find the town where the show was. When we got there, it was quite a surprise to find we were the only whites not only at the show, but in town, period.

But I had no fear and Sam had no fear. We were one with them. It was a great experience being a fan and being in that element. I felt we were embraced by the people in the club as part of Otis's family. It was an amazing night, and one I'll never forget. Years later Otis Redding caught everyone's attention at Monterey Pop, and was soon recognized as the tower of R&B strength that he was. But this was something else.

The money, what little there was of it, was nearly gone, but just as the rent ran out, I traded the Lambretta for a car at a used car lot. The deal was one Lambretta motor scooter for one 1951 Plymouth station wagon. We had decided we would have a better chance of finding work in Key West, but we needed a car to get there. I cannot imagine why we believed that Key West presented more opportunity than Miami, but that was our choice of the moment. We loaded it up with our stuff, and set out at dusk for the Florida Keys.

At the third Key in the chain, a place called Tavernier Key, the fan flew off the motor with a huge bang, and went through the hood of the car. I pulled us over to the side of the road in the darkness. Water was on both sides of the road—the Atlantic Ocean to the left, the Gulf of Mexico to the right. It was quiet and dark, with no traffic in either direction. We waited out the darkness in the car, afraid to step outside for fear of alligators or creatures that might be lurking in the dark.

At sunrise, the barren highway lay as silently as it had during the night. Little waves lapped at the shoreline on both sides of the road. Not much else was happening. A couple of dwellings sat down the road a bit, and what surely had to be the "tavern" of Tavernier Key. After the half-mile walk to the tavern/restaurant, we found out we weren't the only Michigan people in town. The folks who owned the place had left the old homestead years ago for the Florida sun. They kindly fed us a free meal and directed me to a guy who needed some work done, if I was interested.

We were stranded. We had no money and a broken car. How much worse could things get? The guy who needed the work done owned a fishing boat. The hull was covered with barnacles. If I wanted to make a little money, I was welcome to start scraping the barnacles off the hull of his dry-docked boat with a scraper.

For the next two days, I scraped the guy's boat. We could sleep in the cabin of his other boat that was tied up in a slip instead of trying to sleep in the broken car. During the night, a ferocious storm tossed the boat around at its mooring, scaring the hell out of us. We thought we would sink and die, but it stopped in time.

On the third night, the boat guy invited Sam and me to have a drink with him at a bar. We got Robin somewhere safe and went out with him. I started getting pretty drunk after a few rounds, and saw the boat guy dancing with my wife. Sam told me we needed to leave when she came back to the table. I was staggering.

Back at the boat, she was furious. This dude had been hitting on her while I was drunk. She was right. I'd let that happen and right under my nose, this asshole took advantage of me. I felt like a total loser. I had let her down. We didn't have anything. I had to get my pay from our evil benefactor and get us out of there. I confronted him for my money expecting the worst, but he gave me $40 and said he hoped there weren't hard feelings.

My plan was to hitchhike to Miami and find us a drive-away to New York. Maybe there, in Sam's New York hipster realm, we would find a way to survive. I was a good-looking guy, and things like getting rides weren't hard to do. I got to Miami easily and tracked down a couple of drive-away companies until I found a car that was bound for New York: a new Plymouth Barracuda fastback. I made all the arrangements with the contract, which was easy since, I had already done a successful drive-away a month before.

That evening I set out to get back down to Tavernier Key, where Sandy and Robin were waiting without any knowledge of what I was planning. I hauled ass to get there quickly. As I came near the spot where the old Plymouth wagon was still sitting by the side of the highway, I saw Sam holding Robin in her arms. They rushed to meet me as the car pulled off the road onto the gravel shoulder. Tears were streaming down Sam's face as she hurled herself at me through the open window of the car. With black eye shadow and mascara rivers running down her cheeks, she sobbed on my shoulder.

"I thought you were never coming back. I was scared you were going to leave us."

"Hell no. I wouldn't do that."

"I love you," she said, and at that moment I believed it was the truth.

In the dark, we transferred all our belongings into the Barracuda. Luckily, with the fastback hatch, even the easel fit. A new chapter was beginning: onward to New York City and the real world. But if I thought the worst was over, I was mistaken.

2

The Apple Bites Back

It wasn't like we spent everyday building disasters. We were having a lot of fun being unconcerned, as well. Sam and I were playing. At that point in time, all roads beckoned, and anything was possible. The complicating factor was the presence of a small child. It didn't seem to matter to the adults, who weren't acting very adult, that a two year old was affected by their choices and actions.

Robin was a sweet and very pretty little girl. She was as happy as could be, all of the time. There wasn't anything unusual to her about any of the things that were taking place. What could she compare it to, after all? If she was at a jai-alai match in south Florida with two young adults who carried her on their shoulders and gave her things to eat, laughing at everything, how was she to know that was out of the ordinary? We didn't look strange to her, although other people were certainly looking twice at the weird chick with the makeup and the sandals, her mother.

So taking another long car trip with Sam and I, and all our

worldly goods, was just another exciting event in her toddler's world. We were moving on to wherever our vagabond fate would lead us.

In the Barracuda were two leather suitcases belonging to the car's owner. Of course, Sam was going to see what was in them. There wasn't any cash, but there was something useful: a credit card. In 1964, credit cards were available, but it wasn't something I knew anything about. I'd only gotten $50 for gas from the agency. That wasn't going to get us to New York, and we were broke otherwise. We'd use the gas money for food, and charge gas to the owner's card, if it worked.

At the first gas-up, I handed the credit card to the attendant and waited while he went inside to use the little swipe machine that made an ink impression on a receipt of the transaction. When he returned, I forged the owner's name on the paper slip and took the receipt from the attendant. No problem, we were going to make it. Beatnik ingenuity comes through again. Or more accurately, shifty criminal scam slips through the cracks.

We were styling on the interstate in an almost-new Barracuda, on our way to the Big Apple. I didn't know how things would turn out when I delivered the car, but I was fearless, as usual. Maybe it would go down without me having to reveal anything about using the found credit card. That "lucky guy" thing had been following me around for as long as I could remember. It seemed anytime I got into a scrape, I had a knack for getting through a loophole or finding a kind soul to take pity on me. Most often that person would be my father. Even though he wasn't around out here, I had confidence that my charming innocence could do the trick.

If you've ever driven into Manhattan by way of one of the tunnels, you know what a rush it is to emerge into the jungle of people, traffic, concrete, buildings, noise, motion, pigeons, and energy that impacts your senses immediately. The blast is one of total immersion. I once went to New York to visit a couple of chicks we'd met on the beach during a Fort Lauderdale excursion, but this was something else entirely. They lived in Queens, and this was nothing like Queens. At once I became like a survivalist. I likened it to being in the "dodge 'ems" ride at an amusement park.

Sam said we had to look for a place on the Lower East Side, wherever that was. We'd find a groovy little tenement pad that we'd be able to afford; and, after an hour of driving around, we found a "for rent" sign at a building on a very narrow street, East 10th Street between Avenues A and B.

The apartment, a two room with kitchen and toilet, rented for $45 a month, but you had to clean it up. It was strewn with bricks, trash, and unwanted furniture. The tub was in the kitchen, a common occurrence in lower Manhattan. It was a four-story walkup in a Puerto Rican neighborhood. I felt myself being scrutinized by the locals. This was, after all, their turf.

I ran our stuff up the four flights as fast as I could, and got back to the car for the next load. When I finished the very last trip I returned to find the window of the Barracuda smashed with glass all over the sidewalk. Welcome to New York. No one was in sight near the car. It was an eerie feeling. I knew I was being watched for my reaction from unseen places by hidden eyes. I just didn't want to get beaten up. I checked inside the car. The suitcases were gone. Fucking hell, what was I going to do? The car had to go to a place called New Pelham that I would have to find on a map, and then I was going to have to explain everything. Fuck it, I told myself; all I can do is tell the truth.

I located the town on a map and set out with the car the next morning. We had spent the night before cleaning and arranging, and Sam had the little place looking like a cozy little Bohemian nest. Now I was on a snaking freeway with thousands of other cars, all charging toward their known destinations.

I was agitated and stiffened for the confrontation I knew was coming. I found the exit and did my best to stay calm. There it was. I pulled into the driveway and got out of the car. Within an hour, I was grilled for information, accused of theft, and arrested by the New Pelham police. I gazed out the window of the police cruiser as we made our way on this sunny winter day to the small town police station, New York City somewhere off in the distance, and my wife and her child a seeming million miles away.

No one believed my story, true though it was. I had broken the window myself to fake a burglary, and sold the guy's clothes to someone. That was what they thought until I showed them the receipts from all the gas stops along the way from Florida, which somehow corroborated my story.

Although I still don't see how that got me off the hook for the missing suitcases, they let me go. It may have been the real tears I shed when they tried to break my story without success. I was sobbing heavily when one of the cops suddenly said, "Get the hell out of here, and stay out of trouble."

I took a train back to Manhattan, about an hour away, and walked the rest of the way back to East 10th Street. Up the four flights of stairs in the drafty, cold, tile floored hallway with painted metal railings and painted steel apartment doors, voices echoing throughout the abyss. It was some homecoming, in a strange land and a new life with a partner that I still sometimes felt I barely knew, but it felt good to be home somewhere.

The time we spent in New York City was really only about a month, but it seemed like much longer. There were people nearby, on the same block actually, that were "our" people: underground types, street people, druggies, Beats, aimless hustlers with one thought only—drugs.

Rock music was not yet what it would become in a few short years. A band called the Lovin' Spoonful inhabited the East Village, but they weren't accepted as a hip outfit. Actually, the word on them was that they were squares that did a lot of drugs and thought they were hot shit. There were no rock bands whatsoever. Jazz was what people listened to; and, among dopers, there really wasn't any music to speak of.

Sam was always in tune with what was going down—who said what, and what was what. We hung out in someone's apartment in the next building from ours, smoking weed or hash, or taking speed and waiting for someone to show up with a stash of anything.

The drug of choice at all times was none other than King Heroin, a.k.a. duggey, smack, schmack, shit, junk, dope, but that wasn't so terrible.. It was a known fact that junkies were cool, non-violent people. If only society wasn't so evil and capitalistic. Give us the dope and leave us alone.

I moved furniture with one of these dope fiend characters. He was a young black dude named Bartell, a very nice person, easy to be with, funny, honest. I considered him a friend. We did many horrendous moving jobs together for $15 an hour. He had a step-van that we loaded with entire apartments of furniture. From multi-story walk-downs to multi-story walk-ups, just the two of us hauling refrigerators, couches, beds, the whole nine yards. Late in the afternoon, Bartell's nose would start running, and that meant it was time to go cop dope.

The first time I did dope, I was probably given half of what anyone else would do. It was very mellow, very serene, very quiet inside. I felt nauseous, but not uncomfortable. My thinking was literally at rest. I felt almost like I was floating.

It had a strange stringent odor. The "outfit" was homemade rig, a glass eyedropper with a rubber pacifier on the round end and a metal medical needle plugged on the other. The ritual was intriguing. This was serious stuff to these people. This was the holy sacrament of their religion. I felt anxious waiting for the effect, which when it came was so overwhelming that resisting was futile.

One of Sam's "friends" broke into our apartment and stole my acoustic guitar. Sam was so furious, she vowed to bring the motherfucker down. "Nobody steals my shit and gets away with it, motherfucker," she declared. She set about tracking this boy down and locating the guitar by finding out who he was trying to sell it to. The dope community was closer knit than you would think.

When she finally found him, she called the cops. I even got the guitar back, but she insisted on sending him to jail. I remember him pleading with her in court, "Please Sam, don't do this."

She just sneered. "I'll teach you to steal from me," she said, and he was gone. It was my guitar, not hers, but it was her reputation, her credibility, her aura, her venom.

Having moved to Florida to get away from the cold, it seems bizarre that we would then move to New York, straight back into it. At least, it seemed bizarre now we'd done it. And so, after freezing our asses of for a month, walking the streets and absorbing the Village vibe, killing as much time as we could learning the subway system, playing at being street people and panhandling, we decided to move back to Detroit.

I'd sure had enough of New York in the winter, and there weren't any prospects for things getting much better. Two of the degenerate drug types decided they would move to Detroit with us. When junkies move on, they go around and burn all their friends by getting credit for drug purchases, then leave town immediately.

I managed to find another drive-away, and these two native New York creeps piled into the car, making their escape on our ticket. This particular car was a piece of shit old Plymouth that wasn't going to Detroit at all. It was going to Pittsburgh. But it was all that I could find, and I took it just to get out of New York. Once we were back in Detroit, we lost those burn artists by dropping them off at an intersection downtown and pointing down the street. "That-a-way boys, what you're looking for is down there."

I found a small apartment at a flophouse called the Balmoral Hotel, down around Wayne State campus, which served as a temporary harbor for a week before we moved to a basement pad in an apartment building across the intersection. Then we descended on my parents, without forewarning.

Shocked as they were to see us appear from out of nowhere, they welcomed us into their house and fed us. My sister seemed to have grown up in the few months I'd been gone.

They sat and listened to our endless tales of the harrowing road experience. It must have seemed like we were making it up, but we were safe and I think that was what mattered most to them. They were such patient and kind people. And wasn't it just like them to slip money into my hand as we were leaving. Not just one of them, but both of them, independently of each other! That's how they were, always giving.

Sam's influence on me was huge. She was an authority on everything; and, even though it was totally uncomfortable, I had put myself in that position. I'm not sure if I thought I needed to pick up on all her unconventional wisdom, or if I simply committed myself to letting her rule my mind from the start. A strong personality could always take a hold on me throughout my whole life. Even in school, I remember my gym teacher telling my parents that I was easily influenced. "Think for yourself," they would tell me, "you've got a mind of your own." But that wasn't a message that I could hear back then.

"All you have to do is say something, man," Sam would say. "Word gets around that you said something heavy, man. People will notice. They'll say, 'Did you hear what that Mike dude said? Wow, that dude is a heavy cat!' It's all about self-confidence; all this stuff is nothing but self-confidence."

To me, that sounded reasonable. If you were able to throw your weight around and not doubt your capacity, why wouldn't you be able to do anything you wanted? I believed her. She definitely had me under her spell. At 21 years of age, I wanted to be the man, but I had to get past the hippest chick in town.

It looked like we were going to settle into being Detroiters. We set up our new basement dwelling, like all the others we'd had, then people started coming over. One of those people was the girl Becky, who'd lived in the first building we had met at. She came by one night with her boyfriend, a ruddy-cheeked fellow named Rob, who was toting a six of Budweiser. Back in those days, being a beer drinker amounted to announcing you were a straight-up square. The Beats prided themselves on rejecting everything about middle-class

America.

Rob was a nice guy, although slightly nervous. While the girls chitchatted, Rob and I discussed the Rolling Stones' new record. That's something that has disappeared from those days: back then, people took records with them when they went visiting. There were always crazy new things appearing in the record racks, and one way to inspire conversation was to turn people onto your musical discoveries. The Stones record was *The Rolling Stones, Now!*—certainly one of their greatest. Rob and I connected listening to that record and smoking a joint. He also made a point to invite me to come see his band play. It was the start of our musical relationship.

The weather soon changed and the Detroit summer arrived, with lots of people out and about on the streets and sitting on porches, yelling, cars honking, dogs barking—all the hubbub of downtown activity. But Detroit changed something else, too. My relationship with Sam was always on shaky ground in one way or another, but now I knew I couldn't keep on being this clumsy, inept character and having her hissing disapproval constantly. Something had to give. When it finally blew up, I left the apartment to find my own place.

One evening, I stole back to the basement crib and peeked in the window. I saw Sam and her friend Judy, the prostitute from the first night we met, fixing themselves up to go out on the town: laying on the eye shadow baby, glam sexy tight dresses, fishnets, heels, nightclub wear for a hunting excursion.

I hid in my car and when they pulled out, I followed uptown on Woodward Avenue. They drove until they pulled into the parking lot of a big classy joint. I waited, parked across the street where I could do surveillance. An hour later, my wife appeared with a middle-aged man, got into his Cadillac and drove away. Downtown at one of the posh hotels, they left the car with the valet and went inside.

Was I angry? Certainly, but with a calm, condescending outlook that, for the first time, removed this woman from the pedestal where I'd placed her. Not just a common slut, she was a pro! The mythology that had surrounded her exhibition of defiance evaporated at that moment.

But still, when she came to plead with me to come back to her, I weakened and returned. Later, we moved to a house where we spent another couple of months attempting some kind of life together. I even tried, unsuccessfully, to return to school.

We were doomed, though.

Sam went back to New York, for reasons unknown. When she returned, she had my friend Bartell with her. Apparently, they'd hooked up.

Now she demanded that I leave. I refused and, purely to demonstrate how unaffected I was by her betrayal, I stayed downstairs through the night while they occupied the bedroom.

The following morning, I left the house, returning in the evening when they were gone to retrieve my things and anything I wanted for myself. I had lost all respect for her. It was the end, period.

Nothing can kill a relationship faster than poverty. The absence of money creates tension, and tension kills fun. I could handle being broke, but not in the company of a woman. I decided to be single for a while. It seemed like I had my life back, and that freedom was the most glorious thing I'd felt in some time. It had been a year of dark wandering. Though I doubt I was ready for any real relationship, the choice I'd made was wrong from the start, and now I had scars to go with my fascinating stories of the seamy side of life. Now it was I who was dangerous.

I was working at a place called Great Lakes Steel. It was a blasting furnace in Wyandotte, a downriver suburb of Detroit. I worked on top of the coke ovens, where loads of coal are injected into a giant oven to be cooked for 24 hours, then pushed out the sides of the ovens into railroad cars.

My job was to open the lids of the ovens for the coal to be loaded in. It was a filthy, hot and dangerous job, but it paid fairly well for those days. I needed to get money to establish myself somewhere. I was completely lost, but I was still young.

During this time, I was staying with a girl I'd met who had some drug connections, a nice chick with a good cheery smile and a great set of boobs. I came back to her apartment one evening after my Great Lakes Steel shift. With her at her apartment was a black dude named Tyrone, who was in possession of a few hits of LSD. I'd read about the phenomenon of LSD in *Life* magazine, and I was intrigued to say the least. I wanted to try it, being brave and ready for anything.

The next 12 hours re-made my outlook on everything. I realized how arbitrary all of our attitudes, opinions, and ambitions are. I decided I was better than what I'd thought of myself, and that I really could find worthwhile things in life, despite all the damage and regrets I'd endured since I'd chosen to be senseless and fatalistic. It was the single greatest experience of my wild impetuous adventure. By some measure, I was saved.

3

Like A Rolling Stone

I stood in the Florsheim Shoe store on Woodward Avenue, staring at a pair of pointed toe boots with elastic sidebars. A two-inch Cuban heel gave them the vague appearance of cowboy boots. They were a casual-yet-dressy rock and roll style, not greaser, not stiletto hoodlum, not really anything specific, and brown.

I hesitated. I tried on a pair in my size. I looked at them in the mirror. With a shrug, I took them off, put them back in the box, and left the store, having decided it would be pretentious to wear something so inconsistent with my persona. Then I thought about how good they felt on my feet, and how rebellious I felt while I had them on. I went back, plopped down 75 bucks—a considerable sum in those days—and left the store with my brown Florsheim Beatle boots and a very light heart.

I knew the way I dressed didn't really match the boots, but I was driven to keep finding the parts to make the picture feel right. I needed tighter pants and a better hairstyle. I was confused about how to get my hair happening, but it would grow and all come together at some point. I was excited to be rid of Sam, and I was free to reclaim my ego.

I had done a drawing of her on canvas board in Conte crayon and pastel. Her head was prominent in the center, as if it were a playing card. She was the Queen of Spades. Spade symbols at the corners, a winding stairway curled from her breast, around her neck and up the side of her face, disappearing into her hair piled high atop her sneering head. It was a rough piece, but it was accurate. Somewhere, as it all crumbled down, I felt triumphant. She was beneath me, even though she had emotionally devastated me. From here on, things would be on my terms.

Beginning with my the miraculous accident that dropped me into a band of renegades, a nest of vipers, a crew of pirates, a gang of outlaws, a legion of the doomed, enemies of the republic, angels with dirty faces.

It was called the MC5.

We walked into a seedy bar in an ethnic area of Detroit. I had dragged my old frat buddy, Ray Deaver, along for company. He was a lonely guy who smoked Lucky Strikes, and complained about anything you could think of.

A dozen odd patrons sat drinking, while five oddball characters in matching outfits serenaded them with jangling electric guitar music. It seemed absurd to me, but there was my recent acquaintance, Rob, singing Otis Redding's "That's How Strong My Love Is," accompanied by a band who obviously wanted to be the Rolling Stones.

In their white shirts and skinny ties under dark buttoned up vests, they looked like they'd stepped off the cover of *Out Of Our*

Heads. I thought I would look good dressed up like that, with a guitar hanging over my shoulder.

When the MC5— for Motor City, of course—finished their set, I ventured over to say hello to Rob. His bandmates were hanging around in an area to the side of the stage, having Cokes or a pitcher of beer. Rob introduced me around and we had a little small talk about their music and what a weird place this was to be playing.

They weren't a bar band in the usual sense. They were high school kids with the exception of Rob, and much keener on playing for teenage kids at a party or school dance, than anything like this. One of the guitar players, Wayne Kramer, remarked that I had a cool pair of Beatle boots on. I appreciated his flattery and decided to hang out with the Five for the rest of the evening at their invitation.

My friend Ray was feeling aggravated sitting by himself drinking. There weren't any chicks for him to criticize or fantasize about, so he was ready to leave. I wasn't. I was happy to hang out with the rock band boys. I told Ray to go ahead and leave; I'd be all right. He grumbled and strode out of the bar. I never saw him again.

Rob was driving a 1960 Chevy four-door sedan with gull-wing fins horizontal above a couple of bullet-style taillights. I sat in the back seat with one of the guys, the other two up front. The bass player and the drummer had their own cars, so they weren't present. That was prophetic.

As we talked, it became apparent that these characters were no different from any of the people I'd been associated with in my past life. They were crude, rude, and lewd, basically high school guys like any I would've hung around with in my neighborhood, except instead of being ordinary chums, they were a band.

Rob had finished school and had a job at a machine shop.

Wayne and Fred Smith, the other guitar player, were 17, but even at 21, Rob shared their ruthless teenage mentality and aura of juvenile delinquent pool hall humor.

They were awestruck as I told them about the underworld drug culture of New York and Detroit. I felt a surge of confidence talking about this world that was beyond their borders. We rode back to the west side of Detroit and unloaded the amps at Wayne's house, before Rob drove me to my parents' nearby abode, my island in a stormy sea.

By now, my parents were used to being the safety net for their eccentric son. They allowed me to move back into their house without too many requirements, and I fixed a neat little nest under the stairs to the basement.

In my mind, I was able to separate myself from their household and maintain my underground frame of reference, while taking full advantage of their pantry and refrigerator. I even had the nerve to smoke reefer down in the basement, feeling confident that they wouldn't recognize its smell. Everyone at home smoked cigarettes except my mom, so the presence of more smoke didn't set off any red flags. Even a little hash was easily concealed, and if they were to ask what was burning, I would say I put something in the incinerator. My parents backed off easily. Maybe that's why I always felt I could get away with things.

I set about reading a couple of books to enhance my vocabulary of hipness. I needed to redirect my thinking and keep on fascinating my new friends, the rock and rollers. I read a Rolling Stones biography called *Our Own Story: The Rolling Stones* and a Beatles bio, the title of which I can't remember. Then I read the *Tao Te Ching* and a book about Zen Buddhism. Both of the eastern philosophy books were pivotal in defining my attitude. Having had my ego and identity crushed in the past year left me spiritually adrift. Western thinking, the thinking of my parents and the straight world in general, wasn't going to work in my world. The Tao and Zen did. I resolved to strive to behave with humility and presence.

Wayne lived a mile down the road with his mother and two younger sisters. My stories about the sinful life—the intrigue of shifty street dope peddlers and pimps, far from middle class white suburbia and the fate of working in a factory—fascinated him. He wanted to know what I knew, to peer over my shoulder into the abyss and gather what he needed to break out of Lincoln Park. I was no authority, nor was I endowed with any real wisdom; I had suffered from my own poor decisions, after all, and I was still grasping for tools of my own. But I wanted to be as honest as possible in detailing what I thought was true. Wayne and I became friends, or as Fred Smith put it back then, we were going to be "chummy." I felt slightly tagged as a usurper by that label, but I easily discounted it as a spat of jealousy. Relationships within the band weren't of any concern to me at that point. Later I learned that those relationships were the mechanics of the MC5's creative process.

I presume Rob was the cerebral instigator of the band's creativity up to that point. It was through him that the others were introduced to beatnik literature, art, poetry, avant-garde film, or anything else that occurred outside the borders of Lincoln Park. Rob was into the exhilarating world of hot rod cartooning and flamboyant behavior. The other guys were fairly conservative and subdued for the most part. So when I arrived as Wayne's new "guru," I displaced Rob in a sense.

I started coming to band practices, just sitting off to the side and watching. Rob and I hardly interacted. I was now in the clutches of Wayne's obsessive curiosity. I had his ear. We made up a role for me in the band. The fans were going to be told I was the band's songwriter. I was an artist type, a friend of the band who was collaborating with them to write songs. My name was Mick Davies. Of course, it wasn't true at all, but it gave me a fabulous mystique, and most likely, the kids would believe it.

I was immersing myself in pop music: magazines, records, anything about the wave of British bands that followed the Beatles. I was fascinated by everything I saw, and I wanted to crossover. I wanted to reshape myself from a bohemian artist into a skinny-legged, pointy-booted guitar picker. The music I was hearing made my head burst with ideas. I went from being a sullen brooding art misfit to a radiant optimistic troubadour. The whole scene was full of exciting images, young dudes with wild hair and clothes. It was the ideal situation for any single, white, 22-year-old American male in 1965.

I went to gigs and stationed myself at the side of the stage where I could be close to the action, watching all the girls and acting like an important person. With all their cover songs, band suits, and rock and roll hair, the MC5 weren't going to achieve much beyond winning the occasional battle of the bands. The big break of their career was being chosen to open for the Dave Clark Five. It was strange to be hanging around like a fifth (or sixth) wheel, but I couldn't let it go, and I couldn't think of anything I'd rather be doing. I knew that rock and roll was the most important thing happening anywhere, and its time was coming. I fit into it somewhere, but I didn't know where yet.

Living that close to Wayne had me splitting my time between staying under the stairs at my parents' and staying over at Wayne's mom's house. She was a beautician and did hair appointments in the kitchen of her home when she wasn't tending business at her beauty shop.

She told Wayne I had a winning smile, something I already knew and employed regularly. She also was leery of me exposing Wayne to the unsavory vices that she knew were lurking just beyond the nice northwest Detroit neighborhood we were in, and which Wayne was itching to get out of. I was literally the wolf in sheep's clothing; she had me pegged, but couldn't deny her son his companion and new found guru. She told me Wayne had a healthy live-and-let-live attitude, and she wanted it stay that way. I agreed. I had no intention to lead him astray.

It was about nine o'clock in the morning when I was jolted awake by the sound of the Kinks on a small record player in Wayne's room. *"You really got me…you really got me…you really got me."*

"What in the fuck are you doing?" I mumbled in a half-groggy state. The volume was cranked to synapse-rattling level.

"I'm playing the Kinks record," was Wayne's reply, as if that weren't all too obvious.

"It's kind of early, don't you think?" I retorted, as though it might make a difference.

"I don't think so," Wayne shot back, as if to say that my being asleep in the room was irrelevant to anything. He wanted to hear the Kinks record to start his day, and that was all that mattered.

I buried my head in the pillow. What kind of a person is this, I asked myself, who is so inconsiderate as to deliberately cause severe distress to a friend because he wanted to hear a record at nine o'clock in the morning? What a fucking prick.

I had a mind to get dressed and leave this asshole's life forever. I was astonished that someone who clearly valued my company could be so rude. It was like someone waking you up and slapping you. The record played on. Wayne was gazing at the liner notes on the album jacket. It was as if no conversation had taken place. He was oblivious to having disturbed me. I had the feeling I was in the company of a five-year-old. It was the first time I was pissed off by Wayne, and certainly not the last.

My friendship with Wayne continued in spite of it. We were indeed "chummy." It became embarrassing, but I didn't care. Set free from the ghastly grim world of my broken heart and ego, the tutelage of young Wayne had its advantages.

We played records and sang along to Jerry Butler, Smokey Robinson, the Beatles and the Byrds—anything with vocal harmonies. We tried our voices, matching or inventing notes. We had a good thing going, without self-consciousness and self-reproach. We played acoustic guitars and worked on our singing. I was having the time of my life. We sounded great to ourselves, always hitting the right notes, always in tune and in key. The character I was before 1966 seemed fictional, as was the character I was becoming. My life was playing out like an endless surfboard ride, with me struggling to stay up on top.

When Pat Burrows, the bass player, quit the MC5, I was expecting it. Almost like a script in a corny movie, Wayne told me Burrows had quit the band. I didn't care why. It was something I had wished for. He didn't look like a rock star. He was short, with a zit problem and a strange chip on his shoulder, and he had no artistic vision whatsoever, not to mention his very boring greaser hair cut.

None of these things were lost on Wayne, who echoed these same complaints to me all the time. The final straw, however, had to do with the kind of bass Pat was using. The fact that he played great bass lines that fit extremely well into the sound of the band carried hardly any weight at all. It was when he traded in his Hofner knock-off Echo violin bass for a new Fender Precision that Wayne and Pat got into a shouting match, resulting in the final "Fuck you," and that was that.

All of the band's gear, with the exception of the guitars and drums, was community property. An acquaintance from Lincoln Park by the name of Bruce had signed for a complete set of Vox amps—two Super Beatle 100-watt tube guitar amps and chrome stands, plus a 60-watt bass amp and cab called a T60—from a music store in exchange for being awarded the title of "manager." Bruce was a dumpy little fellow and most likely a social outcast in high school, but by supplying gear for Lincoln Park's version of the Rolling Stones, he got to be a member in good standing of the group. As far as him managing the band, nobody took it seriously.

Practice was in the basement of Wayne's mother's house. With Burrows quitting, there was a meeting to decide what to do. Wayne told the others that I was going to be the new bass player.

A tense scene ensued. Rob had tried to play bass before, but it didn't work out. As a five piece, this band was in its element. Neither Wayne nor Fred was going to step down to playing bass instead of guitar. Either they'd have to search their Lincoln Park talent pool for another guy, or go with the untested pseudo-art bum Mark Lindsey lookalike—me. Wayne had decided long before this meeting. Bob Gaspar, the drummer, was compliant. Tyner was affirmative.

Fred Smith was holding out. He felt railroaded into accepting me into the band. "You can't take it upon yourself to make these kinds of decisions, Wayne," he said.

Wayne stood a few feet in front of Fred with his matter-of-fact poker face firmly in place. "So, is he in, or is he out?"

"Well, uh…well, uh…well, uh…," Fred stammered. "Okay, he's in." The tension dissolved. I was getting to live the real life of my dreams, but it felt awkward.

I borrowed Tyner's La Playa bass guitar to rehearse the set until I could get my own bass. It was a little clumsy, very thick-necked and difficult to hit the notes right on. The T60 couldn't keep up with the scorching Super Beatles, but I could hear it.

Those were the days before my eardrums were destroyed by violent cymbal crashes a foot away from my head. It was loud in the tiny northwest Detroit basement room, but I was experiencing a sound that emanated from the windstorms of Jupiter.

Instantly, I went from street life shark to music pond minnow in a whirlpool of decibels, trying to keep my senses together in the giant whoosh of charging sound. By all accounts, the feeling that we produced as a group was good enough to keep going. No one questioned whether it would work. Each rehearsal sounded smoother and tighter than the one before. I was getting it, and the group sounded tough and powerful.

Fitting in as a band member was the toughest part. Smith was so sullen and remote that I really couldn't tell what he was thinking. He seemed more concerned about his image than anyone else, with his ever-condescending air and lack of verbal communication.

He was cagey, measuring his words and never being completely forthcoming about anything. He seemed comfortable with me, but it was hard to tell, because he rarely spoke. It would take a while to get to know Fred, something that would have to happen on his terms and timetable. I liked him, but I was never sure where I stood with him. He preferred to keep you off balance. That was always his game.

Tyner and Wayne talked. Theirs were the constant voices in the room. Bob, the drummer, was very opinionated, but there wasn't anything that made him stand out as a particularly interesting individual. He was a very normal, middle class suburban fellow who happened to know how to play the drums. He was actually a very good rock and roll drummer with a hard crisp beat that made the band sound aggressive. But while the rest of us wanted to explore the infinite possibilities of rock and roll as a form of musical expression, Bob was only in it to make 25 bucks a night.

Rob, Wayne, Fred and I wanted to do the outrageous. We wanted to shock and stun the audience with absurdity. We wanted to be artists on our own terms, without the shackles of conservative pop commercialism. We wanted to be ahead of the curve. Bob was more concerned about getting married, keeping a regular job, buying a house, having a family, and keeping his car and his drum kit polished. For Bob, art belonged in galleries, not in rock and roll. He just didn't see it the same way as the rest of us. He was truly an old school type of band player, very easy going and easy to get along with. I'm sure he thought of me as quirky, but it was okay with him.

I remember the first couple of shows we did together. We played on the floor of a VFW hall or gymnasium at a school where a radio DJ was hosting a teen dance. We played top 40 rock hits, Chuck Berry songs and Rolling Stones covers with girls looking at us quizzically, wondering if we were real or some kind of fake rock band: Fred mysterious as he could be, peeking out from under his bangs; Wayne wiggling his ass in front of embarrassed teenage girls; Rob looking like a space alien refugee with sweat running down his flushed cheeks; and me stood in the middle, gawking at the fretboard of my bass to see where my fingers were while trying to appear as cool and unconcerned as possible.

I believe it was my third show with the band. The reception was a mix of good-natured dancing and bewilderment. As we were about to conclude the performance, Fred started playing a monotone guitar riff we'd been jamming on in practice. It was a high-energy drone in the key of E. It was well known that Bob hated it with a passion. To Bob, it was not a song, not music, nothing but noise.

Fred played and played, though, and Bob sat at his drums with stubborn resolve, refusing to accompany him. Soon the rest of us joined Fred, droning away in this never-ending pulse, Rob shaking his maracas and stepping around at the front like a tribal shaman. Rob began to sing, "Let your love come down, baby, in the midnight hour. Let it come on down, down, down. Let it come on down, down, down."

All at once, with the angriest look he could muster, Bob cranked off a long single stroke roll into the song that sent shock waves through the room, and we were off! It was throttling. As we played, the pulse degenerated into chaos, and the song ended in an anti-climax. Bob was so disgusted at being forced to participate in the mayhem that after it was over, he packed up his kit and announced that he was quitting the band. We had pushed him too far. We knew we had, but we also knew that open-ended piece of musical cacophony was our ace in the hole, our secret weapon, our muscle and our identity. It was a song called "Black To Comm."

Wayne and I went shopping for a good bass for me. There was a small music store in the neighborhood by Wayne's house that had a couple of interesting things. I was considering a Rickenbacker, or a Gibson semi-hollow body, or a Fender. I did like those violin basses, the way they looked, but they didn't feel right, sounded awful, and they were too expensive. After all the comparing and sampling, I was staring at a white Fender Precision in a black hard shell case on the store counter.

It wasn't very trendy looking, but at least it wasn't sunburst like everyone else that had a Fender. It had a tortoise shell pick guard, and the longer I looked at it, the more I identified with it. This instrument would represent who I was as a player; it was me. I decided it was right. The Rickenbacker was too prissy for a down-and-dirty R&B band.

It was going to be a Fender P-bass, the kind of bass that got Burrows axed from the MC5. I didn't have the cash for it, so naturally I asked dad to bail me out once again. It was $265, not bad for a first purchase.

As time went on, I fell in love with the Olympic White Fender Precision. The finish seemed to change from being played and handled to a creamy pearl glowing at the corners. The feel of the curves and the smooth finish was like holding a beautiful woman, and the sound sometimes felt like a deep vibration that rumbled from the floor. It was a thing of beauty. I was happy.

We were now without a drummer. I knew a couple of drummers from former times, but they were jazz drummers, and we weren't a jazz band. I'd never known any rock and rollers. There was one character from Lincoln Park, however, who had once filled in for Gaspar on a gig. His name was Dennis Thompson.

The report was that he played hard and fast, but he was sometimes difficult. He had a fast car, a '65 Chevelle SS, and a nice set of Ludwigs. Wayne would try to get in contact with him to see if he was interested in joining the band. The responsibility of making calls always fell on Wayne by default and by choice. He was the only one who had access to a telephone, and he liked being the contact person of the band. Everyone else preferred to be left alone when it came to the tedious aspect of arranging work for the group. And that included our "manager."

My first impressions of Dennis were exactly as predicted. He was cranky and high strung, always in a foul mood, and he bitched about anything that rubbed him the wrong way. I don't recall him being happy much at any time.

He was concerned about his car, his gasoline expense, his drum kit, his time spent, and so on. What made him so irritable I don't know, except that he was the youngest in his family and had an older brother that played a Hammond B3 organ in a traditional bar band.

He played with lots of gusto, though, and had an intense look about him on stage. Not flashy or show-off, he simply took care of business. He also tended to speed up songs by muscling his way through. All in all, he fit well musically, but he wasn't on the same page as the rest of us social outcasts.

Even though we were doing 98% cover material, with only a couple of originals, it was clear we were going to be a different kind of band than what we had been before. The new emphasis was going to be on power and experimentation.

I believed the only way to be successful lay in being as original as possible; that with all the young stud bands popping up all over the world, a band needed to offer something that was completely fresh. And I believed we were on the threshold of a something that no one had ever seen or heard before. As long as we maintained our originality, we would get noticed.

It was 1966. Life was still being experienced in black and white, stuck in limbo between postwar and Pop art. Stereo was still a new technology. LPs were still being produced in mono. But after years of street rod projects by teenagers and car buffs, muscle cars were appearing in the showrooms of Detroit. Acid was the new drug, and the MC5 were at the doorstep of a breakthrough.

Everybody Must Get Stoned

As a group, the MC5 was fairly tightly knit. We were each other's best friends, but isn't that how it always is at that age? You hang out with your buddies until you find a permanent girl, and settle into something like a family.

Rob was leaning in that direction, but he was still one of the guys, even after he secretly married his girlfriend Becky. Perhaps he feared that the band didn't approve of his wish to marry his girlfriend, and I'm certain his new wife wasn't pleased by the thought of having us at the wedding. But it shouldn't have happened like that. We might have thought he was crazy, but if he wanted to get married, that was his business. We learned of the wedding when our fan club president slipped up and let the cat out of the bag.

At first, Wayne was mortified that we were being deceived. Getting married when you were trying to attain pop star fame was suicidal. Might this mean that Rob intended to leave the band? As expected, we were pissed. It would all blow over quickly, but it was a signal that Rob felt a separation from the rest of us. We chose to ignore it, but it left us feeling slighted and deceived. All in all, Rob's separate life created subtle tension until the day the band came crashing to a halt.

Dennis, our new drummer, also seemed to have another life, one having nothing to do with rock and roll bands and being a musician. In fact, I got the feeling that Dennis was very condescending toward the band in general. He wasn't committed; he wasn't gambling with his future. He liked us, maybe admired us, but he wasn't about to throw his life away trying screw every chick that stared at him at a gig. The band was a minor point in his plans.

But we were still a band, and we did a lot of things together. Like drinking a lot of beer, always the substance of choice among young guys, and even old guys when you come right down to it.

I've been an alcoholic for most of my life. Although I've never called it that or felt compelled to join Alcoholics Anonymous, ever since the time I sat in a parked car with my buddies at the age of 15 and dusted off a six of Pabst Blue Ribbon, the bluesy feeling of being half crocked has been a source of comfort for me.

It wasn't until recently, within the last five years, that I've learned to be sober. I've always found it an attractive way to defuse tension and create camaraderie. I've always been amenable to a drink. In the band, I felt aligned with others who shared my enjoyment of the drinking part of our group activity, and beyond that to bouts of prolonged consumption. I wasn't alone by any means, but it was always my choice to drink as much and as long as there was anything to drink. Do I want a drink? Just ask me, I'll drink with you.

However, marijuana smoking was becoming the vogue substance of the day, and I confess. It was I who turned the band onto drugs of all kinds. I had smoked some crazy hallucinogens; played with ingestible substances like morning glory seeds, pills like Dexedrine, Benzedrine, and barbiturates; injected substances like heroin and crystal methedrine. I had done them all, but nothing really to excess. My experiences were entirely recreational at this point. Oh yes, and there was the acid trip, which I tried again later with astounding results. Nothing was threatening, none of it had been damaging. It was all a little reckless fun, nothing more.

Wayne and I had some incredible weed to smoke. I knew a black guy who sold marijuana in tiny matchboxes. It was clean and it was mean. No sticks or stems, no seeds, just pure bud leaf, dark green, almost black. It was allegedly from Africa. The matchbox cost $10, and when used sparingly—which was normal because it was supremely potent—it lasted a good while. The dealer was a hip young black guy, very smart. He liked us right off the bat and dug that we were two white boys, musicians too, trying to get hip and bring class to the world of squares.

In '66, government propaganda against pot had made the authorities appear to be either liars or complete idiots. We weren't going to be part of the society of dupes. Our presence was going to reshape the stupid world that we grew up in. This created an unbreakable bond amongst people who smoked, one which eventually manifested itself as the '60s counterculture. The smoke was the agent that brought us together—that, and the music. We saw beyond the borders of the pop music medium, and we believed we could create a new dimension there as well.

Rob Tyner was already a smoker. No problem there. I also felt that Fred was eager to escape the drab normality of Lincoln Park as much as anyone, and that getting him to try a little pot would be pretty easy.

One time, Fred and I were driving around downtown in Detroit in my little red Renault R8. We had just smoked a joint of black African weed, the first time Fred and I smoked pot together. People were crossing the street in front of us at a traffic light. I can remember the two of us laughing so hard we couldn't stop. Everybody looked so ridiculous in their clothes, their expressions, and their manner that we just couldn't contain ourselves. It was like being in a capsule, and outside was a zoo of crazy robots. Our guts were aching from laughing so hard, but that experience made friends of Fred and me forever. It was an instant connection. We shared a view of the absurdity of our lives.

Even Dennis came around in the end. Sometime in the summer of 1966, we all gathered at Rob's downtown apartment on Canfield. We were outside in the early evening in front of the apartment building. Rob was strumming energetically on an autoharp, his current instrumental exploration, making it sound like a rhythm guitar, playing a chord progression that sounded semi-R&B.

It was the kind of thing MC5 liked to do, to explore any uncharted territory, looking for that unique thing that hadn't been done yet. Even Dennis was there, having driven himself in his '65 Chevelle down to the city to hang out with his bandmates.

We had been poking fun at him for some time to give pot a try, concerned that he'd never break out of his Lincoln Park suburban bondage. His reluctance was seen as naïve fright, fear of the unknown, ridiculous prejudice, brainwashing. After a while, we went up to the apartment. Rob produced a tray of marijuana and began sifting the seeds out of it. Once a joint was rolled and lit, it was passed to Dennis, who raised it to his lips and took a drag. Everyone cheered and slapped five to commemorate this event. Dennis was officially onboard.

I didn't encourage anyone to go overboard in any way. My new compadres were underage for *drinking*, for Christ's sake. It wasn't in my mind to corrupt them. I only wanted to bring my friends up to the point where I was. It was out of the question that we should try heroin or crystal methedrine. I wasn't looking for any of those kinds of things anyway. Music—learning bass and being a member of the MC5—was number one.

At this point, not much was happening at all for the band. The few gigs we got were spread out and amateurish by any standard. We were paid $200 or less as a rule. Sometimes it was only gas money, but we'd take anything we were offered because once we got on stage, it didn't matter—we were in our glory. The mere chance of performing and hearing our music, wearing our stage clothes, doing our thing was reward enough. If a girl smiled at you, you knew what you were doing was right and you were cool.

The sound of our music was electrifying. We were in training, practicing to become big stars. We worked on our set, trying to arrange the best possible flow. We wanted frenzy and pandemonium at the end. We studied the Stones and were trying to raise the crowd reaction to something approaching the hysteria our heroes inspired. In our minds, the audience was as anxious as we were to be transported to rock and roll heaven. We just had to show them the way.

We played for each other, proving that we had what it took to get over the top. Often, audiences appeared bewildered by the volume, holding their hands over their ears and wincing. Other times, pairs of girls would dance oblivious to anyone else. Every gig, every tune, every note validated the whole trip. The money didn't matter.

The drugs didn't matter. It was all about being in the band, being on the stage, being ourselves: the MC5.

The character of the band was becoming more distinctive. We stopped wearing band uniforms, since it was restricting to have to dress alike. We all had a different idea of how we wanted to look as individuals. Band suits were out of touch with the times. The Beatles' had been the apex. Trying to keep up with that was ridiculous.

Hair was a different matter. Rob had the biggest problem: his was hair that defied all the fashions of the day. Naturally kinky or wiry, his girlfriend Becky took an iron to it as Rob laid his head on an ironing board. When that didn't work, she rolled giant curlers into it to form a perfect bowl. Looking a bit unreal but authentic, Rob would mount the stage with a terrific quasi-Beatle hairdo that lasted until he started sweating, and then it all fell down.

Wayne was trying to manage his pompadour into a cute little puff by pushing his fingers into it and making it fall naturally over the top. I kept pushing mine around, up and down, using hairspray or rollers to get that McCartney look.

Fred's hair was a different story. He had it perfectly shaped, with his bangs hanging over his eyes and sculpted down along his cheeks over his ears. He had the perfect look, and for that, we were thankful. And, oh yes, Dennis the Beach Boy looked out of place completely in his All-American haircut with the front combed down onto his forehead.

I thought we should go up to Ann Arbor and try to find contacts to do fraternity gigs, parties, and anything else we could get to increase our audience. We met Pete Andrews, who was booking dates for bands at frat house parties. He booked us to play the Michigan Union. It was a large hall with a very typical college campus atmosphere, lots of wood paneling, a high ceiling, and hardwood floors—kind of a grand hall atmosphere.

We were scheduled to play two sets. After the first set, we took our break by going to the parking lot to sit in the car and have a beer. There, for the fist time ever, we smoked a joint as a band before playing.

My memory of that second set is that it was totally dreamlike and euphoric. The sound, the music, the feel of the room and the audience, it was almost delirious. The crowd danced in total frenzy. The music soared. We were playing "Gloria," "I Can't Explain," "We Gotta Get Out of This Place," "You Really Got Me." It was charged with energy, musical paradise for sure. We were stoned, and it was slightly astonishing. I think from there, even though we didn't always have pot, we figured getting loaded before a show was a good thing.

Smoking weed back then wasn't like it became later on. We rolled very stingy joints, possibly a quarter the size of a regular cigarette. You just didn't need that much to get a good high going. The pot was really good and clean. We strained all the seeds and twigs out of it before we made the joint. It was a class affair, very cool and focused. Getting high was a ritual of respect. It wasn't about getting fucked up, it was about being intensely involved, to give yourself the advantage of feeling relief from your moods and conventional ways of doing things. Government propaganda and crusading vigilantes created an utterly false impression of "reefer madness" in the minds of ignorant people who had never seen marijuana, let alone tried it. But to us, pot was an embellishment to any activity, hardly a druggy downfall.

The MC5 probably didn't need any weed. Fred's guitar sounded like a beam of electric current coming out of his amp. He was playing a Gretsch Tennessean in those days. Fred got a sound from it that was ultra real. It burned.

Wayne was using a Les Paul and it pierced through anything. Wayne would string all those notes together and make it sound like electric rain from the sky.

Rob was blowing the harmonica like a bluesman with ever-increasing power, and his performance was always bursting with enthusiasm. Even as the instruments and amplifiers changed, each guy still produced same characteristic sound as they had from the beginning. We loved our sound. It was something we prided ourselves on. Every band had a sound that was their own, and ours was more progressive than anyone else had the nerve to try.

We were mixing beer drinking and drug taking on a regular basis, and as it was a time when new substances were appearing out of the blue, we might take whatever was available just to see what would happen. Weird chemicals were floating around, substances like DMT and DET, things that gave you an intense, mind-altering several moments, and left you disoriented for a good long while. They were yellow powders that melted when burnt and smoked, creating cartoon pictures in your head for several minutes.

I can remember sitting around a kitchen table in the apartment formerly occupied by Rob and his wife, where we now all hung out to have a place to stay. Wayne and Fred and I were doing a non-stop psychedelic binge of DET. And, after hours of blasting ourselves silly with this incredible substance, Fred remarked that, for all our trying, we weren't the least bit "high."

In typical Fred Smith fashion, his statement summed up the folly of getting high. After all the smoke cleared and we stared into each other's eyes, we were nothing more or less than what we were when we started. It was all a ruse, a hustle, a con game that we had accepted, taking it for granted that it was what someone had told us it was. Fred had a remarkable talent for gleaning the true nature of things. He could look at you with those steely blue eyes and you would see he was waiting for you to see what he saw. In 1966, Fred was way ahead of the drug culture.

Rob and I had our own weird experience one night, when I suggested we take acid together just for the heck of it.

It happened innocently enough. I was giving the him a ride back downtown to the house where he and his wife were living, which also happened to be the house I had once occupied with Sam. I knew where I could lay my hands on some acid, and I proposed that we do a couple hits. There was no one at the house when we got there, so I rolled a joint for us to get started on, and Rob and I each swallowed a hit of acid.

I put a couple of records on the turntable to set the mood. I recall the record I chose was Japanese koto music. Its strange notations and moody slashes were too much for Rob. He started smoking cigarettes furiously and acting agitated. I changed the record, but when I put on Ravi Shankar's sitar, Rob got worse. All at once, Rob's wife burst through the front door with a bounding dog in tow. Now Rob was on a "bummer."

The rest of the night is a blurry memory of strange guilt and isolation. I was aware of Rob becoming extremely lucid. He laughed and cried, and after several hours of delirious babbling, he began to expound upon what had just happened to him and his view of existence. I guess he thought dropping acid was going to be closer to having a beer than going through an emotional breakdown in the fifth dimension. I was guilty of taking for granted that someone else would have the same experience I had under the same conditions, ignoring the fact that our relationship wasn't on the solidest ground. The shame of it was that we never found a way to address those things. We remained alienated for the rest of our time together.

LSD changed a lot of people's lives back then, including Rob's and mine. What did I learn from my LSD experience? My first trip showed me that life was much more fundamental than I had been brought up to believe, that we humans are much more in tune with animal behavior than I'd ever thought. Strictly speaking, the root of survival was adapting to any condition that faced me.

All of the social processes and behavioral etiquettes installed by modern society were a form of mass brainwashing dictated by previous generations. For me, being enlightened to the greater possibilities of life was the most refreshing experience I'd ever had. I was enthralled to see beyond the borders of my upbringing. The visions I had under the effects of LSD were glorious apparitions, with stupendous electrified trails of glittering images. I was released from a prison of mundane expectations and thrown into a swirling galaxy of unexplored truths. I felt comfort and alignment in my new and wider, wilder universe. I felt relevance in the universe that made infinitely more sense than the stereotypical conditioning of modern America. I was no greater or lesser entity than any other in all creation.

Rob's experience was largely the same, but with the huge difference that he was torn apart by his realizations, slammed to the mat, and forced to wrestle with his free-fall into a strange new void.

Rob closed himself off in his bedroom with his wife for many hours. The exertion of traveling through his layers of predetermined mental state must have seemed like torture to him. There in his tiny room, he slogged through all of his uncertainties with intermittent emotional climaxes, and finally at some point later that night, allowed me to enter and listen as he described the structure of life, as he now understood it.

Rob acted as if he'd been put through an inquisition. He emerged victorious, with a complete analysis of the human experience. The new Rob Tyner was a specimen of raw courage and survival. What disturbed me was how detached he was from me as a companion in the experience. It seemed like he had endured the whole experience completely on his own. I felt like I hadn't even been there, taken a hit of acid myself, and watched as he throttled out of control like a balloon sent flying from a child's hand.

His distance from me was profound. I wasn't sure what I had done that warranted being shut out. I felt as though he regarded me as an evil entity.

The one thing I had hoped for was that Rob and I would become closer, that we would share the highs of the acid trip, and start feeling a creative bond. The result was the total opposite. After that night, Rob and I hardly spoke. Our relationship was strictly superficial and distant.

I don't know what I might have said or done that pushed him over the edge. Maybe I said something that was intimidating or uncomfortable for him. But I decided that he and I just weren't cut from the same cloth. Some people are easy to be with, because you see things from a similar point of view. And then there are those people who feel completely foreign. I can only surmise that was how it was between Rob and me. No matter what it was, I felt distrusted and it hurt; it was a colossal disappointment.

I should have known that our little project was out of joint.

But I had a lot invested in my new career, and I wasn't ready to abandon it because Rob and I were on different wavelengths. At the same time, with him committed to being an alien in my world, it was like choosing sides in an ongoing drama. Who should I be buddies with—the strange, quiet, aloof and mysterious Fred Smith, or Wayne, the mouth that would not stop? I felt that our unity as a group was what defined us, and I wanted to foster that.

I had to get my bass playing up to a higher level, and the music was enough to keep me in the fray. It was that very day, that very practice, that we wrote the song "I Just Don't Know." I threw that bass line in there like a spontaneous reaction to hearing the one-chord Bo Diddley riff that Wayne started the song with. It was up and running, a real solid electrified rhythm barreling and charging forward. There it was, the first MC5 original after "Black To Comm," the interminable guitar stampede that forced Bob Gasper to quit the band. I was an exhausted wreck from not sleeping the night before, and whacked out by the experience of taking acid. I'm sure Rob was feeling a little cranked also. But we still created something great.

If anything gave us an advantage, it was the style of music that we played. Wayne and Fred had learned how to play their guitars by way of Chuck Berry and the traditional guitar standards associated with Chet Atkins, Carl Perkins, Freddy King, Albert Collins, and a wide assortment of blues, rhythm and blues, honky-tonk, and instrumental guitar styles.

None of the other bands around were as well versed in hardcore guitar instrumentals as we were. We could blast off with a version of "Rebel Rouser," slam into "Ramrod," and finish it off with "Pipeline," which we did once for an encore at the Grande Ballroom, sending the audience into pandemonium.

Because we were old enough to be aware of the beginnings of rock music, yet young enough to ride the wave of the British mods, we covered a lot of ground that others could only talk about. We knew what was happening on the West Coast with all the surf instrumental bands—the Ventures and various others—not to mention the rockabilly artists that shaped the entire culture of rock and roll, and the R&B and soul artists with their own brand of pop music. None of the other bands on our circuit had that kind of range.

At the head of the list, though, was Chuck. His brand of guitar playing was perfect for our attack. Of course, the Rolling Stones were also into Berry, and we appreciated them immensely for that.

As for the Stones, they kind of epitomized everything we were trying to achieve, so we patterned our style and sound on theirs. But they weren't the only groups we looked to for inspiration and cool ideas. We dug the Animals, the Yardbirds, the Who, and the Kinks as well. If a band made a great driving groove, we recognized it and gave it a place in our set. Basically, a blues or R&B based tune was what caught our attention. We were very discriminating. While other bands were lulling people to sleep with melody and pretty harmony, we were kicking their asses with punch-you-out rock and roll. At least, that's what we thought.

Amid all this consensus of musical preference, I had radically different tastes. I loved vocal harmony and tended to like things that were unappreciated by the group. We were performing a couple of Beatles tunes that seemed a little out of sync for our shtick. My particular song in the set was "Things We Said Today," which I sang. It's a typical Paul McCartney love song with a tender lyric. We were also doing "This Boy," a Beatles song that I'm sure Rob felt self-conscious singing, as it was dropped after not too long. The propaganda was that I was a great singer, so any time a singing challenge appeared, it was me that was called upon to step up.

When I first joined the group, I didn't hesitate to tell Wayne in particular what quirky things I liked. Things like the Bee Gees, the Byrds, and the Left Banke were among my favorites, and we sang along with the records when we were stoned. I was always looking for that opportunity to throw in a vocal harmony to show off my ability to conceive of a different sound. Mostly, simple harmony on rock records was a two-part affair, a first and a fifth tone. I would look for the third or sometimes a fourth harmony that made the thing sound big like the Four Freshmen, much like Brian Wilson did with his Beach Boys arrangements. It just wasn't a feature that suited the MC5.

After a while, I started feeling I'd better not reveal some of my more questionable tendencies for fear of ridicule. For instance, as a teenager I liked a lot of records that were about being a broken-hearted lover, and songs that were about being sad and crying. I guess it's in my nature to feel insecure.

I loved vocal groups from the '50s. I listened to those songs about lost love over and over, falling hard for the sounds of the harmonies. I suppose that's what I was afraid of revealing to the group, but I don't know why I should have had doubts. Much later, I became a huge Beach Boys fan. I always had the feeling that my weird tendencies were what kept the group on the edge of greatness, that without my out-of-sync input, the MC5 was nothing more than a puffed up bar band. It was a megalomaniacal stance, I know. I was setting myself up for a flawed relationship, but that was getting to be a habit with me.

The MC5 was certainly an odd mixture. There was something

so very unified about us, and on the other hand, with Rob creating a big space between himself and the rest of us, and me being isolated by my tastes in music, a five-year age gap, and a different background from everyone else, the balance was always in doubt.

Dennis was trying hard to fit in, while Fred and Wayne jousted and juggled their way along. All in all, it seemed to be working, and that was always evident when we practiced. The sound of the band leveled anything that might have been detrimental.

The big thing we had going for us back in those days was the will to do things in a new, different and progressive way. When the time came for invention, we all had the urgency to try something never done before, by us or anyone else. When Kramer started the intro to "I Just Don't Know," those first chords were a complete surprise. Every time we played something, it was a chance to invent a new riff, a never-before-heard sound. It was experimentation. If it was a dud, it didn't matter, since it was an experiment to begin with. Of course, it was always better than doing the same old thing.

I wrote a song for the band, but never got around to showing it to anybody. I felt too awkward about my music and lyrics to ever try it out. The music was done on the old player piano in my parents' basement.

I had taught myself how to make three-finger chords, and would spend hours working out the chord progressions of every song I liked. So my playing was minimal and pretty ragged, but I had a lot of fun trying to work everything out.

The song was supposed to sound Beatlesque, but the words were embarrassing enough to make me want to hide it away. They went something like this:

"Night of loneliness, you caught me by surprise, you made me realize, I could be singing and thinking and doing so much better, than I did before. Treasure of nonsense pleasure here to be found, things could be so much better, pass it around....Ah girl, it's so good to have you near me. It's hard to be happy, where people are angry, in bottles of boredom, and life's disappointments surround you....and I think I'll stay for a while."

The music was a cross between the Beatles and the New Christy Minstrels, not even close to MC5 swaggering. I played it to myself and wondered if I could play this for my new buddies. Self-doubt took hold immediately. This was shit, what was I thinking? They would've been wondering what I was doing in their band. What a pretender. So I decided to forget it. That was probably the only time I ventured to write a song for the band. It was enough to scare me out of songwriting forever.

It was a period of discovery for everybody. Just getting to know people was a challenge enough. Add the drug scene, and it got a lot weirder. Things from my high school and college life were distant, and barely memories any longer. I was absorbed with the undertaking of becoming a musician, a rock star, a member of a small band of guerrillas seeking wealth and fame.

And we weren't doing it alone. Astonishingly, the entire nation, indeed the world, was taking a left turn from the ordinary. The road was brand new and beckoned to young eyes to follow wherever it wanted to lead. I was freely letting go of all past associations. It was the brilliant star of revolt, the turning toward an open sea, and a voyage into a promising uncharted life. Rob, Fred, Wayne, Dennis, and Michael, the crew that would make believers of the entire world. Stay alive with the MC5.

5

I Can Only Give You Everything

That first year I was in the MC5, we rambled around the Detroit area looking for bookings, girls, drugs, and general amusements that would keep our spirits up and bring us closer to a reality of being who we wanted to be. For me, that meant a juggling act between having Wayne or Fred as my number one pal. After a few drinking binges, however, Fred became my closest confidant. As Fred probed deeper into the mystique of Michael Davis, we developed a mutual admiration that endured over the next several years.

Our first bouts of drinking took place in an area known as Rosedale Park, an affluent section of colonial homes on streets lined with overhanging oaks, creating an arch. We would sit in the car, swigging our beer, while Fred soaked up the atmosphere of wealth in the surrounding picturesque neighborhood.

To him, Rosedale Park represented the ultimate escape from poverty and the doldrums of the working class. It was a surrealistic garden in the middle of a squalid city. We sat parked in the darkness, discussing the future of the band and our strategies for attaining a place such as this. He believed he had the savvy to make it big, and he thought I would be a good partner in this endeavor.

After a time, we got ourselves an apartment in the inner city, close to Tiger Stadium, a short distance from the Wayne State campus. When we weren't walking around where other "street people" hung out, we went to Detroit Tiger baseball games. The price of admission to the upper deck bleachers was one dollar. You could bring your own beer into the park, as long as it was in a plastic container. A one-gallon milk jug did the trick, holding exactly ten 12-ounce beers, an amount guaranteed to get you drunk, but well within our capacity in those days. Those upper-deck bleachers were filled with pot smokers, and, as is the custom, joints were passed around indiscriminately. Times like those will surely never be seen again.

Perhaps Fred and I were at our closest in those moments, although throughout those days, Fred and I had many a wacky adventure. One late Friday evening, we decided to drive to Chicago to visit Chess Records. We loaded up on beer and cigarettes, filled the tank of my Renault, and drove the 400-odd miles on I-94 to Chicago for the sole purpose of looking in the window of the locked-up storefront at 2120 South Michigan Avenue, immortalized by the Rolling Stones in the title of an instrumental on *12 x 5*.

After staying up all night, we hit the music stores to try out all their gear. Several minutes would pass while the sales clerks listened to Fred rip guitar licks they'd never heard, before someone would ask that we buy something or move along.

Another night, Fred and I, along with Peter Prim of the Underdogs, dropped acid and broke into the Belle Isle Zoo, where we released all the animals from their exhibits. Luckily for us, the Belle Isle Zoo is a children's zoo, so there weren't lions and elephants stampeding around. At dawn, we sat tripping at the edge of the Detroit River as the sun rose and Great Lakes freighters cruised up the river. It was a glorious sight, like a cartoon dream.

Fred and I liked to sit up most nights and hash out our plans for the future. Our idea of success was having two refrigerators: one stocked with Coke, the other stocked with Stroh's Beer. We discussed all the various guitars we would buy when we became successful, as well as cars, and where we would live: Rosedale Park, Grosse Pointe, Polynesia. Ours was a typical rock and roll dream world, except that we knew we had what it took to make it. It was only a matter of time.

Wayne was a big fan of the movies *The T.A.M.I. Show* and *The Big T.N.T. Show* that came out in 1965, particularly the former, which featured James Brown and the Famous Flames, Marvin Gaye, Smokey Robinson and the Miracles, and the Supremes, as well as our heroes the Rolling Stones.

Wayne wanted to be black more than he wanted to be white, and he worked hard at learning how to imitate the stage moves he saw the black performers doing. Fred didn't want to be either black or white. His style was unique, something you just couldn't place. He gravitated toward all things hillbilly, but it was never obvious in anything he did. When Fred started wearing a superhero costume onstage in 1969, it was his own vision of himself—the real "Sonic" Smith.

After months of lurching around the streets of the inner city, we got an invitation to play a party at the Artist's Workshop, which being thrown to welcome John Sinclair back from a stint in jail.

It came about through a friend of Rob's wife, a Wayne State student with connections to the Workshop. We were anxious to make inroads into the art community because we perceived that they were on the same wavelength as we were. We were certain that our raucous mixture of rock and roll, R&B and British pop would provide a unifying vibe, and indeed, we were a hit with the art crowd, who loved to drink and party in their own arty way.

The party was still roaring when the power was abruptly cut by John's wife, Leni Sinclair, who objected to the volume and to rock and roll, in general. The fact that we weren't playing jazz, the music of the Beat generation, was unacceptable to her. We were stunned to say the least, but packed our gear and flipped our hostess the bird on the way out.

Meanwhile, competition was spreading out across the city. Bob Seger, an East Sider, was having success on local radio and building a small but mighty reputation. We respected him. He had a strong voice and his band, the Last Heard, played hard.

Mitch Ryder had a national hit record and another great band, the Detroit Wheels. We'd had a run in with Mitch's brother, Mark, who was trying to promote himself as "Mark Ryder and The Motor City Five." It was a cheap gimmick, considering their family's last name wasn't Ryder to begin with, and Mark disappeared after a short while.

Wayne and I had seen Ted Nugent, guitarist for the Amboy Dukes, at a party on the West Side where he was jumping off of furniture, playing air guitar like a space cadet. We thought he was a poser, but his band was a lot more in tune with the psychedelic radio sound than we ever were. Those were the local heavies; anyone else, we considered inferior. Even on the national scene, there wasn't anyone we stood in awe of. American bands of the time were a struggling bunch of puffers. No one had the sound. And people were beginning to notice.

Sometime in the late summer or early autumn of 1966, our rehearsal space was visited by a local entrepreneur who was looking for a hip rock band to be the house band at a new venue he was opening. He'd been impressed by the explosion of ballroom-style theaters in California, and had access to a suitable venue.

Russ Gibb, schoolteacher and wannabe hipster, came into our lives with the perfect script for the MC5. He liked what he saw and heard, and it didn't take long before he pulled it together. We thought of him as a kook and a slightly perverse eccentric, but what difference did that make? We opened the Grande Ballroom to a meandering crowd of curious stragglers, mixed with several already "experienced" hippies, and pumped out our Who, Yardbirds, James Brown, and Rolling Stones covers with a dash of psychedelic spice thrown in.

The Grande hit the ground running, and for the next few years, it was the epicenter of Detroit rock. For the next several months, we shared the bill with an assortment of bands from around the area. While some of them had small followings, none of them displayed any spark or power. Some of them could even play, but they lacked energy, originality, and a compelling aura. Some of them merely had a weird character as a front man. Some of them plodded through covers. All of them, though, were blessed with a love of rock and roll. Regardless of the state of their art, it was a fun time and everyone loved what was happening.

Rob was back out in the suburbs, in a place called Palmer

Park. He'd found a house to rent, and wanted to base his operations outside the city. Wayne had acquired a girlfriend, who was now living with him in Rob's old apartment on Canfield. We called her "Little Chick." Fred and I were camping at the apartment most of the time, with a few stray girls coming by to hang out and get high. Dennis was living at home at his parents' house in Lincoln Park. The gigs were getting a bit better, with us getting to play some of the more popular teen clubs in the area, as well as the Grande. We felt like we were becoming a part of the Detroit scene, leaving the more remote suburban band scene behind.

Three straights in overcoats, with eyes to invest in the rock music scene, came to see us rehearse at the Grande: Arnie Geller (a.k.a. "AMG" for Arnold Mark Geller), Cliff Goroff, and Larry Benjamin. They thought we had "potential," and gave us a little money to make a record. I don't know why they picked us, because they didn't have any music business experience, nor did they frequent places like the Grande. I think they simply wanted to try to cash in on the band phenomenon. We decided to record our version of Them's "I Can Only Give You Everything," backed with our original, "One of the Guys," a protest song Rob had written around Chuck Berry's "Talkin' 'Bout You."

When had a marvelous time. This was the real deal, being in a recording studio; we were kids in a candy store. The spontaneous harmonies Wayne and I put on "One of the Guys" had us shaking hands and whooping out loud. Fred's rhythm guitar track was particularly astonishing. After the records were pressed, we kept our ears glued to the local radio stations, hoping to hear our single getting played by the local DJs. But that was not to be.

We had a cool band, and now had a record out, but we were

flat broke and getting antsy. Our morale was holding up, but our resources were pitiful. I had the Renault, a gift from my dad, and Rob had a car, a 1960 Chevy Biscayne that he and Fred had once backed into into the window of a music store in Lincoln Park late one night in an aborted attempt to steal a couple of guitars.

After Fred and I left the attic apartment, I lived in a house on Alexandrine Street for a while. Wayne and Little Chick lived downstairs in the front apartment. It had sliding wooden doors at the entrance and had probably been a parlor back in the days when a wealthy Victorian family occupied the house. Wayne and I would sing along with the Bee Gees, and Fred would come by occasionally to sit around and smoke. The old lady who rented out the place had her own apartment across the hall. She liked us, but we drove her slightly crazy with our late hours and noise.

After a while, I acquired a girlfriend who wanted to be known as a witch. She was just another crazy chick that infiltrated my head and wore me out in the bedroom. We lived in an attic apartment that sported gables with windows. I played lots of records: the 13th Floor Elevators, *Between the Buttons,* Donovan, the Who. I made a few drawings in Conte crayon and spent a lot of time sitting in bed, staring out the window. I wondered how it was that sitting and looking out that window was all I really wanted to do. Of course, I was stoned, but it seemed disturbing that I had so little ambition.

I also took up shooting speed. In the next apartment, a crazy guy named Richard carried on doing speed all night and hammering two by fours together. I went to hang out with him and in a short while, I was just as jacked as he was. I built a little rig to give myself injections of crystal meth. This turned out to be nearly a disaster, because after a couple of weeks of being awake without eating, I had to play a TV gig with the band in Lansing.

We left for Lansing in a single car. Without knowing what was going on with me, Rob and Dennis and Fred were quiet and cautious. Wayne had an idea that I wasn't right, but he kept his suspicions to himself. I was trying to be as inconspicuous as possible, but my lips were cracked and bleeding from dehydration. I couldn't look at anybody and I couldn't talk. In the dressing room before the on-camera lip-sync of our record, I applied as much makeup as I could to cover the crack lines in my lips. I wore shades on camera. Afterwards, I asked the guys to take me to my parents' house. I needed to get some sleep.

After two days at Mom and Dad's, I gained enough strength and composure back to make it downtown. What my bandmates thought about me, I don't know. They never said anything, and I probably tried to sound proud of my daring. But I wasn't. I wasn't proud of anything. I felt embarrassed, ashamed, and relieved that I'd managed to slip away without being exposed. I'd let everybody down with my foolhardy drug binge, acting without regard for our career as a band. The incident passed, but inside I felt a little further removed from everybody.

We were about to embark for Detroit's answer to San Francisco's "Be-in"—the "Love-In" on Belle Isle in the Detroit River. The afternoon saw a crowd of curious suburban young people trying to get a taste of the "Flower Power" craze that was sweeping the nation. There were a few genuine hippies, but for the most part, it was a gathering of novices. We started to play our amplified rock music in a small gazebo converted into a bandstand. Near the end of our set, a skirmish erupted off to the side that quickly grew into a full-scale police altercation, complete with truncheon-wielding cavalry detachment and mass panic.

We packed our gear as fast as we could and made for the bridge to the safety of the city. Driving over the Belle Isle Bridge felt good. We got out of there without a scratch. The chain reaction of violence was alarming, and I wanted no part of it. At the same time, however, we wondered if we were responsible for it; if the song, "Black To Comm," had the power to start a riot. Later, though, we learned that a biker had been unruly, and when the police tried to subdue him, they went beyond what was necessary and incited the crowd to protest. In the resulting confrontation, the police were all too eager to enforce "order." It was our introduction to the political side of show business.

Around this time, John Sinclair proposed that he could help lift us out of obscurity by serving as our manager. By moving his people out of the Artist Workshop house—an abandoned dentist's office with a downstairs storefront on the street—the band would have a single place for everyone to reside, and a practice space as well. Situated on a corner facing the freeway, it was out of earshot of neighbors. Sinclair's group, Trans Love Energies—really just a few artists and his wife—would rent another space several blocks away and become the business arm of the MC5, which would be the group's source of revenue.

Without much debate, we flung ourselves into Sinclair's arms like the crew of a sinking ship, clinging to its only means of survival. Wayne led the charge. "It'll be great, man. Everyone will have their own room. We'll have a practice space. John has a van and people to load our equipment." Wayne became John's chief instigator and provocateur. We were instantly transformed from the MC5 into the MC 25.

We sat in John's Trans Love apartment/offices, listening to John Coltrane and a dozen other jazz saxophonists that were creating their own brand of new wave free jazz. We smoked a lot of pot. Yes, we'd been smoking pot before, but this was different. This was religion, and John was taking on guru-like status, becoming our mentor and teacher.

I felt uncomfortable in this atmosphere. I sensed that we were losing our identity as rock and roll hooligans. It was as if we were about to become missionaries. But I couldn't deny any of it, nor would I have wanted to.

For Dennis, the move represented a significant awakening. It wouldn't be long before he'd stop wearing underwear, forget to shave or bathe, and grow enough hair to be mistaken for a derelict. We were no longer five individuals, making up an imprecise singular entity. We were now a community with a strategic socio-politico agenda, a strike force in the name of "the underground."

We immediately benefited from John's organizational ability. We got an old Chevy van, painted our logo on the side of it, recruited a few more people who wanted to be part of the rock and roll milieu, and settled into our new roles as a mobile guerrilla outfit. The transition was smooth. We felt safe and secure. It was only later that we realized how much we gave up to attain that security.

Our rooms at the dentist's office were manifestations of our psychedelic visions. We started taking our experiments further. We played in the dark after smoking weird substances, with the little red lights on the amplifiers glowing in the darkness, the sounds combining to create stupefying, cacophonous epics. In Dennis' room one evening, we wrote lyrics by selecting random phrases from a book. It made sense in our stoned, free-associative mode. Pat Burrows, the bass player I'd replaced, came over one night. He was on a furlough from the Marine Corps. He tried to strangle the cat.

We played at the ballroom often. Our friends told us we were the only real thing happening anywhere. Our show was usually enhanced by strobes and various lighting effects, the aroma of hash in the air, sparkling reflections from a big disco ball, a swirling mass of gels projected on the walls of the ballroom, incense, everyone smoking cigarettes or weed.

No one in the place was completely straight. It was the place to be, and it was the place to be stoned. Our material was taking on epic proportions. We never played a song the same way twice, and most of them normally ran seven or ten minutes. It was a natural progression for us, from bashing out three-minute cover songs to pummeling a riff until it begged for mercy. It was a guitar player's paradise.

The years 1965-1969 were an astonishing time in the world of pop music. For one thing, rock and folk music meshed into a form of popular culture that discarded the past and sought to expand itself as the voice of the generation. The Beatles, the Stones, the Yardbirds, Them, the Who, and the Kinks, to name a few, inspired an entire generation. Every single day was an opportunity to express oneself and spread the word that the old was dead and the new was alive. Our hair, dress, language, personal habits and relationships all contributed to the vast and growing culture of the youth movement. Music was the central feature of the culture, followed closely by drugs and sex.

We listened to the radio all the time in the car. After all, besides the record store, that's where you were bound to hear all the latest sounds from your favorite bands.

The first time we heard "Jumpin' Jack Flash" on the radio, it was like opening a new page in the book of our lives. The song was astounding; it made the air feel like it was charged with energy.

When a new Beatle song would come over the radio, and we'd listen raptly, taking in every note and word. It was a transformation that propelled you into your own personal world of discovery.

I bought records too. After the Who's "My Generation" came *Happy Jack* and finally *The Who Sell Out,* a series of daring thrusts into the frontiers of music. Words can scarcely describe how uplifting those discoveries were for my reinvented self.

In the Midwest, isolated from the coasts with their trends, fashions, and cults, we held a provincial viewpoint that in our minds made our version of the underground a true grass roots experience. We were isolated. We were somewhere else. We were more real, more attuned, feistier, and certainly more hardcore than our coastal contemporaries.

The first time I ever heard the term "hardcore," we were referring to the MC5's most rabid fans. We viewed ourselves as innovators. We had a certain arrogance that we needed to curtail. It wasn't easy. We turned a lot of people off.

We played through the tumultuous summer of 1967, marked by riots in many cities around the country, including Detroit, but once it was over, John Sinclair decided that we should all move to Ann Arbor.

His logic was sound. Detroit was no longer safe. Rob's wife and Fred's girlfriend had been raped along the side of the freeway. All of our guitars had been stolen from our practice room. The Detroit police were constantly harassing us by any means they could think of. We were no longer an anonymous feature in the neighborhood. We had the Detroit Gestapo's undivided attention.

Ann Arbor was a mere 35 miles from Detroit, making the commute to the Grande an easy one, and the friendly environs of the little college town were a welcome change from the cold concrete of Detroit's downtown seediness. Within a month, we'd rented two old-fashioned Victorian houses on a quiet street in the heart of Fraternity Row, and loaded all our worldly possessions for the big migration. I pictured Ann Arbor as a model-railroad town, with little cottages and train trestles bridging a river, and lots of trees. Detroit's mean streets seemed far away.

I chose the room off of the kitchen. It was isolated from the rest of the house, and had a screened-in porch with a private entrance. It was perfect. Even then, I thought of myself as a separate entity from the rest of the band.

Wayne, Fred, Dennis, and Rob occupied the second-story bedrooms with their girls, or in Dennis' case, by himself. John and Leni took one of the first floor bedrooms, Robin Summers and his wife the other. Another couple, Pun and Genie Plamondon, had a bedroom in the basement.

Other people occupied the house next door; the band the Up, John's brother Dave and his wife, and various roadies and girls who performed tasks of all kinds. We rented the houses for $600 apiece. Since John collected any money the band made, it was out of our hands. We were now part of a conglomerate commune, self-contained and stoned.

6

Getting Down

No matter how it appears, at the heart of the creative mechanics of any band are the interpersonal relationships between its members. Even in situations where a single person's energy seems to be the main driving force, what guides and shapes the resulting entity is the interaction of its parts.

In the MC5's case, my relationship with Rob Tyner was so strained that it interfered with our entire creative process. The discomfort I felt caused me to restrict my conversational and creative contributions to the band. If I had anything to say, Rob was quick to step in front, cutting me off in the process. For me, it felt intentional. Maybe he was repaying me in kind. I was terribly delusional back then. Meanwhile, Rob was trying hard to inject his ideas, as it was his duty to write lyrics and be the band's most prominent member, a point that was always contested by Kramer.

Wayne had always fancied himself as the leader of the band, based on his guitar playing ability and his enthusiasm for handling business affairs. But in truth, Wayne spent seven years fighting to maintain his self-image and defend his hill. The real tyrant in the band was Fred Smith. Fred had an uncanny ability to make everyone feel like amateurs. He would listen to what Wayne and Rob suggested, then with a disdainful grimace, shake his head and mutter the word, "No."

Dennis hovered in suspense, pitching his contributions as soon as he sensed the direction the group was heading in. Meanwhile, I waited for a clear point to make, almost never finding a space where I fit in. Ultimately, Fred's stubbornness and reserve, his domineering personal aura, his unflinching deadpan, swayed everyone in the room. He had the upper hand on everyone.

The times the MC5 achieved brilliance, the stuff of legend, occurred in live performance. There, when the cacophony of the sound overcame the tensions between us, total participation produced an outcome of unsurpassed expression. I always had confidence in our chemistry as a group. Regardless of the offstage interpersonal jousting, we were able to put aside our differences and collaborate to create an absorbing picture, greater than anything I had ever seen.

Living at 1510 Hill Street in Ann Arbor was a little like being in the 6th grade, or being at summer camp with a lecherous cabin master. This new balancing act, being a part of a communal family and maintaining our integrity as a rock and roll band, looked good on the surface, but underneath, it was unsatisfying.

We paid the bills, we shared our stories, we treated each other with respect, we had many laughs and warm moments, we toasted and shared dope, and we kept a reasonably neat household. All the roadies and other commune members who contributed their energy and in some cases, personal wealth gave things an air of importance—as in the case of Ron Levine, who bequeathed his entire inheritance to Sinclair as a gesture of his commitment to the cause. Another character came into our circle, Jesse Crawford, better known as J.C., also known to us as the Oracle Remus.

The first time J.C. came to our house, we were blown away by his wit and style. He and his partner, Panther White, put on quite a show, and I guess we were just a little outdone in the charisma department. But instead of bristling with defensiveness, we embraced them and felt like we had discovered an ally. Coming off like a cross between a carnival pitchman, eccentric used car salesman, and a country preacher, he fit our group of showoffs like a velvet glove.

We immediately tapped J.C. to be the M.C. at our live shows, introducing the band as a vehicle to energize the crowd. His good humor offset some of the awkward feelings I had regarding political stances. The elements of satire and absurdity were back in the picture. It felt natural, and I was happily a part of it. It was time to swing for the fences. We dubbed him Brother J.C. Crawford, the Oracle Remus, spiritual advisor.

Panther White, meanwhile, slipped out of the picture. Although he too was a dynamic individual, his talents were not as usable as J.C.'s. He hung out with us for a while, then disappeared from view. But J.C. was indeed a part of the band, a close associate to John Sinclair, and a good friend to all of us. His presence defined our identity once and for all.

I wasn't altogether happy about that, though I liked him a lot. The idea of being a rock band had given way to a mission of creating societal change. The tug and pull of hammering out personal differences was replaced by solidifying the social forms that were in place within the group. Routines became too familiar after a while. Being able to regroup at a distance wasn't an option, and it became tedious to have to see people who would rather not have to see you either: in a word, uncomfortable.

Most of the time, though, life was normal, relaxed, and without much ado. The denizens of the house went about their daily activities, going places or merely hanging around, smoking the omnipresent sacramental herb.

Playing records was a popular pastime and a way of establishing the standards of the group, which was now a communal family. The selection of records was a statement of personal taste, but even that was under constant scrutiny. It was of great importance what the group was willing to accept something they might ordinarily have considered uncool.

I found that the option of secluding myself in my room and playing records on my own little stereo was the only comfortable way out of it. Other household members constantly used the house stereo as a means to foist their personal tastes on the rest of us. Of course, since John Sinclair was orchestrating our agenda, he was mostly in control of that part of the program. Not that any of that was so terrible, it just became a pain in the ass to always have to assent to Sinclair's opinions.

Wayne always advocated Sinclair's positions on everything from turntable etiquette to socio-political sermonizing. In fact, a fierce competition to be Sinclair's number one stooge existed between Waye and Rob. So, when it came to trying to control us hooligans, Sinclair had Wayne by the ear and Rob as the back-up boot boy. The rest of us just didn't get it, or had our own visions of utopia, but for the moment, we regarded the atmosphere of dope smoking, drinking, and fucking as an acceptable default.

I didn't mind us bashing away at the establishment, but I certainly didn't see how we were in line to take over if it all came crashing down. Life went on, and day-by-day, our habits became routine. Our rhetoric became more homogenous, decrying the events of the war and other profound errors of the time. Our voices were loud and our performances were rowdy, challenging the rules of obscenity and decorum. But I only wanted to be in a rock and roll band. This crusade to forge a new world seemed ludicrous, a Quixotic lunge at an imaginary adversary.

Our enemy was ignorance. Our enemy was fear of the unknown. Our enemy was anything that stood in the way of our expression. At times, I thought we were brutes, plowing our way into the mass media. No style, no technique, just pure and simple bludgeoning at the expense of fashion. But like a tidal wave, it all came together as if by Providence.

We played at a sidewalk affair somewhere in the inner city in Detroit. The public at large was our audience. I don't remember why we were there or who promoted the event. I don't think it was for money. It was a community gathering of some kind, and a small group of sidewalk people assembled in front of us.

We jammed our psychedelic rhythm and blues, while a small contingent of black guys whooped it up and slapped fives when we finished our performance. As we were tearing down our equipment, a few of them came over to talk to us. They were impressed with our stuff. They told us we were playing the real shit, badass jams, really sockin' it to 'em.

Then one of them said, "Y'all got high, now get down!" The smallest guy, who was obviously an important member in their group, repeated, "Yeah man…y'all got to get down!"

We were at a loss as to what he was talking about. He explained that getting high was the first step in the right direction. But once you got it up there, once you took it to the top, the next step was to get down with it. That is, to bring it home with power. We understood, and we all started slapping five and laughing. It was a real special event for us. I believe we knew we were the band "of the people" from then on. After that, we started to say "get down" for everything.

Out of exasperation at the absence of anything in the commercial marketplace that met our tastes and requirements, and the fact that we had no money for shopping anyway, we recruited girls from our fan club or our female housemates to sew our clothing. Rob's wife, Wayne's girlfriend, and Fred's girlfriend (later his wife), and a couple of other chicks made our outfits.

We made regular runs to our favorite fabric store in downtown Detroit to buy yards of colorful, outrageous material. The patterns were more or less individualized to size from a universal style pattern made up by us: stovepipe pants with flared cuff-less bottoms and shirts with puffy sleeves. The choice of material was what set each outfit apart. I thought our clothes were such an exciting element of our show, and the sense of individual creativity kept me riding on top of the entire mess we were producing. Somehow things were fitting into place, the mayhem was becoming attractive, and the bandwagon was growing.

I sensed a community feeling emanating from the Grande Ballroom and the various bands that played there on a regular basis. We grew friendly with several of those groups, especially the ones from Ann Arbor: the Rationals, the Thyme, the Psychedelic Stooges, the Up, the Children, the Apostles, and all their respective managers and promoters, people who rode the wave of bands and drug culture that was overtaking the nation's youth.

Even the cops were friendly in Ann Arbor, largely through Sinclair's befriending of Lieutenant Staudemeier of the Ann Arbor Police. Somehow Sinclair convinced the good officer that our intentions were honorable, and he did us the favor of letting us carry on without persecuting us at every turn.

Ann Arbor was a quaint midwestern university town with lush old trees and early settlers' dwellings mixed with mid-century modern atmosphere. In fact, in 1968, Ann Arbor was proclaimed an All-American City, and no wonder; an old railroad station by the meandering Huron River, a fall spectacle of color and annual football frenzy filled the heart with passion.

Enter the MC5, Detroit's refugee bad boy band, stirring up the lazy breezes along the old university streets. Tucked amidst the colonial mansions of fraternity row in two rustic houses, the seeds for the end of conformity were germinating.

I searched constantly for the perfect female. At every show, at every club, everywhere I went, my periscope was always turning in all directions to find "the one." But if any girl even approached my ideal, I was immediately overcome by shyness. While the others freely associated with women, I stood aloof, protecting my vulnerable ego. I was playing it cool. A few of the Mount Clemens babes nicknamed me "cool breeze." I was flattered, but I still would up with nothing.

Occasionally, a girl would attempt to nail me down or I would succeed in luring someone to my bed. But I also wonder if maybe I wasn't over being ditched by my wife. Maybe sex was only a physical exercise to me. Sometimes it seemed the only reason I was in the band was to find sex partners and take revenge for my ill-fated romantic fantasies. I had no qualms about doing someone else's girl. If I could get it, I would take it.

I liked my room. It was cozy and small, filled with my artifacts and color. Indian spreads hung over my windows and above my bed. Multiple empty Kool cigarette cartons littered the floor. I smoked at least one pack every day. Being addicted to both nicotine and menthol made me an excessive user. I had a small globe lamp with an elephant holding a colored ball filled with light, a mattress on the floor and incense in the air. I sometimes read *Doctor Strange* comic books for days on end.

I had a constant stash of weed, and used the porch as a means of entrance whenever it suited me. It also shielded me from howling Wayne and the obnoxious table sessions in the dining room just beyond the kitchen. A clamoring bunch of hangers-on invaded the household almost every night, and the levity of the dining room dope table became a must to avoid. My back porch gave me the perfect escape. I was actually very lonely back in those days, but I don't think anyone was aware of it. Being stoned took up any slack, and it just wasn't a cool thing, being lonely.

I reckoned we were becoming a "guys' band" due to the fact that guys were attracted to our rough and tumble aggressiveness. Though we presented ourselves with a good deal of flash and show, sweetness and light was not what we were about; that, and the fact that Sinclair and Kramer were intent upon pressing the case for sex on demand as a feature of our troupe.

That meant that any female within touching distance was likely to be groped by them on the spot. It was painful to see the crude advances these two barracudas made. Throughout it all, neither one of them felt the least bit embarrassed by their self-serving idea that women liked to be assaulted, but I was. And they drove the women away like a plague.

Nonetheless, despite my misgivings about how things were in the house, the band surged forward in popularity. Our January 4, 1968 recording session at United Sound Studios in Detroit was marked by much hash smoking, a creative production approach (over the engineer's objections), and reckless abandon that produced two startling tracks which were clearly ahead of their time: "Looking At You" and "Borderline."

Though we were criticized for some oddities, mistakes of one sort or another, we didn't care what was said. We'd made ultra-intense music with the tools we had, in control of our unparalleled sound. Sinclair roamed the studio like a mad Merlin with his hash pipe brimming, offering to get the next taker blasted into creative bliss.

I still believed in us as a band. As individuals, we had enormous potential. As a group, we were capable of things others would never imagine. We had the will to take the medium of rock music beyond all borders, on a wild ride into the unknown. This was the MC5 at its very best. All the forces of our energy and destiny were in alignment. We could be unstoppable.

At one point in the session, I remember going into a closet with Sinclair to get stoned. When I emerged, Fred stood with me a moment and provided a little pep talk about all the bass players in the world listening to my track and saying, "Wow, did you hear what that guy just played?"

His sarcasm hit the spot. Something in his words propelled me into creating something I had never played before. Our recording of "Looking At You" from that session has to be the most shocking three minutes of music ever waxed. From the cover artwork of John Coltrane gazing over a collage of band photos to the marijuana leaf on the A-Square Records label, it all worked and gave us an identity to be proud of. It was the MC5's finest hour.

My playing was a bit of everything. I took my cues from the bass players I'd imitated doing cover material. James Jamerson, the Motown great, was probably the one I most admired and wanted to imitate, and although my skills were nowhere near his level, I did my best to mimic his sound. Other bassists I'd slipped into my repertoire included the Rolling Stones' Bill Wyman—whom I'd been told by Fred was the perfect bass player—and John Entwistle of the Who. But altogether, every single song we'd ever played was a resource for bass lines.

Wayne had advised me to try playing bass in an unorthodox manner. He had encouraged me to venture into untraditional approaches to the art. This I tried to do as a rule, but underneath it all, I wanted to convey feeling in my playing. I wanted to add a dimension to the sound of the band that expressed a universal experience. I felt driven to speak from my heart. My goal in playing was to lose my self-consciousness, my self-awareness. I wanted to become egoless. Much of the time when we played endless passages, I achieved a state of suspended presence that could also have been a drug- induced trance.

It seemed that during my entire tenure as bass player of the MC5, I was sorely underpowered. My amplifier from the beginning had a small wattage compared to what the guitars were using. Yet, even as we acquired bigger gear, my rig was never enough. As a result, I stayed planted in front of my amplifier in an attempt to hear my own instrument. With the cymbals close to my left ear and the full-on blast of Wayne's guitar at about the same spot to my right, my bass notes were barely audible. I relied on feeling the air pressure from the speakers just to know I was making sound.

It was impossible to hear the vocals unless we were playing softly, which rarely happened. Things would get so confused at times that we would look at each other with panic and frustration, trying to get back in sync. I can't think of a single show that didn't include some form of musical derailment. Some were momentary, while others were extended lapses into musical chaos. Dennis would become completely unhinged when none of the instruments were playing on the same beat. Yet at times, he was the reason for the fault. Who could hear what was going on?

Regardless of what had happened, I was usually held responsible for the fuck-up; and, for all I knew, it all might well have been my error. Rob had no way to tell what was going on behind him, and though he was singing the lead vocals, he wasn't really leading the music. Wayne and Fred were never blamed for any wrongful playing. They were beyond reproach.

In spite of our inconsistent stage work, we somehow managed to transport audiences into magical experiences through our sheer unmitigated gall. You couldn't deny the results; something was lifting us up and giving the audience a dose of euphoria. Perhaps the mistakes were actually a key part of our act, unintended, but nonetheless a part of the show. The desperation and drama that was created, and the rescue that took place must have had an emotional value that made seeing the MC5 unparalleled. I can't say, being one who was on the stage.

Pun and Genie, down in the basement, fascinated me. To me, they were a sweet couple whose presence was the result of having been Artist Workshop initiates with the task of doing work that involved John's publications and propaganda. I thought of them as our resident hippies.

There was a modest newspaper and art forum that had various notices, editorials and schedules of events. It was called *The Sun*. I assumed Pun was working with Sinclair as an editor, writer, and collaborator with regard to goals that were somewhat independent of our band. Perhaps I was too stoned and passive to realize what Pun and John were up to.

So far as they were concerned, we were all one big happy counterculture, and the band was their willing tool to make political warfare. So far as I was concerned, we were just a band. I didn't feel that we needed to do anything to effect change besides playing our music and being our natural selves. I believed young people would do their own reacting to anything that demanded a reaction, and we would have done the most we could do.

Overt action against the law was an ignorant way to go about getting what we wanted. At the time, the forces that wished to suppress the counterculture were stymied as to what to do about it. Public sympathy seemed to be on our side, and it seemed we held the trump card, the nation's youth. So, in my mind, Pun was simply an eccentric Sinclairite. I didn't realize how dramatic his impact was going to be.

And not only him. There were several people who relished talking about action as a way to confront the powers that be. The band just wasn't enough for them to get off on. They were much more serious about themselves than any of us. We weren't looking for a confrontation. That would happen as a matter of course, we didn't need to push it. So much of which I was unaware was germinating under that roof in Ann Arbor.

Pun was not a loudmouth, nor was he someone who was in your face about what we needed to do. I thought him a likable, modest, and sober guy. He was fairly invisible, as a matter of fact. So I took it for granted that there wasn't any cause for alarm. His wife, Genie, was a soft-spoken, kind-hearted, slender woman with a calm about her that made me feel welcome. She had an all-knowing serenity that I found appealing. They were a married couple, but I wasn't sure what their arrangements were. A bit of mystery surrounded them, but nothing scandalous.

One summer evening as we sat on my back porch tripping on LSD, Genie told me that John had had a vision at some point in the past that was motivating his life. As we spoke, John was in New York, pitching the band to record labels.

The evening passed by; talking, not talking, and just being high together in the darkness. We shared the night together because she and I needed to have a real experience. I was starved for intimate contact. Nothing ever had any meaning beyond the basest elements. Though my life was bursting with importance, I was dying for something real.

John returned from New York the following week, completely discouraged. He was given a courteous reception at several record labels, then shown to the door and told, "We'll call you."

But soon afterwards, one of the people who had seen John's pitch for the band came to Detroit to see what was going on. Danny Fields was working at Elektra Records as a talent development assistant, and his impression of the MC5's performance at the Grande Ballroom changed the course of history. He got on the phone to his boss, Jac Holzman, in New York, and told him that we were a phenomenon and that the MC5 should be signed to a recording contract immediately. As a result, we were signed to a record deal with Elektra Records and scheduled to record our debut album live at the Grande Ballroom on October 30 and 31, 1968.

We all gathered at the Hill Street house for a big signing party, the Elektra brass from New York intermingled with all of the cronies from our tribe. The Stooges were also beneficiaries of our good fortune; they were also signed to Elektra. About 40 people stood or sat in front of the camera for the photo. It was a joyous time in the old house, and when we made the record in October, we were at the peak of three years of being a band.

Our clothes, our hair, our words, our spirit, our fan base, our music, everything was coming together nicely. We had made significant changes in our gear so that the sound of the band was better than it had ever been. I had a new Fender Jazz bass that I enjoyed and was proud of. The new amps were Marshalls. Our girls had sewn fabulous clothing of elaborate and colorful fabric. The set was a conglomeration of many different styles and approaches to music. We really liked everything in our set, making it hard to narrow our choices for the record, but mainly, we had to include as many originals as we could. Great optimism was in the air. We also were representing our hometown of Detroit as a breeding ground for original music.

To make the record reflect our vision, we needed to have an inspired night on the stage. We prepared as best we could without over-working our parts, something we tended to do anyway. Our confidence was in good shape, but always with that nagging bit of doubt. Myself, I consider the edge that insecurity provides to be a positive. It surely gives you a sense of presence, a thing that can work to your advantage if it doesn't upset you too much.

The night of the recording of *Kick Out The Jams,* the air was so completely charged with energy, it was like swimming in adrenaline. I saw sparkles in the light, an intense brightness, and I felt spiritually connected to every individual in the audience.

What kind of drug was I on, you might ask. Well, in truth, as a group, we did what we normally did, which was smoke copious amounts of good quality smoke, hashish or whatever was offered. We didn't, as a rule, carry our own. It was unnecessarily risky, and as everyone else provided anything at all times, we were quite well taken care of. So, yes, we were pretty well tanked on everything. The sound of the music was as crisp as anything I've ever heard in my life. Every note and tone rang through like a beam of sound energy. The clarity was incredible.

We burst onto the stage of the packed house with all the lights up and brilliant. After a few seconds of plugging in and checking string tuning, we faced the raucous, intensely charged, tumultuous crowd. Their eager faces told everything. They had been chanting "M-C-5!" for 10 minutes. J.C. Crawford stepped to the center microphone and began his introductory rant. The crowd was delirious. I felt like I was on air. "I give you a testimonial, THE MC5."

The glory began with Wayne's guitar intro to "Ramblin' Rose." As the whole band joined in, the assault of the music was like a wave of charging energy. This was the moment I'd been seeking. We were launched in an unbelievable surge of our own creation. We were airborne. I heard the E string of Wayne's guitar hit the second verse with a flat thud. His guitar was out of tune. "Oh well, fuck it, we're the MC5," I thought to myself, I didn't let it faze me.

"And now, it's time to…" Tyner ran across the stage to the

center microphone decked out in skin-tight striped pants. Then, the immortal words blazed throughout the room and the world and the universe, *"kick out the jams, motherfucker!"* The pitch, the clarity, the crispness, all at once the room erupted in joyous chaos.

It had been our big 1-2-3 punch to start the set. The last song of the opening triptych, "Come Together," a Smith riff that vaguely resembled the Who's "I Can See For Miles," was one of those open-ended pieces that might be shorter or longer on any given night. We purposely cut it to a reasonable four minutes for recording considerations.

The spontaneous aspects of the evening were holding up, and I think the fact that it was a do-or-die moment worked to our advantage. It was a glorious event, the kind that can only be had by much dreaming and toiling, for such things don't come your way by accident.

The New York Minute

Once the record was completed, with all the vocal filler and embellishment the studio could provide—things we felt were needed to recreate the live feel of the performance—we sat and waited for the test pressings, eagerly anticipating our ascent to greatness.

What a shock, what an anticlimax it was when I played the thing on the stereo in my room. Oh Jesus, was that it? It sounded flat and garbled. I tried to shield my senses. I really never expected it to sound like that, distant and contrived. Just who was it making all that random vocal blurting and banter?

I don't think I had ever felt so disappointed over a piece of recorded music, but it was what it was; there was no getting around it. Elektra had made promises that if we weren't happy with the live recording, we could go into the studio for a retake. Truth was, the trip to the studio to re-track vocals and add embellishments was all we were going to get in the way of second chances. It was a done deal. The next issue was the artwork and packaging. Our friend and honorary MC5 brother Gary Grimshaw's burning flag/marijuana leaf sunset, a combination of glorious psychedelic images, hit the Elektra planning room trash basket and was promptly replaced by a carnivalesque collage of live photo shots with Bill Harvey, the Elektra art director's image inserted in the upper right hand corner, without the band's approval.

A jolly red, white, and blue circus script MC5 logo topped the layout, giving the album a cheerful glow that must have somehow pleased the marketing brains that were putting up the money for all of this. We felt powerless to do anything about it. Even John Sinclair was powerless to sway the situation in any way. We bitched, to no avail.

On the whole, our spirits remained high. We were on the brink of getting our sound and our vision out to the entire world. We had a great label with really cool bands on it, and a label that I had been fascinated by previously for all its delving into Baroque music. We had a live recording and the chance to break out of all the local restrictions. Shit man, we were going to New York.

I started feeling cocky, we all started feeling cocky. I wanted to embody what the record was about to be, bright and bursting with energy and color. It didn't matter that it wasn't really dedicated to the revolution. We had product; that was the point.

There wasn't a whole lot of kick-up-dust rock and roll around as 1968 turned to 1969. There was the Who, of course, but they were off on a tangent with their "rock opera" *Tommy*. Hendrix was a factor, as was a new up-and-coming band, Led Zeppelin. There were some white-boy blues bands, but none were doing the blast-you-silly kind of ballsy rock we wanted to play. We also had the ace-in-the-hole of the psychedelic, experimental, improvised space sounds of feedback and distortion we were conceiving. Yeah, we felt good about where we were headed.

To me, the whole idea of talking about revolution was a tactic to align us with a global awakening. But by no means was it something that I thought we needed to dwell on as the "theme" of the band. We packed off to New York to introduce the band to the industry and New York media.

The next thing I knew, we were sitting in someone's apartment in Manhattan, being interviewed for a national magazine. Rob and Wayne were trying to explain how the "revolution" was going to be carried out. Each time someone spoke, they produced a lengthy stream of jargon and expressions that we had invented, endless explanations that clarified nothing to a dumbfounded writer who was probably wondering just what these intense, revolutionary cats were talking about.

Certain band members were so obsessed with being the center of attention that there was scarcely a second when someone's mouth wasn't moving. Rob was expected to do a lot of the talking because he was the lead singer of the band and as such, he should have a lot to say, but Wayne Kramer was never comfortable playing second banana, either on stage or in a written piece about the band.

The conversation was rife with mindless jargon and cliché. "Off the pig," "all power to the people," "capitalist honky pigs must die," and other remarks of that nature filled the air with received righteousness. I tried, as the schooling of the interviewer took place, to think of a statement that summed up the gist of what we were concerned about, but I couldn't. Every time someone made a statement, someone else would feel compelled to interject his own viewpoint.

The result of that interview and every other interview we did was a crock of mindless political irrelevance without merit. As the band tried to detail every little thing that was wrong in America, I became intensely unsure about what to say. So I said nothing, because it was all so irrelevant. Everyone slapping five and saying "right on" only made me feel ever more alienated. All I wanted to do was get away and get drunk. Rob used to say "You can take the boy out of Lincoln Park, but you can't take Lincoln Park out of the boy." And, right then, I was rather glad about that.

We were invited to a few parties where the New York movers and shakers would be scrutinizing our talents. People in the music business, artists, agents, press, and also the politically astute were available to us at once for their first viewing of the new kids in town. I suppose we needed to make our opinions known, if only to make people aware of whom we were. But in our enthusiasm to reveal the basis of our agenda, we presented ourselves as an extremely politically charged group with radical action as our central point.

Of course this clashed with the music business' agenda, so the media were understandably anxious to hear how we intended to reconcile one with the other. But we were completely unprepared for the conflict that we threw ourselves into. Sinclair was pushing the radical side of what the MC5 said and did, while we as a band were thrown to the wolves. The record label was nervously standing in the wings hoping we could handle it, but in truth, we had no idea what was going to happen.

The New Yorkers seemed hopelessly mired in their own social rituals, while we acted like goons from outer space. To them, we must have looked like a bunch of hicks who lacked any sense of how we were embarrassing ourselves publicly. But they were very interested in using us for whatever we could give them, style-wise.

The Invisible Theater, a consort of actors who did improvised performances, approached us. They wanted the MC5 to record a soundtrack for a film of their performances.

We gathered at a small recording studio in Manhattan to lay down an improvised track of musical chaos. The studio, tiny as it was, was crammed with people, with barely enough room to stand without tripping over someone's feet. Tape was rolled and we attempted to play amplified noise while the film of naked people leaping around was screened. It was an incredibly pretentious scene. What might have been an auspicious piece of artful creation amounted to a bust. Everyone was stoned, but the atmosphere was stultifying.

It was disappointing. No one said anything about the mediocre result, but it was apparent to me that no connection had been made, and the fact that it was the New York underground art and theater people made it all the more disturbing. That was a terrific missed opportunity. Maybe, had we been better prepared ourselves, things would have been better, but it just didn't happen.

The Invisible Theater was not an especially big item, but it still would've been a good connection for the band.

But we put the disappointment behind us, and went on to the club scene with eager appetites.

We went to Steve Paul's club The Scene in Soho to see Slim Harpo. Hanging out with the elite and celebrated was as important as anything else. Upon seeing Jimi Hendrix seated at a table close to the stage, Fred slipped up behind him and gave his hat a bump. It was typical of Fred to challenge anyone. His hoodlum audacity was a trademark, and he could never resist any chance to bring a rival to his knees. In this case, however, nothing came of it.

Up at Elektra, we must have seemed like an invading crew of Vikings someone mistakenly let in the building. Holzman was slick behind his walnut desk, holding a brief audience and having a few chuckles with us before sending us with an escort to meet the staff. Our gracious patron Danny Fields took us around the to the established hot spots, one of which was Max's Kansas City, a well-known midtown eatery and show club. In the back room at Max's, we had steak and lobster with horrendous amounts of beer and Jim Beam bourbon whiskey, the band favorite.

It was good to relax like this; the drinking was not John Sinclair's favorite band indulgence. To him, drinking was a habit of squares and in direct opposition of the consciousness-enhancing effects of pot smoking. In fact, he frowned upon our alcohol intake severely, but was unable to quell our dysfunction.

We were constantly on the move to meet more contacts. One of those was a photographer lady named Raeanne Rubenstein, who was doing *Village Voice* and *East Village Other* work. She was fairly well connected with the underground and the real business types. She did a photo shoot of the band for *Circus* magazine that is well known. Also, she did a photo shoot of me for the *East Village Other* that she called "Apocatastasis," a Greek word meaning "return to the source."

She also told me a friend of hers who was very savvy about band survival in the business had the opinion that the MC5 would be around for about six months. I'd say we lasted a bit longer, maybe not in the public eye, but in terms of notoriety the MC5 is still around.

Of course, the Fillmore East showcase gig has to be counted

as the crowning misadventure of the season. Unknown to most of us, a volatile situation was brewing in the neighborhood where the Fillmore East ballroom was located, having to do with free tickets and a confrontation between Graham and the leaders of the Motherfuckers, a radical group of hippies.

And Elektra naively walked into the situation.

We arrived at the theater anxious to reveal our rock and roll power to city of New York. Everything was cool as we lounged in the dressing room, sucking down smoke and beer. Out on the floor, at tense situation was unfolding with Graham withholding the promised free tickets and the Motherfuckers threatening to burn the place down. I can still see John Sinclair seated in the dressing room lighting up another joint for the band while we took our time dressing and getting blasted.

About an hour and a half past the scheduled stage time, we decided to go out and play. In the space between the curtains at the side of the stage, I saw figures at the center microphone on stage who were not part of our or the theater's crew. The stage had been taken over by rowdy members of the audience. Security was nowhere to be seen. The crowd was incensed.

J.C. tried to introduce us, but was booed, yelled at, and drowned out by the noise. I heard people yelling, "Where the hell were ya?" Our absence during the early confrontations had not simply been noticed. We had been expected to be out there, fighting the man for free tickets like the rest of them. It wasn't the Grande Ballroom.

Wayne started "Ramblin' Rose," but it sounded dull. Rob ran out to scream "Kick Out the Jams, Motherfucker," but something was missing. A person from the front row mounted the stage and stood next to him. One of our roadies rushed out and pushed the guy off the stage, not knowing he was the leader of a neighborhood gang. The song ended and Rob shouted to the crowd, "We came to play music, not politics." The audience was yelling obscenities at him; things were sailing through the air and onto the stage. We played on as though everything was cool. I was afraid something really dangerous was about to take place. We were on the verge of a riot with any band member a likely casualty.

Slogging our way through the set, we finally closed the show with as much bravado as we could sum up. Amid mixed boos and cheers, the band retreated to the safety of the upstairs dressing rooms and bottles of whiskey, our New York entourage crowding in to witness our reaction to what had just happened. Then somebody mentioned that something was happening downstairs on the floor of the ballroom.

J.C. Crawford was engaged with a small group of hippie types, who were arguing that the MC5 had sold them out for stardom. Immediately, Wayne entered the fracas with endless explanations, trying to justify our position.

I stood by with not a single idea how to solve the debate. It was a helpless mess. After a while, the theater staff insisted we should leave through the back door, and out into an alley. Once there, the spirited debate resumed.

Looking to my right, I saw the blade of a knife in someone's hand. Two stretch limos idled nearby, sent by the record label to drive us to our hotel. It came down to this: If we got into those limos, we were the Enemy.

No matter. As calmly as I could, I walked to the closest limo and got in. Wayne and Jesse weren't far behind.

We arrived back at the hotel a very disturbed bunch of rock stars. I hadn't ever felt the disappointment that I felt after that show. Everyone was somber. In the moment, the significance of the event was hard to understand, but the real question was: Who were we, *really?*

I don't blame Danny Fields for sending limos to pick us up. What were we supposed to do, ride to the gig in people's cars, take the bus, walk? Maybe these days that would be appropriate, but when we were on display as the record company's newest acquisition, chauffeured limos were the right thing. No, it was because we had made such a fuss about being revolutionaries that we brought this type of scrutiny upon ourselves. Revolutionaries are always subject to purges.

I am amazed that John Sinclair was so passive about the entire debacle. It was mainly his indoctrination that brought us to these circumstances. Between his influence and Wayne's complicity, Rob's verbalizing hypothetical causes and the rest of us responding like a herd, we placed our necks firmly on the chopping block. But it wasn't over yet, not by any means. It was just beginning.

In spite of all of the bungling, we were gaining friendships and fans. We played some out-of-city appearances with our label mates, David Peel and the Lower East Side. They were a nice bunch of New York kids with an anarchic sense of humor. Elektra had released their debut album with a song entitled "Up Against the Wall, Motherfucker." Their album was called *Have a Marijuana*. So, Elektra's Holzman was definitely trying to score with the radicals. He just wasn't prepared to stick his neck out very far.

When we played less critical gigs, we did much better at winning people over. It was a dubious initial coming-out party, but I'd have to say, we were still in good shape to capture the flag. The record hadn't hit the streets yet, and New York isn't all there is. The thing that impressed me was that New Yorkers want to be won over as much as anybody; you just have to prove you can handle the attention. If you falter under the microscope, they will reject you like a turd on a dinner plate.

I loved New York, missed it when we left, always felt important when I was there, and couldn't wait to go back. Plus, having lived down on the Lower East Side a few years before, I was coming back to a familiar place.

But getting back to Ann Arbor and Detroit was good, too. Our fans were getting super hyped up now, as the record was soon to be released. Despite everything, or because of everything, this period was incredible for its energy.

We had an extraordinary amount of publicity before the record release. That didn't really help our cause as much as taking the public by surprise might have, but we were something different, and it drew attention. *Rolling Stone* wanted to run a story about us before we did our record; it appeared as the cover story of their January 4, 1969 edition. The media heard about the Detroit phenomenon and was on top of that. Everyone was waiting with bated breath to hear the sound of the MC5. When the record came out in February, it was an inevitable anticlimax.

The reviews were mixed. One in particular was an obnoxious description written by the late Lester Bangs, *Rolling Stone*'s eloquent reviewer and ultimately, an arch MC5 fan.

To my amusement, he described our sound as a perfect sound track for the satirically hilarious cult film, *Wild In The Streets*. But his smearing of our record put a stigma a mile wide on the band, one that we couldn't shake. Since we took every single part of our identity so seriously, it made things a bit sticky. Luckily I didn't feel particularly slandered, but I had less to lose, I guess. That the best critic *Rolling Stone* ever had didn't think the MC5 was the greatest thing he'd ever heard was a stinging rebuke to the egos that were. Elektra may have bitten off a rotten piece of jerky. We'd have to go out and prove we had the right stuff.

I had very weird perceptions of things back in those days. Probably from drug-induced fantasy, I thought my energy was connected to very dramatic situations involving all of creation.

I saw New York as a heart through which all energy flowed. I pictured the universe as an imperceptible body, of which we were all merely a minuscule part. I thought of every individual's energy as having the potential to alter cosmic events beyond our perception. I thought that as a mass of beings, the human race was involved in a struggle of forces represented as truth versus falsehood, positive energy flow opposing negative energy flow. I viewed our lives as agents of greater forces, somehow recognized by instinct.

Does any of that make sense? At the time, it did. It is what I believed, but rarely did I speak of any of it. Especially my belief that my purpose was of such great magnitude that to fail meant certain doom for all. It was a lot of responsibility for a person to account for. And I saw what we were questing for as a most noble task. The MC5, the guardians of the gate to truth, the shamen, the ultimate soldiers armed with guitars and entrusted to bring the rest of humanity to the Promised Land. We had our destiny and it was real big stuff.

Certainly the events of the day were challenging everything that had ever been thought before. Values about sex, drugs, family, religion, virtually all established thought was under attack.

We believed we represented the new breed of citizen. I was always seeking the big breakthrough. As an individual, I had to exorcise myself in order to be worthy of the quest. Everyone depended on me. I wonder if some of the guys who went nuts during this time period had similar notions. No drugs were bad, sex with anybody was good, and in the cause of freedom and justice, all things were created for the taking.

We went to the West Coast in the summer of '69 to play a short series of dates that stretched from Seattle to L.A., with a stop in the Bay Area. In Seattle, we played with Jethro Tull, who seemed very professional to me, compared to our very amateurish assault. Eggs and a bottle or two went flying by as we kicked out our jams. Apparently the west hadn't been briefed on our virtue.

Once we hit Frisco, things changed for the better. A houseful of young nubile hippie girls greeted us and made us feel like a hot item. Things were on the rise. There were at least five or six girls who intended to become part of our party from the time we arrived. They were wholesome, pretty, and scantily clad. Things were not quite this open back in Detroit. These chicks were not playing hide and seek. I found a particular girl that I liked. She had an assumed hippie alias, something like "Jasmine," and was prone to dancing in public without underwear. Hordes of Asian guys with cameras stooped down to get up-the-skirt shots of her pubes while she twirled away unconcerned. She was a top-of-the-line hippie seductress. We became friends and more. All of the girls were open and receptive to anyone whom they liked. It met all expectations of what was happening in the Haight-Ashbury.

In one particular incident, a friend of ours took a picture that depicted several members of the band having sex with a lone female.

It appeared as though we were in the midst of a "gang bang." The picture appeared on the front page of a student newspaper, just a bit of devilish behavior, nothing that wasn't enjoyed by everyone present, soon to be a big problem. I only even mention it because of all the trouble it caused. Otherwise, it was a minor incident without further consequences.

Our stay in the Bay Area was high drama. The gigs were very intense, our entourage of panty-less hippie girls swirling away while we shattered everyone's eardrums. We caused a sensation of audacious freedom that people were not quite ready for. I believe most were impressed, but we offended many as well.

On a Friday evening, we were pulled over on the Bay Bridge by the San Francisco police with a minor female in the car. I suspect they were out looking for us, because it seemed like they knew who we were. After searching the car and checking all the IDs, we were hauled off to jail for the weekend, causing us to miss one gig. In court, the judge admonished the police for holding us without cause, and fined us for the half can of beer that was our only transgression of the law.

I remember so much happening during those few days we spent in San Francisco. I can scarcely believe it was only a week or less that we stayed there. We took acid with Tim Leary at his house in the Berkeley hills. We lived in a motel located on the ocean shore, where all our hippie freak females shacked up with us in rotation. We played at least two gigs, but it might have been three. We played at Speedway Meadows in Golden Gate Park, where thousands of people were lounging in the sun, getting stoned and drinking Red Mountain wine. On acid, I took a cab from Tim Leary's house to the Avalon Ballroom, where I saw Santana, ran into a girl I had met the night before, then spent the rest of that night with her. It was certainly a more intense thing than we were used to having in Michigan.

We finished the trip in L.A., playing one night at a mall, and the next in San Bernardino, opening for Janis Joplin. She was debuting her new group after the dumbasses at her record label decided she should be made a solo celebrity, firing her original band members from Big Brother and the Holding Co., except for guitar player Sam Andrew.

I made some distant eye contact with her, hoping she might think I was cute enough to hang out with after the show. It might even be possible to get laid, but at least I thought it would be fun to get high with her. She smiled back at me from the stage when I stood in the wing.

After she finished her set, she came over to ask me what was happening afterwards. I told her she should come with us. We piled into the station wagon we had rented, with Janis, Wayne and me in the far back seat, facing backwards. Then we stopped at a store to stock up on liquor. At the checkout, we made her pay for everything. Once we got back in the car, Wayne started acting crazy and boisterous, shouting obscenities and making weird faces. She said she wanted to go by her hotel to tell her people where she was going, but when we got there, she literally leaped through the back window of the station wagon and ran full speed across the parking lot to safety. I don't blame her one bit; we were being real assholes.

At least, that's how I remember it.

Our California trip had netted us two stompings at the hands of Jethro Tull; sex with a bevy of nubile teenage hippies; an acid trip with guru Dr. Tim Leary at his house; a glorious assault of high energy rock and roll music on 10,000 drowsy hippies at Speedway

Meadows in Golden Gate Park; a blasphemous photo published in the local newspaper; three days in the San Francisco city jail; some unforgettable one night stands; a disastrous encounter with Janis Joplin; and a new mob of riotous MC5 fans. Otherwise, you could say we had offended most everyone else.

I can still see the reddening sky as I looked out the window of the plane on the flight back to Michigan. It felt like we were leaving a paradise vacation, never to return. As the orange and red faded into purple and darkness, I could feel the darkness setting in on our world of rock and roll. I had no idea what was happening across the country, far from California and deep in the affairs of MC5.

The little photograph of the groupie intimately embracing us in Berkley had hit the wires and gotten the attention of the promoter in Florida, where the MC5 was booked to play at a big teen event.

Consequently, the governor of Florida banned us from entering the state. Should any member of the MC5 be so brazen as to cross the state line, he would be subject to immediate arrest. At that point, I believe our record had entered the *Billboard* Hot 100. We were getting some airplay in the major markets.

Then, the bricks started falling out of the wall. The Florida gig was cancelled, of course, and the RKO radio stations across the nation joined in the witch hunt by removing the record from their play lists when it was discovered that the album version of the song "Kick Out the Jams" had an obscenity in the intro.

Shortly thereafter, the J.L. Hudson Co., our largest local department store in Michigan, refused to stock the album for the same reason.

Our response to that outrage was to post an ad in the *Ann Arbor Sun* proposing that our fans kick down the doors of Hudson's, followed by the words, "Fuck Hudson's." And the ad was paid for by Elektra Records, who were unaware of any of this and had not been consulted by either the band or our manager.

The end result of that was the canceling of our contract by Elektra Records. We got fired. Where did we go wrong? Who was keeping the watch? We had blown it.

The mood around the Hill Street house was a mixture of panic and bewilderment. Almost immediately, John was off to New York to seek a new deal. Being free of a record label had its advantages, but we didn't even actually own our record. Elektra owned it. Starting over wasn't that bad, if you still believed in the band and thought you could make something happen regardless.

It happened fast. Atlantic Record Corporation picked up our defunct contract and all recordings owned by Elektra. The band was rescued from the dustbin of history. The bigger fish in the pond swatted the small fry out of the way and opened their great big arms to welcome us by slipping us a cool 65 grand for an advance.

How this fit in Sinclair's revolution I can't fathom, but somehow we were now locked into a corporate entity that made Elektra look like a flea market operation. Meeting Ahmet and Nesuhi Ertegun, Jerry Wexler, and all these guys who were legends in the business, plus being signed to their label was almost too much to fathom. The signing photo says it all: happy are those who have a rich daddy. With a big-time showbiz manager in Dee Anthony, a crack booking agent like Frank Barsalona from Premier Talent, and the boss record label, Atlantic Records, how could things be any better?

In response to the bad reviews of the live record, Atlantic was going to send a character named Jon Landau to produce our next album. Jon was also an important writer at *Rolling Stone*, well respected and sharp. He would give us the right slant for the band's first studio effort. It was all set.

Sinclair, meanwhile, was growing more distant as he prepared for an upcoming marijuana bust trial. In fact, I don't think he even realized he'd signed us over to the legions of Caesar.
But he had.

8

The Promise Is Broken

We moved out to the country. It was a little not-on-the-map sort of place called Hamburg, Michigan. Okay, it's on the map, but there wasn't anything there except a Dog-N-Suds, a convenience store, and a gas station. We rented a house down a blacktop road in the middle of the woods, someplace where we could practice without irritating neighbors, and shoot off guns.

Did somebody say guns? What the hell was that all about? Somehow during the preceding months, it had been determined that an armed confrontation with the authorities was imminent. I guess I was too preoccupied fucking pretty hippie girls and dropping acid with Tim Leary to realize the imminent danger of the government moving in on us.

A real shift was taking place within the cozy stoned walls of Trans Love Energies. Some of us had adopted the Black Panthers as a role model, and being armed was part of it. I wasn't into that type of shit, but as the house band of the revolution, we were expected to fall into line. The people back at the Hill Street house were stockpiling weapons. Everyone was talking in cliché terms about how badass we were and what we had to do.

Sinclair was just as defiant as ever, but the bottom line was, he was on his way to jail anyway. Who and what was he managing? Meanwhile, we were handed $1,000 each as our personal allotment of our $65,000 advance. We were calling ourselves "thousandaires." After a time, Fred bought himself a Corvette, Wayne bought himself a Jaguar, and Rob acquired a leased station wagon for his burgeoning family. Dennis had to match Fred with a Corvette of his own. This revolution was going to be riding in style!

I bought a Guild 12-string acoustic guitar with my thousand. It seemed a bit odd, but nobody was going to tell the MC5 how to spend our money. I'm sure our former housemates were talking counter-revolutionary trash on us to no end.

In the new house, we were down to just the band members and their spouses. Rob was a father by now, but it was still basically communal. Dennis and I shared a large loft, the bachelor penthouse. During this time, Dennis and I became much better friends.

The biggest change, however, was the absence of Sinclair. John had organized all our activity that concerned business, a responsibility that now rested on our shoulders and required someone to step up to do it. In the first days of the band, that had been Wayne's domain, and now with us breaking away from the large family setup and Sinclair's casual overseeing, things returned to the way they had been in the beginning.

We were writing the new music for the first Atlantic sessions. Some of the material was astonishing and I was very excited about the record. We still followed the methodology that we always had: someone would play a riff, and the band would jam until the music took shape. It was very chemical. If someone did something that worked well, it would be kept as part of the song.

That was what I liked best about the band: the way every guy felt ownership and pride in what he'd contributed. It was what made the song. It was what made the band. Without any one part, the song would be something entirely different. That's what made the MC5 the special band it was. Without that, the MC5 would have been just like any other band. We were an equal opportunity employer, five individuals creating one sound.

We didn't talk much. Everyone was more or less self-contained with their "ol' ladies" in their respective rooms, and came out to use the kitchen at times. Wayne was around in the house, playing records on the stereo or fussing around in the practice room. Fred was fairly reclusive, only coming out when it was required. We were pretty good at taking care of ourselves and showing up on time for business, again with the exception of Fred, who always made everyone wait.

Rob took the brunt of abuse during those days in Hamburg. Probably at Wayne's instigation, it was determined that every member of the band except Fred was too fat.

We all had our share of pudge, but in Rob's case it was unacceptable. Poor Rob was the victim of multiple defects: the gap in his teeth, the kinky hair, the glasses, the weird body; he was the anti-glamour-boy. Hard to imagine it was such a problem, but when you start taking everything about yourself too seriously, there's no escape. His weight was of prime concern, although when I see photos of him from back then, he hardly looks overweight at all.

As a group, we went on the protein-only diet. Steak, cottage cheese, salad, yogurt, eggs, and eight glasses of water per day were the limits of our sustenance. I can't believe we actually did that. We must have substituted whiskey for beer too, because I can't imagine us not drinking. Rob was also required to jog around the house 50 times every day. After just two weeks, I felt incredibly weak from lack of a balanced diet, and promptly mutinied.

I remember taking Chairman Mao's *Little Red Book* into the bathroom one day for reading material. All of our former housemates were always quoting from the book. I read through the first few pages, and that was all it took. It was suddenly apparent that this directive was made for a regiment of ants. If you happened to be an ant, here was the plan and you'd better not deviate.
Back at the Hill house in Ann Arbor, Pun Plamondon, the official Minister of Defense of the White Panther Party and Sinclair's right hand man, had written an article condemning the concept of the individual. In it, he said that individualism was a disease of capitalism, and must be eliminated.

It was at that point that I personally relinquished any sympathy, identification, or participation in any activity coming out of Hill Street house. The path of our former colleagues was against all my beliefs and had no place in my plans. I still loved John Sinclair, but I was disgusted. We really had a mess on our hands.

Jon Landau arrived soon after we moved out there. He was slight of build, slouchy, nerdy, someone who wore brown instead of black. Wayne immediately swallowed him up. I think Wayne was as frightened as anybody about what to do with Sinclair's bunch. That guy was still technically our manager. He and his stoner comrades were running around taking on the establishment like Christ defying the Romans, going down with a stick of dynamite in their teeth, building bombs in the basement, and they wanted us to follow right along. I had no wish to become a martyr. The arrival of our producer presented a fresh conspirator, and as was Wayne's habit, he claimed the advantage for himself.

Jon Landau, rock writer, Brandeis University alumnus, rookie music producer, now working for the Atlantic Record Corporation and the MC5. He had a slippery way about him, a little conceited like you might expect of an Easterner with hipness founded in the rock press, but that's beside the point. Our immediate concern was how to reclaim the path to success. Here was our ticket, but he was going to learn on the job. We hung out for some time, listening and arranging, and all seemed to be going fine, despite the usual MC5 randomness in the music.

We selected a studio on the Northeast side of Detroit. It was so new that the main tracking room with the 16-track recorder was not yet finished. There was a smaller room with an 8-track that was available until we could get into the bigger room. The place smelled new: floors, panels, wiring, baffles, it was all spanking new, without an ounce of vibe. Our engineer was a large character wearing a toupee.

It was going to take a month to do the record. Anxiety built as we struggled to get the songs ready. So much was in limbo, the management issue being the most perplexing. How were we supposed to maintain the kind of unity we'd had the year before, when we were hitting on all cylinders? It would be different for sure.

I think by and large, we felt compelled to let things play out however they were going to. We knew John Sinclair was going down, so whatever happened, we'd be in new company and that was fine with us. The bungling of the Elektra contract and the mishandling of the previous dilemmas left us believing Sinclair wasn't able to take the band anywhere but down.

Once we got better acquainted with Landau, he was quick to disparage and demean Sinclair and his revolutionary mission. He told us that John's ideas were laughable. Sinclair was using us to play out his fantasies, Landau said, and if we stuck around for it, we wouldn't get anywhere. That struck a chord, with Wayne particularly. At one point during the first week in the studio, John stopped by to see what was going on. He stood just inside the doorway of the room we were playing in while we rehearsed James Brown's "It's A Man's, Man's, Man's World." When we finished the song, John chuckled and said emphatically in his gruff stoned voice, "It sucks." It probably did. I wasn't feeling much, and everyone was stiff as a board. Regardless, John's comment was indicative that we were no longer together on anything.

Within a few days, a meeting was arranged at our house for the purpose of firing John Sinclair as the band's manager. J.C. was also present.

Sinclair was outraged that we refused to give him any royalty from the new record. He maintained that, as the broker of the Atlantic contract, he was entitled to a percentage.

However, Landau had informed us that word had spread that the MC5 was available through industry channels, and Sinclair had merely picked up the telephone. He really hadn't figured in the negotiations. A very stone-faced Wayne denied him his claim; so much for brotherhood. I wonder, if we had given him a point on the record, would he have written all those nasty letters about us from prison? Clearly, as a tactical move, this might have been not our wisest.

John sat there at a corner of the table across from me, his jaw hanging in astonishment.

"Nothing? Nothing? I don't need a lot, but…. nothing?"

"We don't think you should be compensated for anything further. You got most of the advance, so that should serve as severance compensation."

Wayne's air was one of complete detachment. The rest of us watched the reactions in that paralyzing moment. A brief argument ensued, without resolution. John and Jesse Crawford rose from the table and left the house.

The whole affair filled me with shame. While getting rid of Sinclair might have been appropriate, J.C. was a different issue. He had brought an invaluable completeness to our performance, and besides that, he was an incredible friend. I felt such fondness for him and it pained me to treat him like a bum. I felt like a two-faced piece of shit. I felt like we had used him, and then blown him out the door when we were through with him. I knew I would miss him. He was a quality guy.

John Sinclair was convicted of distribution of marijuana in a Michigan courtroom, and sentenced to 10 years in state prison. A benefit rally was held at the University of Michigan Student Union to raise defense funds for his appeal. John Lennon and Yoko Ono appeared and recorded a song dedicated to Sinclair. The MC5 were not invited to participate. The vicious onslaught of John's letters from jail took its toll on our morale. It wasn't easy to explain away the harshness of our separation. Now what had we done? It seemed like we were stepping off a plank in outer space, starting all over again, without a foothold. We still had a record to make, and a host of new enemies to deal with.

Wayne and Landau were locked in strategic conference, Landau telling Wayne how it should be, Wayne taking it all in, relating his new revelations to the rest of us in his matter-of-fact persona. We had no real manager, but our producer was filling in. I may have blocked much of that time out of my mind because of the confusion I felt, being under scrutiny at all times.

They were isolating my bass track, so all that played back were naked bass notes. I'd only been playing for a few years at that point, and it was painful to listen to the fumbling and jerking, misplayed notes, arrangement goofs. It wasn't fun, and it wasn't musical. My guitar apparently had a ground buzz or some noise issue that made it necessary to bring in a replacement bass. A semi-hollow body Framus replaced my Jazz Bass, and instantly gave me fits. The neck was too narrow, and the body was enormous. I complied as best I could to get the job done, but my confidence was suffering and I was losing heart.

We didn't feel like a band. We seemed like robots on an assembly line. Landau was well aware that we suffered from inconsistency, his point being that things on the record had to be "correct." He had made Wayne agree with that premise from the outset.

But the MC5's strength wasn't correctness, ever. The MC5's strength was invention and spontaneity. It was this fundamental contradiction that eroded the progress of our band. What occurred during the *Back in the USA* sessions was an overhaul of the elements of the band. It was, in a sense, a makeover: from mean to clean. After struggling with a couple of numbers, I regretfully relinquished the bass chores to Kramer, who methodically plunked out the most impotent bass lines ever laid down.

I wasn't the only laboratory rat. Actually, everyone had a turn under the microscope. Second most notable was Dennis's tempo and meter. At first, the challenge of playing with a click-track almost proved too much, but little by little, he came through with complete takes.

The guitars presented tuning difficulties, those being the days when guitars were frequently tuned from string to string, and rarely together. The vocals were a horrendous obstacle. In fact, Rob probably had the hardest challenge of all.

The one thing I did find easy was doing backup harmonies. I was always confident I had a good singing voice. I never doubted that I could lay it down. I finally got the bass down on several of the songs by the end of recording.

The result of the month of commuting from Hamburg to East Detroit boiled down to a breakdown in morale. My self-esteem was diminished considerably and the music really wasn't anything extraordinary, in my opinion. I felt about as detached from the record as I felt from everything else. At this point, I would have been happy to leave the band, but I had a problem. I had nowhere to go, nothing to go to, nobody to be with. I was trapped by my own choice to be unattached. I did the next available thing: I turned to drugs. The '70s were hitting hard. Things were changing all around. Many people were taking harder drugs as a result of a shift in the smuggling policies of the people in the drug business.

Cocaine was showing a large presence, with other types of mood-altering affairs like Valium, Quaaludes and some heroin getting play. The old hippie staples of hashish, marijuana, acid, mushrooms, and so forth, weren't getting it any more. In general, there was a mood of getting fucked up physically rather than mentally.

Clothing was drabber and less celebratory. Before long, the

MC5 decided it'd had enough of communal living and sought to go independent. Jimi Hendrix, Janis Joplin, and Jim Morrison all became casualties of drugs and alcohol shortly after the decade began. People connected with the music scene in Detroit shockingly expired. The tide of rock and roll turned decidedly degenerate.

Did we do it? Did we betray the gods? In my delusional state from a year or so before that, I would have taken on the blame. I would have imagined that the universe was directly responding to a misdeed that was completely my fault, like karma or something spiritual. But these times were different, and I had given up on spinning celestial designs in my imagination. If I was the problem, I wasn't alone.

I guess I was getting desperate to have anything other than the band as an outlet. The first thing that came along was a brazen blonde chick that stopped by as we were leaving the studio one night to invite us to a party.

Getting fucked up every night was pretty much a routine, but this time I had to drive to Detroit, so I got Dennis to go along with me. Dennis and I had a little menu of treats we used to complement our chemical attractions. Boone's Farm apple wine and Beer Nuts were one favored combination. Stroh's beer and Slim Jims were another. On extreme evenings, about once a week, we'd do pints of Jim Beam and a six of beer.

We went to this party in Detroit where the blonde chicks were. A crew of rock party people were hanging out, doing regular party things. In the kitchen, a guy a bit older than the crowd was sitting at the table, cutting lines with a pocketknife. There was a brownish powder on a mirror. I was invited to have a hit. It was heroin. Almost immediately I felt warm, at ease, and comfortably detached.

Dennis didn't hesitate to get a snoot full for himself.

On the drive back to Hamburg, we spoke about the "blow" with approving adjectives. Probably for the first time in years, I had a sense of calm that had been missing since joining the band. I don't know if Dennis shared that feeling. I think he had a lot of anxiety about throwing his fate up to chance by going with a life of being in a band. I know he was hesitant about it all in the beginning, but then he got caught up in it, and let's face it, it was a life that was full of unbelievable chances. So, anyway, if he felt that same sense of relief I felt from getting high on heroin, I completely understand.

Her name was Sue, Blonde Sue. She was brash and independent, kind of tomboyish, with lots of laughter and that in-your-face bluntness. In addition to being confident, she could instantly turn on a female vulnerability that I found alluring. That sort of female bravado must be my weakness, for it was just this sort of thing that attracted me to Sam. Throw in the dope quest and I was right at home.

After seeing her a couple more times, I must have decided to make a move. I wanted something more permanent than the helter-skelter aloofness that I was living. Connections with Wayne, Fred, and Rob were remote, and Dennis was really a moody one. Sue got me out of Hamburg, out of the sphere of annoying MC5 interaction, alone with a pretty female, and back to the familiar ground that I'd played on in the first years of reckless abandon: dope.

In a sense, doing dope was a way to step away from the bullshit of the band. It gave me an independent side that made me feel superior, elite, elevated, the effects of the dope canceling out the disgrace of having been incompetent at the recording session. Sue and I got along well enough, but when a relationship is about doing drugs,

drugs *are* the relationship.

By and by, the rest of the band followed me into the drug abyss as if it were the next big thing. We met some really downtown characters. There were two black guys who were brothers and dealers: Ninny and Junie Boy. They lived deep in the inner city of Detroit. Imagine the MC5 all sitting around eating chitlins in a dingy apartment with cockroaches crawling up the walls. We fascinated them, white dope fiends playing rock music at big time rock shows. That's how it started, the MC5's drug spiral into total destruction.

Not everyone in the band was drawn into heroin. Rob was keeping his hands clean, and his choice of indulgence remained typical of the Beat society, e.g., cigarettes, coffee, beer, and weed, things that inspired conversation. He loved talking. The rest of us, though, were well away.

The record *Back in the USA* came out to a mixed lot of reviews. People were generally amazed and dumbfounded by the squeaky-clean production and lack of bass guitar in the mix. While most reviewers couldn't or wouldn't argue with Landau's production, there was a sense of unfulfilled expectation that made it clearly questionable. Where was the bass? Was the MC5 now a mainstream product? Could this really be the same MC5 that was heard on *Kick Out The Jams?*

Inevitably, the reception at live performances was riddled with insults and heckling. We had sold out, that was obvious. All attempts to pacify, quell, or power through our dilemma felt dishonorable and trite. But after a fashion, the agitators, unable to spur a mass lynching, cracked open another beer or found some weed to smoke and melted back into the background. So much for the revolution. Shortly thereafter, we split up as a communal entity. We left Hamburg, each man going his own separate way, dividing our household possessions by drawing slips of paper with the co-owned items written down on them.

My bounty was the Electro Voice stereo speakers and a share of the record albums. I was happy with that. My dad helped me get a car: a Buick Riviera, suitable for a stylish cat like myself. I promptly set up living arrangements back in Detroit with the little junkie chick, Blonde Sue. I succeeded in fooling myself that I had a real relationship with her, and for a while we pretended to be a couple. Band gigs, some of which required travel, occurred at fairly regular intervals. One such gig was an outdoor festival in Toronto. Sue, one of her girlfriends and I drove up to Toronto in the Riviera, my new Rickenbacker bass in the trunk of my beautiful gun metal grey car. I parked in the open field behind the stage, took out the bass and set it down by the side of the car, where the girls were relaxing after the drive. I went to find out where our dressing room was to be, and upon returning, found the car parked in a different place.

"What the hell, why has the car moved?" I asked.

"We decided to move it up closer," the girlfriend replied.

"Where's the fucking bass?" I retorted.

They both looked at me quizzically. I looked back to the area where the car had been parked before. Nothing but open ground stretched across the scene. My heart sank to the bottom of my stomach. I had traded in my Fender Jazz with the alleged noise for a brand new maple-glow Rick bass, and at this moment it was a goner. Things were not looking good.

The girl named Blonde Sue left for California after we'd shacked up for a couple of months. During our couple of months, she cheated on me regularly, crashed my car, stole my practice amp, a black-faced Fender Bassman, and pawned it.

A guy was murdered in our presence, and finally, she told me she was pregnant and going to California to get an abortion. I was heartbroken, and I reveled in it. I was swallowing barbiturates like they were jellybeans, pretending to be in the band.

The other band members were tolerating it, sort of. I scared Rob so badly one afternoon, driving him to practice, that he swore he'd never get into a car that I was driving again. My life was careening out of control, and I knew it, but I was helpless to change my way. We flew to Salt Lake City to play a gig. It was a short flight to L.A., so I bought myself a ticket and went on to L.A. after the gig to visit Blonde Sue. She was staying in Laurel Canyon above Hollywood in a house where lots of dopers hung out. We had been hanging with some guys from a band called Blues Image. They were cool and liked to play with dope, so I felt sort of comfortable. Sue was working at a massage parlor down in Hollywood, and I wondered if she was giving blowjobs, but being a trusting fool, I didn't question. We went around to see people with Sue showing me off like a trophy rock star while we got stoned and drunk.

The last night I was there, I borrowed someone's car, drove down the steep-as-fuck canyon street, crashing through the barrier at the bottom of the hill. It was a Cadillac. I injured my ankle in the crash and hobbled back up the hill to tell the guy where his car was. The next day I got dropped off at the airport and made my way back to Detroit, where I holed up in my parents' basement for the second time. Things weren't going very well.

It was winter, cold as hell, snow falling, and I was feeling a head cold coming on. Sue and I had had a little regular dope house where we were welcome. It was on the order of a blind pig, a residence where you knocked on a back door and were invited to come in and buy any sort of thing they were serving, drugs or alcohol. You could order a beer and a bag of mixed jive, heroin with a cut on it. It didn't cost very much to get loaded, so it was fun to go down there and relax. When I knocked on the back door, it was snowing and the temperature was about 15 degrees Fahrenheit. I stayed down in that little basement bar for a couple of hours, drinking and having a bag of dope.

Upon leaving, I discovered that it was still snowing, freezing as before, but as I entered the outdoors, I felt warm and toasty. The night weather was not at all unpleasant, my head cold symptoms had disappeared, and the freshly fallen snow amused me. Not only that, my thoughts about that distant love interest had all the trappings of a movie that no longer appealed to me. For the moment I was free, free of physical, mental, and emotional weight.

I spent a couple of months down there in my parents' basement. I rigged a bed and a small arrangement of furniture. With the cost of getting high so cheap, it was easy to allow myself to trot off to the dope house whenever I had the notion. There was even parking behind the dope house. Fate was inviting me to help myself. I was driving a Buick Riviera and going to the speakeasy house regularly. The band was my only social life, and not much of that other than going on road trips for gigs.

We were in Florida for a big show with Alice Cooper and Bob Seger. The morning after the gig, I awoke at the hotel and went outside on the balcony. Something was not right. I felt melancholy and the air had a peculiar smell. I couldn't figure out what it was. What was that weird smell?

I started to cough and hack from a tickle deep in my throat.

I felt clammy and uncomfortable. Jesus Christ, could I be getting a cold? The crazy smell in the air, and the flakey dark mood, what was going on? Was it what I thought it might be, dope sickness, a sign that I was developing a habit? I was missing the bitch that dissed me for a life of crime in California. A stupid song was playing on the radio, Elton John's "Your Song." I tried to ignore my discomfort, but everything was making me feel miserable. Yes, it was definitely symptoms of withdrawal.

I had a choice: stay the fuck away from any drugs until it went away, or go looking for something to end it now. Every addict faces that choice every time the dope runs out. Most often the choice is to go get something. That decision becomes the way of life that goes on and on interminably. It was the first of a couple of trips to Florida that had me looking for a heroin connection.

One of those trips actually reunited me with my ex, Sam. She was living in Deerfield Beach and mooching off her parents. I spent one night with her, scoring a bag of jive that wasn't cool. But I had no intention of doing anything with her other than getting high, and it was the last time I ever saw her.

She called me up out of the blue at my parents' house one night wanting to borrow a couple hundred bucks to retain a lawyer because she'd gotten busted with drugs down there in Deerfield Beach. I told her I'd send her something, but I had no intention of actually doing it. She was on her own. My life was turning in that direction where feelings are pushed back out of sight. It is a common feature with drug addicts. All that matters is getting the dope.

Returning to Detroit was always most satisfying. I knew where to go, whom to call, what to expect, I was going full tilt into the character of a drug fiend. I really didn't care what anybody thought about me, I was on my own and determined to play out my hazardous games.

Actually, I didn't feel that out of step. Keith Richards from the Rolling Stones was getting busted, and it was obvious the crazy drug-addled lifestyle was a popular fashion. Where would it all wind up? In my head, I imagined the band was forever. We were all so committed, I couldn't fathom there not being a band. We still had a ways to go.

Atlantic Crossing

The MC5 benefited from its members inspiring each other. As individuals, there were different traits that set each guy apart from anyone else. To say Fred Smith and Wayne Kramer both played the same style of guitar would be to so oversimplify what they actually did that it would be misleading.

Sure, they both played electric guitars, but that was where the similarity ended. As a member of the group, I constantly appreciated how diverse we were, that we created something no one else was capable of. Rob's vocals were unique, yet when combined with all the music, his voice became another instrument.

All together, when we invented music, it rang with a strong heart and created an enchanting aura. Structure never was the MC5's long suit. Spontaneity and surprise, backed up with heaps of power, is what set us apart.

Once *Back in the USA* became the main body of our set, we

abandoned those areas where we had gambled musically. Those were the areas where audiences lost their self-consciousness and became mesmerized by the band.

The MC5 had stolen a glimpse of the truth through a crack in a very frosty window that others would never even bother to look for. It became legendary when others glimpsed the light through us, a light so bright that it was blinding. If you were there, you told other people about what you'd experienced, but no words could ever really convey what had happened, nor could it be duplicated. Sometimes ragged and disturbing, sometimes obnoxious, sometimes incredible, the face of the MC5 always changed. One thing was constant: it always provoked a response. If no response were provoked, the MC5 would have figured out a way to make one happen.

With Sinclair and his cult lobbing shit balls at us any way they could, a music press trying to write honestly about the band without pissing anyone off, and the band imploding under the weight of drugs and alcohol, it's amazing that we carried on, but why not? We still clung to the hope that things would turn in our favor, in spite of everything.

The one thing that determines anyone's life expectancy in the music business is sales, and the one thing that we couldn't change was that ours were sliding.

The record company was banking that the Landau-produced MC5 would go through the roof with sales. But rock writers don't necessarily make good producers. I don't hate *Back in the USA*. It's a great record, a classic by a great band. I played the bass guitar on "Teenage Lust," "High School," "Let Me Try," and "Shakin' Street." Kramer did the bass on all the rest. I sang all the principal backup vocal harmonies. To say my heart wasn't in would be untrue. I was compromised, but if I could do it again, I would in a heartbeat. Playing rock music is the love of my life. It is what I was meant to do.

I guess we were rock stars. We wore flashy clothes on stage, played in front of thousands, flew to distant venues, drank heavily, had roadies, stayed in nice hotels, rode in limos occasionally, and opened shows for very big acts. I can't say we were aware of being on a downward spiral. The only thing that might have seemed uncomfortable was the audience response at the end of our set being subdued. Instead of sweaty, exhilarated, hyper-sexed crazies, a zombified group milled amongst themselves waiting for the real end of the set. "Alright…alright….we're the MC5. Thank you and goodnight!" Rob was the only one sweating.

Had we not experienced those delirious Grande days of hypnotic strobes and flickering images on the walls, I might have taken the lackluster in stride. We had good connections, and the band was tight, maybe too tight. Several times we returned to New York, usually playing at Ungano's, a club on the Upper West Side that showcased aspiring record label acts. On one occasion, we opened for Weather Report, after which we went around the corner to catch the Elvin Jones group's set.

Then, in 1970, the record label sent us off to England for a few shows. I remember reading in the *Melody Maker* on the plane that the legendary MC5 were about to make an appearance in the U.K.

"Legendary," that was a laugh. How did we achieve the lofty status of legendary? Just being in the land of our hero groups was exciting. Here was where the Stones and Beatles had cut their teeth. The Yardbirds and Who had throttled audiences with unprecedented original music there. The Davies brothers of Kinks fame were out there somewhere.

I looked at the street below my hotel window. It was early afternoon. The sounds of men shouting to each other in their British accents echoed through the air. Small trucks were stopping with their deliveries, and pigeons flew from the rooftops. It was like a dream. Though so much had transpired in the life of the MC5, it seemed that it had all been a prelude to this moment. We had finally arrived on the shores where it really mattered, the Avalon of rock music.

The MC5 were primarily night people. Fred was hardly even seen before three in the afternoon, unless we were traveling. I preferred sleeping until afternoon. Dennis slept in as a rule. Because of late hours, but regardless, sleeping in late was normal. I pulled the window curtains closed, turned down my bed covers, and got into bed to sleep off the first trans-Atlantic flight of my life. I was in England at last.

For a few days, the record label took us around to popular pubs and eateries, pitched a nice reception party at their offices, and introduced us to the hot after hours spot known as the Speakeasy Club. As we filed into the club, a drunken Keith Moon was seen hollering obscenities at some people from the open door of his white Rolls. Inside, the atmosphere was intensely chic, dark and warm, alive with conversation, with almost every table occupied. We were seated in a semi-circular booth amid the curious glances of extremely condescending faces.

"Oh gawd, Yanks!"

Somebody nudged me. "That's Jeff Beck sitting behind Fred."

"Damn, really?" I replied. I could only see the back of someone's head, so I just accepted it.

We sat there looking at the menu, feeling like we were on the menu. Our label guy knew the important people, of course, so no one was overtly rude, and we were treated respectfully by anyone who had any real clout. Being Americans and very conscious of our macho responsibility, we all ordered steak. Bourbon and Coke, the band favorite, was immediately served so we could relax a little bit while the London elite scanned our credentials and our behavior.

After dinner, a dessert menu was produced, with several mysterious items.

"Whatever Peach Melba is, I'll have it."

Shortly, I was treated to one of the most fabulous flavors ever in my life: French vanilla ice cream with peaches, covered in caramel sauce.

Our hotel was up by Paddington Station, a bit off the main drag, in a neighborhood with a lot of those flats with white door stoops. Drinking was what the MC5 liked to do best, so we tried a pub or two before settling in at the hotel pub as our primary meeting place. Then out of the blue, a telephone call came from a person named Twink, from an MC5-like band called the Pink Fairies.

"How bout a going out for a loon?" he asked.

"What's a loon?" I replied.

"Oh you know mate, a bit of crazy fun." His voice was bright and uninhibited.

"Yeah, sure, come on over."

When they arrived, a couple of us piled into the tiniest car ever, a Mini, with three Pink Fairies and a blonde German girl high on acid to drive around London, having sex in the car in the middle of the afternoon. From that point, the MC5 and Pink Fairies became brother bands.

The fun was just beginning. On another afternoon, a group

of rock-looking guys came walking down the sidewalk as we came out of the hotel. As they drew closer, they started waving at us like they knew us.

"Hey, what's happening, you're the MC5, how're you doin'? We're from Detroit too. We have a band called Sky. I'm Doug."

We didn't know them at all, but they were there to do some recording. Eventually, they would become the Knack, and have a hit record called "My Sharona." It was a shock to meet Detroiters from a band we'd never heard of on a London street.

Our roadie, Steve "The Hawk" Harnadek, decided to get a tattoo while in London. At that time, tattoos were unheard of among rock and rollers. Tatts were still the badges of bar room toughs, military guys, or degenerates and drunken sailors. Naturally, he wanted a hawk on his arm, but after emerging from the sub-sidewalk tattoo shop, his tatt resembled a parrot more than a bird of prey. We chided him endlessly.

We played the Roundhouse, an old train switching building converted to a venue. It was big and full of people. We did pretty well, I'd say; not the pandemonium of a Detroit show, but for the reserved Londoners, it was good.

Then we flew to Basel, Switzerland, in a DC3 prop plane, to be met by a bus bound for Lake Constance in Germany. I was fascinated to be in Europe, the land of my ancestors, far from the Northwest Detroit suburbs of my parents. Geeky languages and accents, very different food, but always plenty of beer and cigarettes keeping me from feeling too far away from reality. There were two young blonde girls on the bus besides the driver. I didn't know why they were there or whom they were with. They might have been there to be available for the band, but no one ever made any attempt to find out.

Once we got to Germany, it was like a fairy tale. The shop windows displayed Alpine goods, the beer came in steins, and to this Detroiter, it felt like being at Disneyland. It was an outdoor festival, and the day we played, it rained for eight hours straight.

When we took the stage, a completely delirious and rain-soaked crowd chanted our name. It was phenomenal—a totally foreign audience singing along with our music. We were exhilarated. That evening in the hotel tavern, we celebrated in a sing-along with old German regulars sitting around long wooden tables. Rob sang "Georgia On My Mind" a cappella, to tumultuous applause from the astonished Germans.

Word was that *Back in the USA* wasn't doing as well as the first record had done. Even with all the production and team players, its chart level was far below what the live album had accomplished. A sense of anxiety came over us, and I couldn't help but feel we had blown it. We had a good band, no, we had a great band, but we were stepping in shit trying to be a big band.

As a quick remedy, Atlantic sent us into a London studio to get started on the next LP. We assembled for a rough band track—meaning rhythm guitar, bass, and drums—for a new song by Fred called "Sister Anne." After overcoming the initial difficulties of arranging, and inventing a bass line for the song, we went for a take. Once again, my bass had noise issues.

So our label guy called Chris Squire from the band Yes, and asked Chris if he'd so kind as to bring his Rickenbacker down to the studio to help out a distressed label mate. Within an hour, the "Rickie" was there and pressed into service. It didn't take long to get a hot band track. Once we were satisfied, Fred and Rob dubbed the harmonica duet over the basic track, and we had our first song of the next album in the can, minus vocals and overdubbed guitar solos. It was all we had time for, but it was a great start.

We returned to the States and got started looking for a studio in Detroit. Somehow we came up with a place called Artie Fields. Artie had been a swing band guy from the '40s, and the idea of being somewhere esoteric was cool.

It was a good sized room with a nice old-timey atmosphere, and it was inexpensive. Atlantic recommended Geoff Haslam as a producer, an English cat with a relaxed, flexible manner. Had he been assigned to the band for *Back in the USA*, things definitely would have been easier.

I was able to shift in and out of heroin use by staying off it for a few days until the effects of withdrawal stopped. But the attraction was always present, and it didn't take much irritation to spur me back to the dope house. We were meeting an assortment of people. Through drug dealers, we met people of various backgrounds and interests. There were business people, criminals, bikers, crazies, flakes, photographers, writers, and fringe people.

One strange episode was meeting a group of gays that wanted to hire us to play their gay picnic bash. They had a bar on Woodward Avenue, the front of which was totally plain—no windows, no sign and no light, just a wooden door. Inside a dimly-lit bar room, gay men seated themselves in booths and at the bar, talking and drinking, while music played from a jukebox. We didn't look out of place at all. I don't remember too much about the picnic, except for being so drunk I fell off the side of the stage, landing on one leg without missing a note, and kept on playing.

The recording proceeded extremely well. All the new material was happening without problems. I had no trouble laying down my tracks and no one was saying, "Hey, this guy can't play, let's call in a session player." The change in mood was remarkably productive. Blonde Sue called me from California on the studio telephone. She was due to have an abortion the next day, and she was having second thoughts. "What should I do?" she asked. She was distraught. "Should I go through with it?"

By this time, I would not have known if she was pregnant by me, or if she'd even fabricated the whole pregnancy. "Yes, do it," I said, not wanting to deal with it or her anymore. I was numbed by the whole experience. Now, I was using drugs without having an accomplice. Why would I want to mess that up? Plus, I had no inclination to try trusting her. She was history.

The record got finished, and I was proud of it, but apathy had replaced former ambitions. It had been decided that Fred would have control of the album's thematic elements. He would design and supervise the production, and be credited as co-producer of the record. The Landau experience had left us insecure about handling ourselves, and we all thought Fred had the best chance of making things stand up to the test.

Meanwhile, potential managers were courting us. One guy actually flew to Detroit to meet with us and lay out a management proposal. It was a good chance to resolve loose ends and get back on track business-wise. To my dismay, the band rejected the offer and decided we would handle our own affairs, meaning Wayne Kramer and Fred Smith were going to decide everything.

Right there, any chance of pulling the MC5 back on track was eliminated. Fred wouldn't commit to anything, and Wayne's decisions were all bad.

The rhythm section had been maligned whether rightfully or not, with such contempt it would never stand with any degree of self-esteem again, at least not in this band. Rob had endured prolonged ridicule. His body, his voice, his stage presence; just to hang onto any inspiration left from those early days as a rock and roll singer was hard. None of this was obvious, and the band continued to approach the future as if everything was in check. I felt gloomy and alone.

High Time, despite being the most accomplished work that we'd done, received the least attention from the public when it finally hit the streets. The reviews complimented us, but nothing could bring back the sense of imminent breakout that once prevailed regarding the MC5. Going back to England helped our general morale, but in the wake of Fred and his wife losing their newborn son in a sudden infant death syndrome incident, things weren't at an all time high.

I decided to take a bus to the Albert and Victoria Museum. The entrance was crammed with every sort of animal taxidermy. Somewhere on the second floor, I spotted Rob wandering through an exhibit.

"Hey Rob, wow, isn't this an incredible museum. I'm so glad I decided to come check it out." It was great to see Rob there. Thinking we were on a shared wavelength, I tried to start a conversation, and even imagined that he and I might hang out together and go through the exhibits.

But I was wrong. He quickly turned his attention to another direction in the vast galleries, and wandered off by himself. I was confused and hurt. It really hit home that he and I didn't share much of anything, even though we had been partners for a number of years. You might say it was yet another kind of bad trip, resembling the schism that had appeared between us in '66. I was so much on my own I didn't care one way or the other.

With my hand a little deeper in the dope scene, I got myself educated to where I could score in London's Chinatown. A one block-long street close to Charring Cross Station, Shaftesbury Street, was the place to score. Junkie solicitors stood in the shadowed doorways, easily recognizing a would-be dope seeker.

I quickly found a Limey bloke who would then go to his "chink" and return with a small packet containing the drugs. It was cheap and very strong—raw, brown, unrefined heroin that reeked of vinegar. The atmosphere on the street was seedy, like a movie about opium dens where evil characters and strange human traffic flourished in secret subterranean cellars. I was taking care of myself.

Things at the record label weren't as hospitable as they had been. We weren't front page news any longer. I remember playing a very small venue in Wales, and there was an outdoor thing at or near Brighton. The English band Slade was getting some press, as was the Move, and a ratty looking character named David Bowie. Things were morphing all around, with a new emphasis on costume and drama. The MC5 was becoming darker and darker. Then it happened. Fred took the call; the Atlantic Record Company was dropping the band. There would be no third album on Atlantic. Our sales numbers indicated a definite descent in the band's popularity.

We had played a fair amount of big venues, medium venues, even got to open for huge acts like the Who, Led Zeppelin, and some others. Played countless times with Alice Cooper, Bob Seger, Ted Nugent, Ike and Tina Turner, Frank Zappa, and Joe Cocker, but we had hit the rut where no matter where you play, it's not going to bump your career. We were spinning our wheels, and they had decided to pull the plug. Bye-bye, limos.

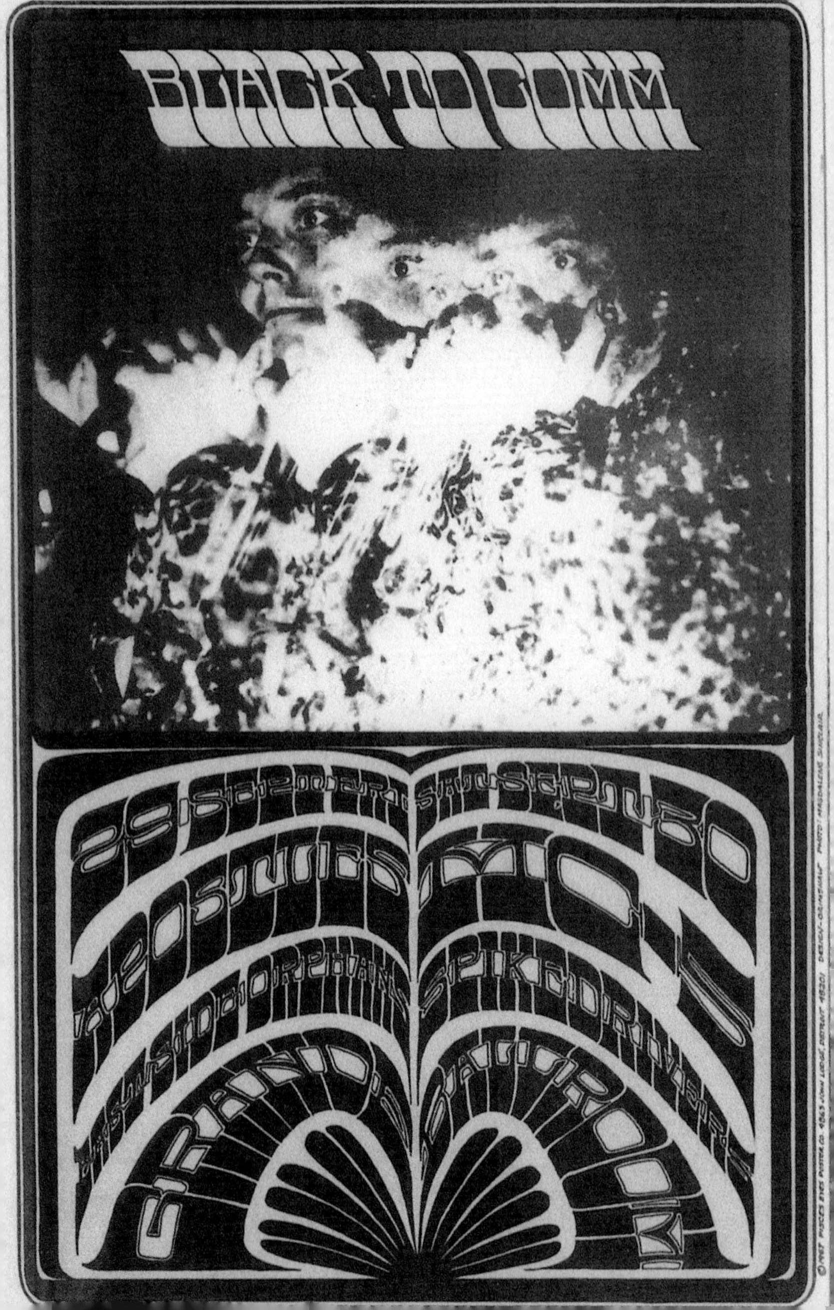
BLACK TO COMM
©1967 PISCES EYES POSTER CO. 4863 JOHN LODGE, DETROIT 48201 DESIGN-GRIMSHAW PHOTO: MAGDALENE SINCLAIR

10

Out Of The Frying Pan...

These days, when it comes to talking about the MC5, I remain just as tongue-tied as ever. In all the years during, and all the years since that mighty troupe took the stage, neither my words nor my explanations seem complete. Scores of reasons and dilemmas play with my memory of what might have been, but nothing really defines what made it so formidable or why it all came crashing down like a burning dirigible.

Looking at the big picture, I try to imagine what it was like for the fans, because it was the fans that gave us the reputation that survives to this day. If I'd been a fan, coming to an MC5 show that balanced on a tightrope, pitting the power of law enforcement against the raucous energy of a crowd of hormonal teenagers and psychedelic rabble rousers wearing spangled colors, draping flags over their amplifiers, blasting high energy beats and screaming liberation anthems, then I would have been just as spirited and carried away by the event as any young person could possibly be. In that atmosphere, anything would have been possible, and I would have left with a powerful and lasting impression.

Imagine the heaving mass of sweaty bodies, the colossal electronic guitar distortion, delirious energy, and partially naked people moving in unison with each other. Imagine the cops trying to put a stop to the revelry. The MC5 must have seemed like a squad of angels battling the forces of a repressor tyrant. As heroes, as martyrs, as saviors, as victims of circumstance, it becomes classic human drama and the source of myth.

No wonder it all came crashing down. Regardless of what the band produced in the wake of switching our allegiance, modifying our strategy, or retooling—however we might try to rationalize it—nothing could be enough to fill the void left by the MC5 that was. Nothing could replace the nightly drama of being sacrificed at the altar.

The MC5 gave up its status as house band of the revolution to save its own ass. We traded in our destiny of getting nailed to a cross by the contemporary Romans we were baiting. That might have been an exciting prospect. Martyrs always draw a good crowd. When we laid down our weapons of war to make a bid for conventional success, we torched our own balloon.

Things were in a state of decline. We'd had a couple of offers from management professionals to take charge of the group. In one case, the person made multiple trips at his own expense to meet with us and discuss managing the group.

I think we might have been spoiled by our time under the

Atlantic umbrella, but any connections arranged by Atlantic evaporated the minute the label let us go. Kramer and Smith determined that we weren't going to sign with some upstart out of New Jersey. The shell shock of our business catastrophes made us leery of any approaching scavenger. We weren't biting on anything unless it was wrapped in green. We no longer had confidence in each other, and that spelled doom any way you look at it.

In 1971, after recording *High Time*—conceptualized by "Frederico Smithelini," but really a return to band consensus production—a minor tour was booked, followed by another minor tour, somewhat suspiciously arranged for the purpose of meeting and intertwining ourselves with the entrepreneur, Ronan O'Rahilly. He was trying to secure us a deal with Phillips, a reasonably significant label, offering a decent cash advance for recording.

Without a record label or a manager, the band had undergone a complete meltdown in terms of business. Ronan was a great prospect for taking up the MC5 cause, being a staunch rebel himself with his pirate radio station, Radio Caroline, broadcasting from a ship in the English Channel. He was the kind of charismatic fellow that fit the MC5's image.

At the time, however, there was a second interested party in the form of the notorious Roulette Records, helmed by the shady Morris Levy. They were offering a fraction of the advance money that Phillips offered, and were a smaller label to boot, but it was a guaranteed deal.

Wayne and Fred, after suspending their silent competition to become the de facto management team, decided to pass on the Roulette offer and pursue the Phillips advance. Result: the Phillips deal fell through at the last minute, and the Roulette offer was rescinded by the time the band decided to backtrack.

I didn't care. Heroin saw to that.

I often hear people wonder what is the attraction of heroin? What is attractive about becoming a heroin addict? As a long time junkie, I should be able to answer that question at least partially. I will try.

The drug is a painkiller. It kills pain of any kind. It deadens the nervous system. In the absence of signals from the nervous system, the brain is filled with a euphoria that is simply not possible at any other time, except during sleep, but sleep is unconsciousness. Heroin is like a waking dream.

I had a girlfriend who told me she had been obsessed with syrup of ipecac, a potion that induces vomiting. How could that possibly be enjoyable, I asked? She had no precise answer; only that every day she went to the pharmacy to buy her ipecac so she could have a private vomiting session. This woman became my drug trade partner for the last year I was in the MC5.

I'm not trying to draw a correlation between puking and drug addiction, but we do know that painkillers create nausea as a side effect. One of the tell-tale signs of addiction is the absence of nausea when taking painkillers. To get maximum effect from a shot of heroin, nausea is the standard of a measurable dose, the one that pushes your tolerance beyond its limits. Puking means two things: your body is rejecting the substance, and the shit is good.

Being alone in a car on a Detroit freeway, feverishly searching for a gas station with a lockable men's room where five minutes of privacy would give me enough time to feel comfortable in my mind and body once again, is not the picture of a rock star I would want my fans to see. Yet, I performed this sordid activity daily. In the squalor of a filthy gas station toilet, I would cook my dope in a tarnished teaspoon, draw up the liquid in a disposable syringe, tie off my arm with my belt, and inject the dope.

James Brown called it "King Heroin," and this is why. In spite of the humiliating degradation of living this way, I was determined to continue. Maybe more than anything else, it's a control issue. When everything in your life has funneled down to the barest thread, controlling your blood pressure may appear to be the only place where you have the final and uncompromising say. It's your world and you alone are the master, which is the irony.

I used to tell myself that junkies were the most resourceful people in the world. I considered my ability to obtain dope and find locations to do my thing a strength that set me apart from most people, because of the difficulties I had to overcome. My delusion validated what I was doing. When I succeeded in getting high, I thought well of my accomplishment. I had my shit together and nothing could stop me.

The ipecac girl came into my life as one of many people who came to MC5 shows to have a good time, dance, get high with friends, parade around and be merry while the bands played. She was a Midwest hippie, by which I mean she and her people dressed like hippies, took psychedelic drugs, smoked a lot of dope, acted like tribal people, and were of course, music fans.

While the MC5 weren't particularly fond of hippie culture and ridiculed it more than related to it, I personally didn't see any reason to be hostile. I liked the hippies' general attitude, and the women were happy to have sex. The hippies were all right with me; they were peaceable, and so am I.

Adele—for that was her name—had joined a Hare Krishna

temple after becoming disenchanted with hippie lifestyle, and after some time, lost interest in that as well, divorcing her husband in the process. She was looking for a new game, and there I was floating like a leaf in the wind, with nothing but empty shadows for my current outlook.

She took to riding her bicycle over to my parents' house, where I was holed up in the basement as a displaced resident. She was met by my father, who, admiring her highly motivational effort, announced to me at 8:00 AM, "Hey Mike, there's someone here to see you."

I was deep in a self-induced coma from a dope run the night before, and my usual waking hour was after three in the afternoon. Seeing her at that hour of the morning, in my parents' driveway on a bicycle, put me over the edge.

"What the fuck, what are you doing here?" I was beside myself with anger.

"I just wanted to see you," was the demure reply.

"You have to leave, I'm not seeing anyone right now." I was livid and disgusted. I sent her away, I hoped for good, returning to my tomb to sleep the day away undisturbed.

She was persistent, calling me on the phone, offering to take me to any number of activities she thought might be enjoyable. I was firmly in her sights and nothing was going to stop her. She thought that maybe taking me to the beach would be a good way to get me in a good mood. So one fine day, I agreed to go with her to Lake Saint Clair, a large, vile public beach between the Detroit River and Lake Huron.

While sitting in the sand on a blanket amidst a couple hundred people who were tanning up to lose that Michigan chalky complexion and try to appear rich and happy, all I could think of was getting dope. I offered a proposal to Adele.

"You can give me some money to buy a bag of dope and I will hang out with you for a while, or you can take me home." I had no idea what she would say, but I was pretty sure she might go for it.

"I don't have very much. How much do you need?" she said as she pulled out a $20 bill from her little beaded hippie pouch.

"That will be just enough," I said, claiming the green and feeling slightly disgusted with myself.

Adele had a little daughter who was around three years of age. Why she thought being with a junkie rock and roll star was appealing is a mystery, but when a woman gets her mind set on something, she will pursue it relentlessly.

After that, she accommodated my appetite for heroin often, and we soon set up house on the East Side of Detroit, where we would live and sell drugs. Adele was very streetwise for a hippie/Krishna girl. She had good deal-making sense and a knack for acquiring cash.

She bought a Volkswagen convertible, put down the rent and security deposits for the house, and somehow made connections for a steady stream of drugs. She could get pot, hash, coke, heroin, pills, whatever there was. It didn't take long at all before the phone was ringing constantly with people looking for drugs. Actually, it became the dope Mecca for all the area rock and rollers.

One evening, out of the blue, Iggy, the singer from the Stooges, knocked on my door looking for a fix. I had a very strong bag of dope that evening and I wasn't keen on letting him shoot up without warning him how dangerous it might be.

He insisted on doing two bags at once and I pleaded with him to stop fucking around or he was going to kill himself. Apparently, he though I was being a pussy for being so cautious. He didn't want to miss out on the strongest rush he could manage. So, he cooked up the potion.

I pleaded with him once again to inject it ever so slowly, because he wouldn't be able to assimilate the whole amount without going under and possibly dying. Without so much as a blink, he pushed the plunger down all the way and smiled at me. It only took a few seconds. His eyes rolled back into his head, his mouth dropped open, and he was gone. His breathing stopped, and so did his heart. I was panicked. I shouted at him, to no avail. Adele slapped him across the face a few times, also to no avail.

I yelled for Adele to get the bag of coke I had stashed in the other room. In a minute I had it ready in a syringe. I went for a vein in his limp arm. In went the coke, but nothing happened. Just as I was wondering where a convenient dumpster might be, I thought I would try the cold water remedy.

I carried him into the bathroom and laid him down in the tub. On went the cold water from the shower, but nothing happened. It had been a few minutes since he had lost consciousness and stopped breathing. He was dead, gone, expired, overdosed.

I flashed on my lifeguard senior lifesaving training. There was one last thing: the dreaded mouth-to-mouth resuscitation. I pulled his mouth open, tilted his head back, pinched his nostrils together, and blew a lungful of air into his chest.

Once, twice, then on the third breath he sputtered and gasped for more oxygen. It was like a car engine trying to start on a cold day. Finally, he caught the rhythm, and was breathing on his own. He gave me the shittiest grin I have ever had the pleasure to see, and said, "Wow."

At that moment, the ever-opportunistic Adele, standing in the bathroom doorway, took a picture. In it, the look on my face is one of disgust and frustration. I had warned him repeatedly. I had wasted a half a gram of coke I'd been saving for myself. And I was completely removed from my own euphoric high that would now have to be replaced. He continued to be smarmy and lovable. He actually asked me if he could have some more. I refused, of course. I told him to get out.

When the band decided to go back to England, I was all but isolated from them. I had no wish to leave my house, let alone leave the country. I had a pocket full of cash and an endless supply of drugs. I was cashing out people's guitars when they were hard up for dope money, and actually had a .38 mm pistol I kept close to my person.

Band affairs were dreary events, full of posturing and empty jargon. I opted to get my own ticket and meet the rest of them over there a day after their arrival. Wayne, Dennis, and Fred were regular customers at my house. Rob never did get involved on either end of the drug trade. He had his coffee, cigarettes, and stash of weed. He also had a family, something that none of the rest of us had.

I packed what I needed in terms of extravagant stage outfits and stuffed assorted drug paraphernalia in the deepest recesses of my suitcase. In those days, airport security was very lenient. Random searches were a rarity, with simple screening at the gate before entering the aircraft.

In a real show of arrogance, I had to drive at outrageous speeds on the freeway from Detroit to make the flight at the last possible minute. Once at the gate, a security officer asked me to place the contents of my pockets on the conveyer belt. As I reached into my pocket, I felt the tip of a disposable syringe I had forgotten to get rid of.

Knowing it was going to cause a scene, I asked the officer if we could check my pockets in private. He asked what I had, and I told him I had a needle. That set off a chain of events that caused me to miss the flight. As two agents escorted me to the airport security office, I managed to slip my finger into the key pocket on my jeans and remove a packet of dope I was carrying to enjoy on the flight while I traveled. Ever so nonchalantly, I dropped it on the floor as we walked and talked. After a lengthy interview, I was released. It seems that possessing a syringe at an airport wasn't sufficient cause for arrest.

I called Adele to come get me, since my flight had departed without me. I would have to take the same flight the next night. In an unparalleled show of further arrogance, I went back to the spot where I had dropped the bag of dope from my pocket and, as discreetly as possible, picked it back up before leaving the airport for home. Since the first gig of the tour was the next night at the London School of Economics, I knew I had fucked up beyond reason. I was going to miss it. I knew I was in big trouble.

When I arrived at Heathrow, Dennis met me outside with a van that the band was using. He was shaking his head. "Everyone's pissed," he told me with a stern face. He wasn't kidding. He knew things were probably beyond repair, but he wasn't giving me the whole scoop.

"Where's the dope?" I asked him without bothering to ask what was in the works.

"Same place as before, Garrard and Shaftsbury," he said.

"Let's go," I responded. I didn't care about anything.

The mood was muted. Nobody was saying much about the missed gig. Someone had filled in and it was over with. We went out to meet with Ronan at a vegetarian restaurant. The MC5 were not vegetarians. Going back to Ronan's place, Fred and Wayne were conspicuously having thoughtful dialogues with him, while I lounged away the time drinking.

The entire tour would last a few weeks or more, with gigs spread out every few days. Each day I would haul myself down to Chinatown to get a bag of dope. I almost bought the farm one day in the Charring Cross tube station toilet. I cooked up a bag of the stuff, shot it into my vein, and felt the life going out of me. The lights were going dim and I struggled to maintain consciousness. I knew if I let go, I would pass out in there, and probably be found dead or in a coma. I held on, concentrating on remaining awake. After a long moment, the wave of death passed. I decided to take a cab back to the hotel, and be safe for a while.

I missed my nice comfy East Side bungalow and the certainty of having plenty of dope and money. Adele wanted to come to England, so I told her to get herself a ticket and come on over with a decent stash. In the meantime, I asked her to send me a package with something in it.

It was February 1972. I remember it because she sent me a Valentine's Day heart-shaped box. The "candy" was inside. It finally got to my hotel the day Adele herself arrived. We actually opened it together.

Dennis was waiting for the "candy" too, because I had told him about it, and he asked me every day if the mail had come. She and I holed up in a small room in the hotel. We got loaded and took pictures of me in my "duke" outfit, a Mardi Gras costume I had bought at a thrift store in New Orleans. My isolation from the band was complete, even on the road.

London was very wet and rainy most of the time. The radio had bizarre soft pop rock, the likes of Marmalade and Mungo Jerry. Slade was happening, a kind of cartoon version of hard rock, but a definite preview of things to come. All in all, I was enjoying the trip.

As we were set to leave the hotel and travel to France the next day, I started my packing. Adele would stay behind at the hotel until I got back. Dennis knocked on my door to tell me there was a meeting in Rob's room on the next floor. We assembled in the small room and everyone took a seat. Wayne stood and without hesitation, announced that everyone felt that I should leave the band.

My immediate reaction was not one of surprise or panic. In fact, I was hardly fazed by the notion of it. As a matter of form, I asked why. Fred was the one to speak. "Everybody thinks you just aren't into it."

I paused a second and said it would be fine with me. "After we finish the tour, I'll leave and you guys can find a new bass player." "We already have," Wayne retorted with an air of seriousness.
"But I want to go to France and then I'll leave," I said with some resolve.

Wayne shook his head. "We've already taken the steps to replace you." The air froze for a second or two. "We'll take a vote. Why don't you go back down to your room? We'll let you know what we decide."

I left the meeting and returned to my room. "I just got fired from the band," I told Adele.

"Those fuckin' bastards," Adele exclaimed. "That fucking

Wayne Kramer. What a fucking creep. They're not getting anymore freebies from me, or credit either."

"Actually, I don't really mind leaving the band. I'm not happy in it."

"Those sons of bitches! Fuck them!" She was taking advantage of the opportunity to say how she felt toward the others and defending me from the hurt she must have thought it caused me.

Within five minutes, Wayne and Fred appeared in the doorway. Wayne entered the room and stood at the back wall, facing the bed where I was reclining.

"Well…it was no," he said matter-of-factly.

I shrugged like it was all the same to me. "OK," I said, and after that, no words were spoken.

Fred gave me a wry grimace as he disappeared from the doorway. Wayne meandered toward the door, paused and looked around the wall, and then at the floor. He looked up, then looked down, then moved off out of sight.

The awkwardness of that moment did not belong to me, although my nerves and emotions were drawn tight as a bowstring. Once Wayne left my line of sight, I felt an immense relief from the stranglehold of being in the band. An overwhelming weight was immediately lifted from my shoulders. I was free of it.

The flight home was as relaxing as could be, especially after I had to fight and claw to get the band to pay for my return, since I couldn't use my original ticket. After much telephoning back and forth between Ronan, Fred, and myself, they finally relented and paid my fare.

The sky looking down on the gray-green and brown of the city of Detroit was a beautiful thing to my eyes. Without the clangor of MC5 propaganda, I felt like a real person again: anonymous, but real. I had only been back for a few days when I read in *Rolling Stone* that the MC5 had been booed off the stage at Wembley Stadium. "Ha," I beamed inside, "There you go!"

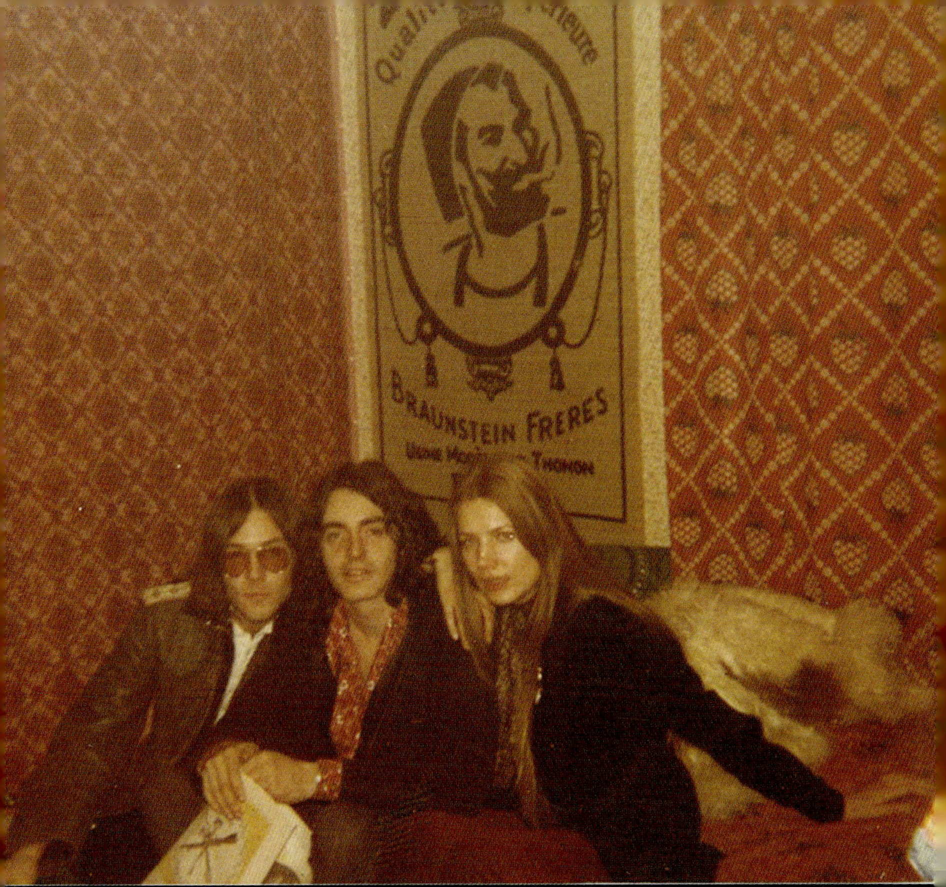
BRAUNSTEIN FRERES
THONON

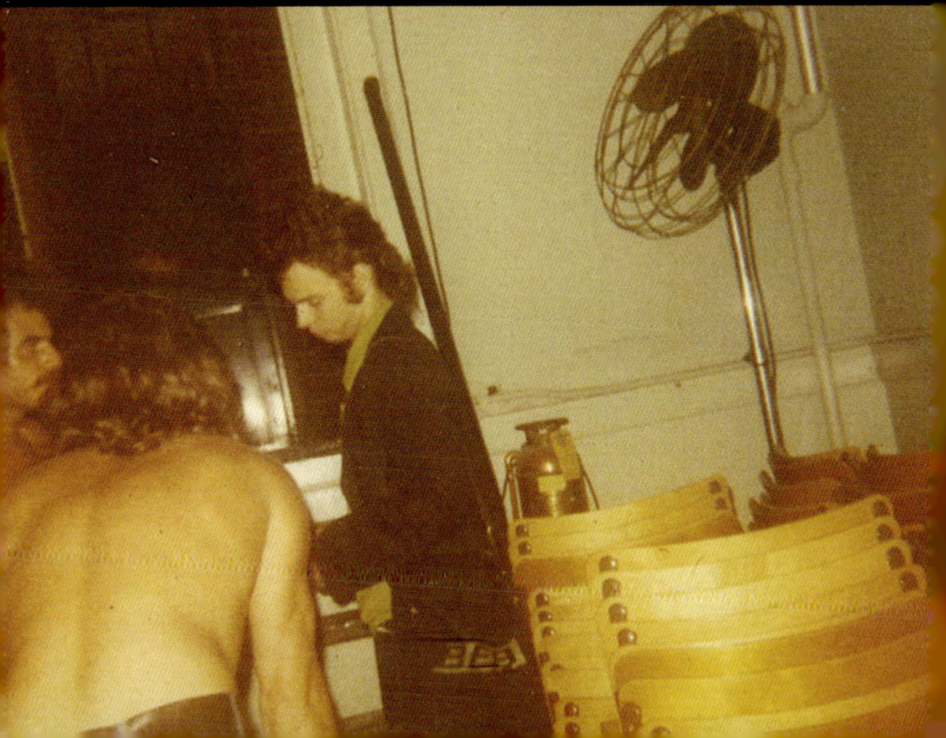

YRC

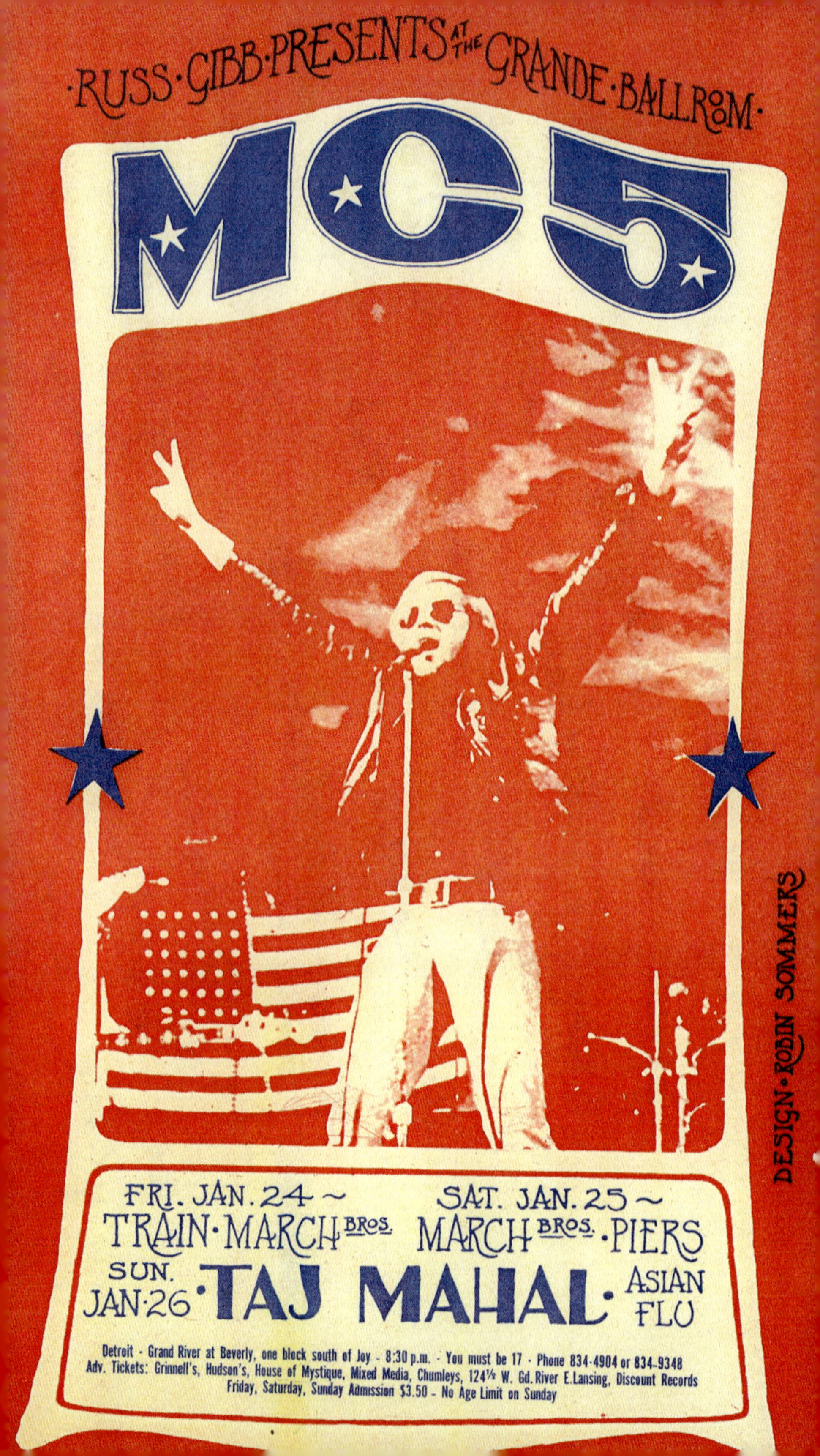
·RUSS·GIBB·PRESENTS AT THE GRANDE·BALLROOM·
MC5
FRI. JAN. 24 ~
TRAIN·MARCH BROS.
SAT. JAN. 25 ~
MARCH BROS.·PIERS
SUN. JAN·26 ·TAJ MAHAL· ASIAN FLU
Detroit - Grand River at Beverly, one block south of Joy - 8:30 p.m. - You must be 17 - Phone 834-4904 or 834-9348
Adv. Tickets: Grinnell's, Hudson's, House of Mystique, Mixed Media, Chumleys, 124½ W. Gd. River E.Lansing, Discount Records
Friday, Saturday, Sunday Admission $3.50 - No Age Limit on Sunday
DESIGN·ROBIN SOMMERS

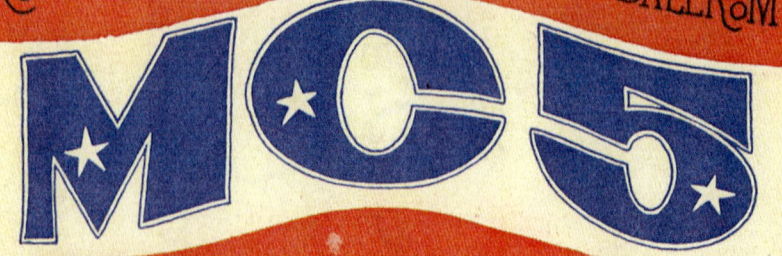

11

...Into The Fire

My next few years were a headlong dive into drug addiction.

Adele and I returned to the East Detroit neighborhood where we'd rented the lower floor of an old house. Ironically, our upstairs neighbors were a Detroit cop and his wife. A stream of customers flowed through the front door, not outrageously, but steady enough to be noticeable. The quiet residential city block seemed shuttered and unconcerned.

Piles of white powder sat in dishes atop my dresser; a measuring spoon ring with teaspoon and tablespoon measures was always close by. I'd survey the bounty and ask myself how long this could last. I knew that I was living in the lap of drug luxury, and that something was bound to send me tumbling back to reality.

It was surreal. Besides always recouping what I needed to re-cop, I was amassing enough disposable cash to go out and buy a Harley, a fanciful dream of my teenage years. I'd awaken in the morning or afternoon and prepare a fix to start the day.

After an interlude, I'd decide I needed a cocaine rush to pick me up. Depending on the strength of the coke rush, I might prepare another hit of heroin to calm my metabolism down. All of this was by intravenous injection and the process would continue endlessly.

Alcohol was also a steady feature, but not as dominant as the drug consumption. Back and forth, down to up, up to down, and very often together at the same time; those particular potions were called speedballs. As the day or evening wore on, my apparent mission was to deliver my body the maximum shot of coke without going into cardiac arrest. This was followed by a shot of heroin to relax my blood pressure. I was literally a maniac. Curiously, I seemed to function socially as if I was in absolute control of the situation.

Adele was getting slowly into it, but only occasionally, so she could share some of what constituted my life. She still had her little girl to care for, although television and toys managed the job a great deal of the time. Besides, her mother lived a few blocks from us, and the child was always welcome to stay there for extended visits.

I had completely let go of any interest in the MC5. No word of them came my way via either publicity or the grapevine, until one day a few months after my separation from them, Dennis came by as a surprise visitor.

"Holy shit, man, what the hell are you doing here?" I ventured.

"I quit," was his reply. "There's no love in that fucking band, man. Fred and Wayne are running the whole show like they fucking own it. Rob's not happy, either. He's going to quit pretty soon, too. Mark my words."

I was relieved to hear him validate my feelings. I knew what he was going through, and yet, I was really surprised he threw it down. Dennis always seemed to be trying to fit in the mold, but now he was proving to me that he was his own man. I was proud of him.

Wayne and Fred had been on a roll ever since we had become manager-less. They somehow thought they were the only capable decision makers, when in fact it was their decisions that were ruining every chance the band had to be real. Rob was the perennial whipping boy by default, and he was the person most likely to have something better to do than wander the world, trying to be a rock star. You knew they were going to push him too far; it was just a matter of time.

Dennis told me that the vote back in the hotel room in London was three to one. I didn't ask him then, and I've never asked him since who was the one. I just surmised that he was always on my side. But what Dennis really wanted that day was dope.

The most important piece of equipment in my house had always been the record player. I had won the Electro Voice studio monitors in the raffle that divided up the band-owned gear when we separated at the Hamburg house two years before. I had an amp and turntable of some kind, and a voluminous collection of great records: Motown, soul, R&B, jazz, pop and rock. I'd spin records all day and night. The sounds were always happening at my place. I was learning who was the real deal in the music world. More than ever, without prejudice, I sought out my favorite artists. It was, besides an unreal time of drug use, a time of unrestrained self-appeasement. I actually don't regret it in the least.

But like the man said, "Someday it'll all come crashing down." And so it did. One evening, as we casually sat in the dining room, a loud bang sounded at the front door and a chorus of men shouted, "POLICE! OPEN UP!"

Just then, a side window shattered and a body came flying through the opening. Within the next minute, a dozen men with drawn pistols entered the living room in a frenzied state, shouting obscenities and bellowing orders. I was thrown up against a wall with two fellows holding my arms, my face pressed against the wall. The hyperventilating crew of Detroit police officers and plainclothes agents was frantically tearing through all of our belongings and furniture, looking for the crucial evidence that would support their breaking into our house. Adele was struggling with a cop or two, screaming insults at them.

"You have no right to do this, you fucking bastards! Fucking cocksuckers, I have a lawyer, and you fuckers are going to get sued!" Then, with a cop holding her in a hammerlock against the wall, our eyes met. She gave me a look that said, "Don't worry, we'll get out of this."

I watched as a cop counted my Harley cash. "Twenty-two hundred and fifty-one dollars. Is that correct?"
They had a baggie with a small amount of dope in it, and some disposable syringes. We had been at the end of a supply. So, the evidence was minimal. The "real" evidence was that sometime, somewhere, I had sold a bag of dope to an undercover cop. Someone who'd been busted had sent the narcs to me to lighten their case. That's how the game works.

We were transported downtown to the Detroit police headquarters lockup, 13th floor, Beaubien Street. High in the building, overlooking the wintry street below, six large cells held the arrests of the night. Steam heat rising, the ancient radiator pipes knocking and clanging while prisoners sat, lay, stood, paced, shouted, or rambled insanely.

"Tricky Dick don't like it," one drunken man kept repeating throughout the night.

At 8 AM, we assembled to be transported to court. There was some panic that we wouldn't be arraigned until several days later. Had that been the case, I would have been in deep trouble from withdrawal, but luckily, my name was called.

When I entered the courtroom, the first thing I saw was my parents, whose faces wore mortified looks. The black bailiff read the charge of "possession of *hay*-ron, with intent to distribute." Like a smartass, I feigned confusion at his incorrect pronunciation. He repeated it the same way, until the judge corrected his pronunciation and the arraignment continued. I was released without bail on personal recognizance, meaning I gave my word to show up.

"What the hell?" my dad said, a phrase he often used.

"I have a drug habit," I told him, matter-of-factly.

"How can I help you?" He was sincere and always wanted to give me whatever I needed to straighten up. He knew about going down the hard road. Without his ever giving me the whole story about his brushes with the law (and I'm sure with a variety of illicit things), I suspected that he'd corrected the attitude of his youth not a moment too soon. He had the face of a tough guy, an immigrant with deep survival skills. My only thought was of getting home to the wreckage of our house and obtaining a fresh supply of dope; I was getting sick.

It didn't take long for people to tell me about hearing of my bust on the local news. Apparently, it had been reported that night on CKLW radio. The report said that the MC5 wouldn't be playing any gigs for a while, because the band's bass player, Michael Davis, had been busted for drugs and was in jail at the moment. A lot they knew; I hadn't been in the band for six months.

The police had destroyed our home. We decide it was best to move. We found another house, loaded all the stuff that was salvageable into a van, and set up housekeeping at the new location. Along with the change of location, I decided to join a methadone clinic as a way to show the court I was attempting to deal with my addiction by choosing legal help.

Unfortunately, methadone is not only a free and legal means to appease a dope habit. It's also an even more addictive substance, harder to quit than heroin, and can serve as an enhancement to an ongoing heroin habit. No one quits dope until they are ready to quit all of it. If an addict were to use methadone for exactly one week, without using any heroin, he'd avoid heroin withdrawal and likely be able to stop the methadone before becoming addicted to it. But of course, every addict commits to the program, which goes on indefinitely and keeps him or her chained to the clinic interminably.

I continued using heroin and selling it to support my use. In the span of less than a year, I got busted again for selling dope to a cop. It might have been the same one that set me up the first time. Like Sinclair, I blinked and wasn't on my guard. Drugs will do that to you. It put me in the position of having two cases on the docket at once for the same offense. With the city and the state eager to process minor drug offenses quickly, I was fortunate to get concurrent probation.

We moved again, this time to the inner city, a neighborhood

close to the Wayne State University campus. I was back in my old stomping grounds. It was all too familiar, and it felt good. Adele was pregnant, and I thought I would try to go back to school. I wanted to be done with dope. My probation officer would be taking samples of my urine when I reported and the last thing I wanted was to go off to Jackson State Prison.

My mind returned to thoughts of art. I registered for school, scheduled a couple of classes, and started the fall term, still in good standing with my prior credit hours.

Three nights a week, I went to Old Main, the oldest building on campus, where there were studios to do oil painting. The entire semester was spent doing one painting. In my case, it was a three-by-four-foot canvas abstract of the fetus that Adele was carrying. I didn't know what I was doing until the last session, when it dawned on me that was what it was.

The class was filled with a few middle-aged women exploring their untapped lack of talent, a couple of serious-but-confused younger arty women, a couple of guys looking for a new angle to their boring lives, and me, a refugee rock musician who had once roamed these same hallowed halls before I jumped ship. Our instructor was a bearded, seriously dedicated painter, working the young wannabes into an awareness of what painting means.

At the very last session, His Holiness critiqued each student's painting in front of the whole group. When he got to my abstract, richly colored, straight-from-the-tubes apparition of a fetus, he paused and sighed.

"When I first saw this painting," he began, "I thought, 'This person is either onto something, or they are one hell of a dilettante.'" Not knowing what a dilettante was, I immediately felt flattered that he thought I was similar to Bob Dylan, but then I began to suspect that I was being ridiculed. He finally vindicated me completely by announcing it was one of the best paintings he had ever had a student do in one of his classes. I glowed a little bit, feeling redeemed from my dismal failure in the music profession. At the end of the class, the prettiest girl student, of whom I was mildly aware, came over and said how much she liked my work, and that my painting was fabulous. The Casanova deep inside me smiled.

I thought I was through with the MC5, but like a bad penny, the band reappeared in my life. After a few personnel changes and attempts at touring, the group broke up permanently. I was unaware of the desperate measures Wayne and Fred had taken to keep gigging as the MC5, but Dennis updated me on the latest dramas.

The very last thing we did together should not have happened at all. We were asked to play on New Year's Eve 1972 at the Grande Ballroom as a farewell performance.

Each member or former member was called and asked if they were willing to do the gig. Since everyone needed the money, the answer was "Yes." As we were all dope addicts, except for Rob, no one was in very good shape physically, mentally, emotionally, spiritually, or musically. A couple of hundred people showed up at the Grande that night, and we went on looking and feeling like a ghost of our former selves.

Sometime during our set, Wayne Kramer, the guitarist who stood on my side of the stage, turned toward his amp, switched it off, fetched his guitar case, which was conveniently by the side of his amplifier, packed his guitar in it, jumped down off the front of the stage, and set off across the dance floor through the crowd of curious watchers while the rest of us played on.

As I saw him disappear into the darkness, I felt hurt, angry, empty, and relieved. If that was his statement, I didn't know exactly what it meant, but I knew what it felt like, and I didn't like it. If Wayne hadn't gotten paid before the set, I'm sure he would have stuck around for the money.

Adele and I moved again, to a duplex further in the inner city. I completed my probation and gradually returned to using drugs. I found a new connection that claimed to be a brother of one of the Temptations. He had a small storefront on Woodward Avenue that served as a front for his real business.

There was a bar next door that he claimed he partially owned. He was a cagey old devil, preferring to deliver the order to your location. He drove a ratty old Falcon and wore dark blue work clothes and an old ball cap. He was kind of an eccentric, a bit of an oddball for a dope dealer. He liked to have me sample his latest bag. He was always available; I had the feeling I was his favorite and maybe his only customer.

Fred Smith had kept in touch with me. We had managed to stay friends despite the falling out I had with the group. He had a notion that I might be better equipped to sing than play bass guitar, and I had those thoughts myself.

We decide to form a group with a different bass player, Dennis as the drummer, and me singing lead and hammering on a small Casio keyboard. I think we placed an ad for a bass player, which was answered by a fellow named John Hefti, whom we hired without trying anyone else. We played mainly cover tunes. After a couple of weeks of practice, we got booked to play the bowling alley bar in Lincoln Park.

The contract called for four or five sets per night, three nights in a row. By the second set, my voice was beginning to have a gravelly deep sound to it. By the third set, I was hoarse from straining. The second night was pure panic, and I was gargling with clove throat elixir to numb my abused vocal chords. Some of our former fans came to see the phenomenal new group with Fred, Dennis, and Michael. I could sense their skeptical stares as I tried with all my strength to entertain them.

I struggled in the upstairs room of my house to write a song on the Casio. I had an interesting part, but I couldn't put two parts together to make a song. I was losing confidence and I was very afraid of disappointing Fred. We got together with another guy named James Allen, who was an accomplished keyboardist. He was a nephew of the famous union leader Jimmy Hoffa.

Practice shifted over to the attic in Dennis' house. He was a newly married man. We had gone to his wedding reception to get drunk and party with him. Dennis told us Wayne was playing at a bar not very far from the reception with Mitch Ryder. We took a ride to drop in on Wayne at his new gig. As we walked into the club, a place called Sexy Sadie's, we caught Wayne sitting in a chair, playing guitar while the rest of the band stood on the stage. Mitch greeted us with a salute. "Brother" Wayne was drunk and not so pleased to see us.

We called our new band Ascension, after the John Coltrane album. It was pretty much organized by Fred, and mainly featured Fred's latest originals. He was coming into his own with writing, picking up where he had left off at the end of the MC5.

The one person we deliberately did not want in the band was Wayne. Wayne's attitude had been more than anyone wanted to have to put up with again. He had Kramer's Creamers going with some local junkies. Rob was trying, too, with his own quasi-MC5 outfits. My drug use had decreased somewhat from the year before. I might get a bag every couple of days, a less intense obsession, but it still had a hold on me.

We played a couple of gigs locally, but we didn't ever gel as we had hoped. After a line-up change or two, Fred came up with the name Sonic Rendezvous. I played at least one live show as Sonic Rendezvous, trying to sing Fred's songs and play keyboard, but I didn't have what it took at all. I think we both decided to let it go. Of course, a couple of years later, Fred put together Sonic's Rendezvous Band with Scott Morgan, Scott Asheton, and Gary Rasmussen, to considerable acclaim in the Detroit/Ann Arbor area (and in years to come, the rest of the world).

Adele and I moved one last time, to a neighborhood on the West Side of Detroit, not far from my parents' neighborhood. I restarted my drug dealing and using, and visited the methadone clinic daily. I was not in a band, although there was always talk of jamming or starting a project with any musicians I knew. I had a blue Epiphone solid-body bass that had survived my MC5 days, but any amplification was forfeited when I was dismissed from the band.

Aside from keeping a revolving supply of heroin by selling a portion of what I bought, my activities were few. Sitting on the porch with my neighbor, drinking beer and punch made with MD 20/20—sweet port wine mixed with Kool-Aid—and smoking a joint, kept me occupied on hot summer nights. I did little else. Other time was spent alone in the basement of the house, chain-smoking Marlboros and building model car kits. I sold dope to a few people. It was enough to keep me in stash.

On a bright, crispy cold day in January 1975, I answered the front door, whereupon two smartly dressed DEA agents announced they had a warrant for my arrest. I had sold dope to a federal agent recently—it didn't matter when or how it happened—and they were politely going to put cuffs on me and take me to the federal building for booking. An astonished Adele looked on as I was led to an unmarked car and placed in the back seat. It was the end of the road. With two prior felony convictions at the state level, and now a federal rap for the same thing, the strike count was three. Word was that almost any federal conviction resulted in jail time, regardless of prior history. The best I could hope for was a light sentence of, say, two or three years. In any event, my life as a rock and roller, a family guy, and a dope fiend was about to be terminated with extreme prejudice. It took about six months for the clock to tick down to zero. During that time, I reduced my drug activity, but I still continued to use, and did so right up to the last day. Junkies are hard-pressed to ever deny themselves anything.

    As the court date drew near, I became more anguished, particularly in regard to detoxing from the methadone clinic. It seems that I spent more time being dope sick and getting a shot to relieve the symptoms than having any pleasure from it. It was an ongoing nightmare, but I was determined to stay the course.

    The reality of leaving the children was too much to bear. My little girl was barely two years old, and although I was an abomination as a parent, the two of us were bonded unlike anything I'd ever known. As a family, the four of us felt completely comfortable and devoted together. Adele and I weren't what you might call a happy couple, but after four years of being together, we had something. We were scared, that much is true. Not knowing what would become of us held us in suspense, waiting for the final axe to fall.

My court date came in August. I pled guilty to a single count of possession of a Schedule 1 narcotic. It was a plea bargain. The U.S. attorney dropped three other charges in exchange for a guilty plea. It was the legal business-as-usual formula. A pre-sentence examiner interviewed me to determine what sentence to recommend to the judge. At sentencing, on the advice of my public defender, I blamed all my crimes on my heroin habit, and asked that I be remanded to a facility that rehabilitated addicts.

My mother and father sat in the courtroom as the U.S. district judge delivered my sentence: "Three years of incarceration at Lexington Federal Correctional Institution. Prisoner will be given A2 status. Good luck, Mr. Davis. I hope I don't ever have to see you in here again. Get yourself together, son."

I looked around at my parents to see my mom holding back tears and grimacing. My dad sent a sad but sympathetic gaze back to me. It was the best I could hope for. Three years wasn't a lifetime, but being a junkie could be the end of my life. Then, my public defender made one last request.

"If it pleases your honor, Mr. Davis would beg the court to grant him a stay of sentence so he can completely detox from a methadone clinic that he currently is attending."

Judge Damon Keith peered at me over his glasses. "Defendant is granted two weeks stay. Two weeks from today, Mr. Davis, you will turn yourself in to the U.S. marshal. Next case, please."

I was free to go—for two weeks. Mom and Dad took us out to eat and to talk about our feelings. But as usual, our feelings were a little too ambiguous to speak about. Conversations with my parents were always difficult. So difficult were they, that most often they weren't attempted, and if attempted, the outcome was much too awkward. I was sick, and that might have been what made things difficult for everybody.

The two weeks soon became two days, and then one day. I was down to five milligrams of methadone. I developed a manic attack of pacing from the front of the house to the back. It was uncontrollable. Back and forth, back and forth, I paced rapidly from one end of the house to the other.

My father tried to stop me. "Get a grip on yourself, Mike!" I tried to quell the compulsion. I forced myself to relax. It was like when I was a little kid, and couldn't stop twitching and contorting. On the last day, a couple of my friends took me to a local bar in the afternoon to get crocked as a going away present. After several rounds, I fell over some chairs and landed on my face on the bar room floor. My head was spinning.

September 8, 1975, I did a last shot of dope and got in the car to go downtown. Adele and the kids came along to say goodbye. We sat in the car at the curb of the Federal Building. There were tears and hugs, and promises.

"Write as soon as you can, every day. I'll write to you everything that happens. Don't worry, we'll be all right."

One last hug, and I stepped out onto the curb. I waved, blew some kisses, and turned to the steps. Well, I said to myself, here we go. I passed through the big heavy doors with brass handles and onto the elevator to the office of the U.S. marshal, for better or for worse. I didn't know what was going to happen, but my life was about to be out of my control.

SAT. AUGUST 28
MC 5
SPRINGWELL
INSANITY'S HORSE

8-12:00 $3.00

WAMPLER'S LAKE PAVILION

12

The Bridge To Nowhere

I once heard it said that prison will either make you a stronger person or turn you into a total pussy. I don't believe that it does either, but it does lay obstacles in your way that force you to figure out how to survive without being destroyed.

Basically, you are thrown into a population of outlaws that are only mildly subdued. Like any group, large or small, most individuals are moderately behaved, and a few are abominable monsters. Those are the individuals you learn to avoid at all costs. Establishing a peer group will give you relative peace and keep you out of trouble. I was sentenced to a medium security facility, where the inmates are permitted to wear street clothes and move about the compound freely. These are the facilities people refer to as "country clubs."

About the hardest core prisoners at Lexington were bank robbers, who were sent there because the court deemed them qualified to receive help for their substance abuse problems—the alleged reason they took to robbing banks.

Therefore, the atmosphere of cruelty and gangsterism was not a factor. These are drug dealers without violent behavior records. In some cases, white collar criminals like income tax offenders and defrauders of the government are sent to Lexington as a result of plea-bargaining deals. In general, it's a higher class of felon.

I spent two weeks in transit from the time I turned myself in at the Federal Building in Detroit until I arrived at "Lex." It consisted of an overnight stay at the county jail and a 12-day wait at Milan Federal Correctional in Milan, Michigan. Milan was a hardcore joint, with all the usual stereotypes one usually associates with prison. However, the holding block was separate from the general population, where the gruesome jail hierarchies and treacherous inmate initiations occur. My conditions were more bearable.

I knew almost instantly when the cell door in Milan slammed shut and I scanned the tiny rectangular room, dimly lit by a single bare bulb, that this was it, the place I was going to have to accept, and I knew I could. Aren't we creatures of survival? Aren't we capable of almost anything? It would be a long time until things were back to normal, whatever that was going to be, but I knew I could get used to it, because I had to.

I remember the sound of a distant train whistle crossing the landscape in the night, as I lay awake while 100 guys snored. I remember my cellmate, an elderly Mexican man who was being deported after living in the U.S. for 12 years, leaving behind a wife and family. I felt like I was in a Hieronymus Bosch painting of souls descending into hell, but it was only as bad as it was for me because I was going cold turkey from methadone.

After two sleepless weeks of agony and waiting, my name was finally called, and I was loaded into a white passenger van along with eight other convicts and two U.S. marshals. Brief as it was, the trip was a godsend after being in stir for longer than I'd ever been confined in my life. And before the day was out, we were pulling into the main entrance of Lexington FCI.

Lexington's façade was similar to a typical old time hospital. In fact, Lexington had been built in the 1930s as a naval hospital. However, once converted to a Bureau of Prisons facility, it served as a treatment barracks for drug addicts with jail time. Some famous celebrity heroin addicts had stayed there, giving it an aura of dubious degenerate prestige. I didn't count myself as a famous person, but I relished the association with the likes of Billie Holiday, Lenny Bruce, and anyone else whose name lent a patina of glamour to being a junkie jailbird. Whether any of these people actually served time in Lexington I don't know, but I'd heard rumors.

The separation from my family left me feeling empty and cast adrift. With them hundreds of miles away and three years being taken from my life, it seemed like I had died. All my thoughts resonated with abandonment. My spirit was flat, my pride evaporated. I struggled to invent a plan to overcome the dilemma. There was nothing to be done.

I was given a job in the bakery. It was ridiculous, but I had to accept it. I awoke at 4 am, went to the job site, kneaded dough for five hours, cleaned pans, and went back to my barracks for the rest of the day. After a couple of weeks, I asked to be transferred to the paint crew. I was a better painter than a baker.

Sometime in my first month at Lexington, I met a new arrival in the lunchtime chow line: a stocky fellow wearing snakeskin cowboy boots and a fringed suede jacket, smoking a pipe. He had been a pilot (smuggler), an actor (hustler), a Marine (badass), and an artist (poseur). He was the first person I had met in jail that I could communicate with. We became friends right away.

Paul was a very intense, enthusiastic individual with a great talent for self-promotion. He once told me that he was always selling himself. He was from Charleston, West Virginia, and he told me that the first thing he did when he left there was to lose the accent. After serving in the Marine Corps, bouncing around Sausalito, and having a go at being a soldier of fortune, he wound up running dope loads from South America to Florida in a Cessna. That got him to Lexington on a four-year bid.

One day, Paul brought me a magazine to look at. It was a travel magazine with a story about Native American medicine art called "Sand Paintings." It had several pictures of sand paintings, and some explanations of what was being done. A "singer" or medicine man creates a picture on the ground, using pigmented sand. He makes images of animals, plants, natural phenomena, and spirits. The patient stands inside the sand painting, and ceremonially transfers his illness to the images. The sand painting is then destroyed, taking with it the patient's malady.

Paul reckoned we could do replicas of sand paintings in acrylic or oil paint on canvas, and decorate the visiting room with them. It was a far-fetched idea, but one that I thought was feasible. We took it to the warden, who was intrigued, and immediately ordered that we be given all the means to execute the work. Thus, began our prison job that lasted the entire time I was locked up.

We converted a storage room into a narrow studio space, large enough to set our canvasses against the wall. The prison wood shop made the stretchers, which we prepared with canvas. The institution purchased two complete kits of painting supplies, consisting of a dozen brushes and tubes of colors, to get us started.

It took me two weeks to complete the first painting, the only one I did in oils. This wasn't the kind of painting where you freely express whatever comes into your head. This was replication of an already executed work, methodically copying the original. Since we didn't sign our work, it was not plagiarism, but a faithful reproduction. In any event, the pieces were stunning, and everyone concerned was so pleased with the results that a green light was given for us to continue for as long as there was a wall with an empty space. My whole prison ordeal took on a new aspect. I didn't have to be like everybody else and we were allowed to work whenever we felt like it (but every day, of course).

We established a routine that made each day interesting. The institution was co-ed, with an almost equal ratio of men and women. Just like in high school, I had my sights set on several females, but lacked the audacity to be aggressive.

Physical contact beyond holding hands was forbidden, so you had to be careful or you could get in trouble. If you got written up for an infraction, it could cost you your furloughs, and a series of write-ups could affect your parole status. Getting caught having sex would get you sent away to a maximum security place like Sandstone, Minnesota; Terra Haute, Indiana; or Leavenworth, Kansas—bad places where people got beaten up, or worse.

After a while, I had my bass guitar sent to me. Good thing I did, I'm sure it wouldn't have been locatable when I got out if I hadn't. I played music with a few different groups. There was a rock outfit, a country outfit, and a jazz group that met every so often. Occasionally, we played in front of our fellow inmates at arranged concerts. None of it was serious, just a recreational diversion from routine prison life. That's how it was: once you get there, you resigned yourself to the fact that nothing that happened while you were there had any merit, or mattered after the day you were released. You forget about being there and let the days peel off the calendar unnoticed.

My former band mate Wayne Kramer came to Lexington after I'd been there a while. He sent me a letter out of the blue, telling me he was going to court in the near future for delivery of cocaine. He was shitting his pants about going to jail and wanted me to instruct him on how he could get to where I was. He had a federal case, so I simply told him to blame everything on drug use and ask to be sent somewhere he could get some help. About a month later, there he was in military fatigues, standing in the chow line. We greeted each other and after that, I hardly ever saw him.

My only unfortunate episode at Lexington was an incident that left me with a broken nose. I was hurrying over to the cafeteria for lunch. I was late getting up and wanted to make it before they closed the doors. Grilled cheese sandwiches were on the menu: my favorite. Being the last person to arrive and with no one behind me, I asked for a second sandwich off the grill.

The large, ugly bastard on the other side of the counter then told me I got only one. I grabbed the closest one I could reach off the grill while he hacked at my hand with a spatula. As I was walking away with my tray, he stormed around the side of the counter and with Mike Tyson force, leveled me with a shot to the face.

I woke up in a mop closet with blood splattered everywhere and down the front of my shirt. I picked my disoriented body off the floor, staggered into a bathroom and gaped at my image. My nose was lying sideways on my face. I splashed water over my face, took a hold of my nose with two fingers and cranked it straight. The sound in my head was deafening crunches. After a few minutes, a couple of correctional officers appeared, and escorted me to an isolation cell upstairs. I remember hearing the sound of the other inmates sarcastically commenting about the "late police," as if it were a powerless entity that only shows up after anything has already happened. It struck me as funny.

Later, after the warden came around to see me and get my version of the incident, I was released to my regular quarters. I was then sent to a hospital in town to get my beak set, stayed overnight, and came back with a big white nose wrap. A couple of weeks after that, my attacker got shipped to Atlanta. Apparently, violence over a grilled cheese sandwich was not tolerated at Lexington.

Paul was released in June, the year after we arrived. Our plan was always to imitate the old cartoon of the guy who paints himself into a corner, by painting ourselves out the front door of the institution. In his case, it worked as planned. When I tried to get the parole board to see my case in the same light, they denied me because my guidelines called for me to serve more time. In fact, my guidelines called for more time than I had actually received as a sentence. I was disappointed, but I shrugged it off, knowing I was completely at the parole board's mercy.

My friend and fellow bass player, Tim Shafe of the band Detroit, arrived and was placed in my unit. He was a natural, fun-loving guy with a great sense of humor and no fake airs about him. He and I got along very well. Since Paul had left and I was still doing the decoration thing, I got Tim made my new partner, and he and I continued to occupy the painting studio. We carried on by inventing new things to paint and decorate the walls of the institution, shifting over to quilt designs and astrological symbols, moving our hangings inside the hallways of the main building.

Finally, in September, I received word that sentencing judge had reduced my term, overriding the parole board's inflexible standards. With that done, I had a mere two weeks left to serve before my release. It was almost unbelievable, an incredible weight lifted from my being.

The best thing about Lexington was leaving. The second best thing about Lexington was that it allowed me to recuperate from the inner tragedy that got me to that point. I decided to abandon drug use. I didn't want to keep repeating the script of addiction, arrest, and prison, not to mention the likelihood of overdosing or being murdered. So, it wasn't hard to make a resolution to change my behavior. My problems weren't so severe that I couldn't handle them without drugs.

Frankly, doing drugs is a rather luxurious way to avoid facing difficult problems. No one forces us to retreat into addiction; we do it on our own, with purpose and volition. And we abandon everything we supposedly care about in the process. We do it because we are unsure but we think we know what we're doing.

I left Lexington in the fall of 1976. I'd been incarcerated for a year and a month. I had every reason to be hopeful, but virtually nothing to come back to. I did have my family. My mother and father were there to welcome me, and my sister lived close by with her boyfriend and their two kids. I had an aunt who lived not too far from my parents, but that was all. Adele, the woman I'd lived with, had succumbed to a life of dope. She was living with an escaped convict, doing and dealing drugs, having lost custody of her two children (one of whom I'd fathered), and as far as I was concerned, she was completely out of her mind.

My mom and dad were glad to have me home. They were hopeful, as was I, that I could start a more functional life, having had a year to regroup.   Back in the same old rooms that I grew up in, with the old familiar furniture and the art on the walls—some of which was mine—I felt at ease. No pressure, no demands, nothing but that same old familiar place and my people. They had a dog, they had a cat; it was just such a normal life. At the age of 32, fresh out of jail, a blank sheet for a future, not looking back, not looking ahead, I tried placing myself in the safety of their home for the present. There was food, beer, warmth, comfort, and that same old lack of things to talk about.

What was it that kept us from sharing our real feelings? I don't know. After the initial greetings and obvious conversation, it seemed that an impasse always occurred that propelled us off in other directions.

Generation gap? No, I think that something in our shared past had placed impossible walls in our memories, but no one was able to recall what had happened. We talked all right, but some horrendous lack of confidence always chained us. How could I not love my parents? Then, what held me back? I wish I knew. They cared for me; of that I'm sure. What, then, made us such awkward company? The word was out, apparently, that I was back on the street. A couple of females were calling the house. My mom would ask me, "Who is so and so?" I would say, "Oh wow, when did she call? Is she going to call back?"

Soon, I was being picked up and taken on evening forays to bars or clubs or even to people's homes for socializing. One particular lady was a promoter of rock and roll shows, and a friend of the Tyners.

213

"Is it cool for you to go over to Rob and Becky's house?" she asked me.

"I guess so," I said. "I don't have any hard feelings, really." I had known Rob and Becky the longest of anyone in the MC5, and without being sensitive, I must have thought we could share some insights or common feelings about all that had happened. Also, after my year of incarceration, I was a tad confrontational, as is often the case after someone has had the experience of jail. There was a brusqueness about me.

We arrived at a sedate brick house in a sedate Palmer Park neighborhood and went to the door. Becky answered and showed us in with a look of controlled dismay. We sat down on a couch. Becky glared at me and said, "Like a thief in the night, eh, Michael?" I was taken aback. "What do you mean?" I was serious. I had no idea what she was referring to.

"Come on, admit it, like a thief in the night."

"No...I, I just stopped by to say hello."

"Come on, admit it." She was pressing me, and I was feeling like I'd opened up an old wound, or was about to experience a new one.

"Where's Rob?" I ventured, wanting to escape the present interrogation.

"He's in the kitchen," she said with a wry tone.

"I'm going to say hi to him," and I rose to get myself out of the room with the two females who went on talking about some mutually shared tidbit.

Rob was seated on a stool with his legs crossed shaking his foot a million miles an hour. A cigarette dangled between his fingers, which he constantly flicked at with his thumb. A cup of coffee sat on the table in front of him, and he gave me a strange look, as if I were a six-foot lizard.

"Did I come at a bad time?" I asked him.

He took a drag off his cigarette, blowing the smoke out as he replied, "I don't know if there's a good time."

"Well, what's happening?" I asked him, still trying to break through the stultifying resistance.

"It's kind of weird, don't you think?" he replied.

"No, I don't think so, what's weird about it?" I said. But I was thinking like a convict, someone who faces any challenge straight away.

He flicked at his ashes once again. "It is, man, it's totally weird, you just coming over here uninvited."

I guess it was. I believed him. I turned and headed back the other way. "See ya," I said, and returned to the living room, where my escort was already standing in anticipation of departing.

"Ready to go?" she asked as I came into the room.

When we got in the car, she turned and said, "I thought you said it was all right for you to go over there."

"I thought it would be all right, but I had no idea it would be like *that*," I said. "Why didn't you check it out?"

"Becky didn't seem to mind when I mentioned it to her," she said.

We went downtown to the Lindell A.C., a famous Detroit sports bar where many of Detroit's pro athletes sometimes hung out. The girl behind the bar recognized me and gave me a warm and cheery smile.

"Hi, Michael, how're you doing, what'll you have?"

We stayed at the bar for a long time. It was fun being back and having sweet young babes give me positive vibes. Later, we all went to the barmaid's house for late night partying, but this was no ménage a trois. I had to pick one, and that made for a problem. Welcome back; no sooner did I step off the dock than I had a mess on my hands. All the while I was in Lexington, I never had a funky entanglement. Almost instantly upon my arrival home, I was up to my ears with girl trouble.

Another close encounter took place. The ex-girlfriend of a former acquaintance started calling my house and having conversations with my mom. She came to get me one afternoon. She had a nice car, she was pretty, and she had ambition. She assured me she was going to be successful in business, and was thinking of relocating to Austin, Texas. We dated a while and all of it was great, but I just wasn't ready to mate up.

I had an encounter with Adele and her fugitive boyfriend. It resulted in a brief rumble, with Adele pulling her best friend's hair and trying to throw her off a balcony for bringing me there. The kids were in the custody of her mother, far on the east side of Detroit. Adele was pissed off about it, but not enough to straighten up and reclaim them. She was living the life of a criminal outcast and relishing the danger. It was seedy and disgusting, and I'm glad the kids were somewhere else.

I was communicating with Paul, my partner from jail. He was living in his hometown of Charleston, West Virginia. Flying was cheap back then, so I booked myself a ticket to Charleston to catch up with Paul. He had pitched the idea of us doing the same type of thing in the Charleston Public School system that we had done at Lexington, and we had an interview with some government people about securing funding.

I landed on a chopped-off mountaintop near Charleston and took a cab to Paul's mom's house. For the next few days, we tooled around Charleston sampling the taverns, talking about our project, and enjoying his mom's biscuits and fried chicken. Though the project fell through when they found out we were ex-convicts, it was a valiant attempt and a fun trip.

Then a weird thing happened. I got a phone call at Paul's mother's house from a girl whom I only knew as Wayne Kramer's "walkie" at Lexington. (A "walkie" is someone you walk the yard with at the institution, a quasi boyfriend-girlfriend.) She was on furlough from the institution and had somehow found out I was in Charleston. She wanted to come over and pick me up, so I said OK.

We went to a couple of bars, and finally she suggested we get a hotel room. I was stunned. I barely knew her, and had only seen her a couple of times with Kramer. We shacked up at an old hotel downtown and said goodbye the next morning. She was due back at Lexington. I never saw her again and I don't know if she ever told Wayne about seeing me. I skipped out on the bill when I left, and for years I got postcards from that old hotel, telling me I owed them 50 bucks for the room.

Up the road from Ann Arbor is a place called the Hilltop Inn. It's basically a roadhouse set out in the country, a typical redneck establishment. I went up there one night to see Fred Smith's band. I didn't know it, but this was the beginning of the next three years of my life. On this night, the place was filled with the area rock crowd, all leather clad and primed for loud music.

I stood at the bar, waiting for my beer to arrive, when I felt a tap on the shoulder. I turned my head to see Hiawatha Bailey, my little buddy from prison.

"Whoa, Hiawatha, I thought you were still in the joint."

"Michael no, I got out a month ago. Hey, we have a table right over there, come on and join us…Pam's here."

I didn't know who Pam was, but I went over to the table and sat down with a group of people. Hiawatha knew everybody. Everybody knew Hiawatha. We had met at Lexington the previous year, right after I arrived. I was sitting on the couch in the TV room when a soft, whispery voice spoke into my ear from behind. "Are you Michael Davis?"

After checking to see if any strange looks were being made in my direction, I turned to see a young effeminate black man with inquisitive eyes, starring at me affectionately. No one had taken notice. I responded, "Yes I am, what's up, how do you know me?"

Hiawatha proceeded to tell me how he was from Ann Arbor, had roadied for the Up, was in the Rainbow People's Party, and was a huge fan of the MC5. Then he said, "I'll talk to you later."

We became everlasting friends, and still are today. Here we were on a cold winter night in Michigan at the Hilltop to see Fred's band, Sonic's Rendezvous.

After the show, Hi (as he was called) asked me to come over to the house he shared with Pam out on Plymouth Road. They still had a half keg of Molson from New Year's Eve. How could I possibly say no?

I learned that Pam and I had had an encounter at some time in the past. I didn't remember it, or her. She was acting very sweet and demure, and it was apparent she was into resuming something. It was Pam's rental house we were in, and it was on Pam's dime everything was supplied. Hiawatha had a knack for setting himself up in cozy situations.

Some of the people from the bands arrived to party, and as it was an old farmhouse surrounded by fields, anything went for as long as it might last. I stayed on for a few days, and then decided to make my whereabouts known to my parents by going back to their house in Detroit.

Two days at my parents' was as much as I could tolerate. I was hankering for mischief and party games. While I may have said "no" to drugs upon leaving jail, I did not say no to alcohol. In fact, the very first thing I did on my reentry to free society was to march into the liquor store next to the bus station and buy a pint of Jim Beam. It was probably a good ten minutes before I finally decided, "Aw, what the hell am I waiting for?" and cracked open the seal to take the first swig. Thus, my inaugural hours in the free world were a quick-start drinking bout, followed by passing out until the bus pulled in at my destination.

I didn't want to be responsible for having my parents' car, so I had Hi come get me in Pam's Opel GT. As we pulled away from the curb and left the northwest Detroit neighborhood, it rivaled the feeling I'd had not that long ago when I was released from prison. The adventure was on.

The "farmhouse" on Plymouth Road was a turn of the century two-story structure with a small front porch, similar in lots of ways to the MC5's Hill Street house in Ann Arbor. It had small rooms, a Franklin potbelly stove in the living room, oak doors and hardwood floors. About 40 acres of land out back gave visitors ample space to wander, and aside from another house just like it across the road half a mile down, we had no neighbors.

Pam and her son, Jared, age 10, occupied the house. Hiawatha had his own room. An endless stream of people came by to visit, staying for any length of time, bringing an endless supply of beer, wine, liquor, pot, and so forth. There was always someone else there besides the four of us. Sometimes, it was a full-scale party. Often, people simply hung out there as a convenient place to get loaded and, because Hiawatha liked to hunt young white boys for sexual conquest, his targets were always there, awaiting their fate.

For me, it was an opportunity to slip back into society without having to so much as think about looking for a job, making new friends, or locating old ones for that matter; sooner or later, everyone came around to the farmhouse.

We slept in till afternoon, rose in time for supper, then started drinking and continued to drink until we were so wasted that we passed out. At first it seemed unreal, but one wintry day while stocking up at the beer and liquor store late in the afternoon, it occurred to me that living that way was a perfect holiday, one that might last a long time. I would stay with it as long as it was available.

Pam was in love with me. She was a sweet angel of a girl who drank a lot of cheap table wine. Shame on me for taking advantage of her, but that's what I did. Hiawatha was all for it. He coached Pam constantly on how she could bring me under her control. He relished having me in the house as a lure for the rock crowd, for one thing. He also had strong feelings for me as a friend, for another. The three of us got along as well as anybody could, even with all the drinking and weird scenarios. We were birds of a feather.

Pam's son was a little hellion of a kid. He was audacious, emotional, and a little bitter about his mother breaking up with his father. He ran around the house and jumped up and down on the furniture. He had a record player in his room that blasted the first Kiss album over and over. "I…wanna rock and roll all night…and party every day." He'd leap on his bed with a toy guitar and go fucking crazy to that tune. I didn't think he was very happy about me sleeping with his mom, or that I had a free ticket to be at the house for that matter.

He and Hiawatha had a uniquely strange relationship. Jared insulted Hi all the time, calling him a stupid faggot and things of that sort. Meanwhile, Hi acted like he was Jared's aunt or a nanny. It worked quite well, all things considered. Hiawatha treated me like a rock and roll version of Hamlet. I reveled in it.

Months went by. I kept my appointments with my parole officer when they came up. I remember him pressing me to provide statements of places where I'd applied for work. I always managed to make the right evasive maneuver. I had to provide urine samples occasionally, but I wasn't messing around with narcotics. So, although nerve-wracking, I wasn't fucking up the terms of my parole. It seems that even though I maxed out my time, they had some technicality whereby they could pull you back on if you slipped up.

I had vaguely decided on trying to become an artist, and playing in a band was at the top of my not-to-do list. At the moment, all I wanted to do was nothing. The farmhouse routine was working for me. But the punk movement was exploding—even Hiawatha was getting his own band, the Cult Heroes, together from the people that were stopping by. I should have seen it coming, and maybe I did: inevitably, someone was going to approach me about getting a band together.

On an early spring evening, Ron Asheton, guitar player from the Stooges, arrived at the farmhouse with an interesting proposal. I listened to him while he extolled the exciting possibilities of the two of us teaming up to play in a band together. Ron and I had always gotten along really well. He and his brother Scotty were fun people, very smart. Of all the local cats, they were the ones with whom I was most comfortable.

Ron was very enthusiastic. "Come on, man. It'll be great!" He was proposing that I join with him and several other people, two of whom he had brought with him to the house, in an already existing band called Destroy All Monsters.

I was skeptical, but intrigued. We were all a little drunk, but that was par for the course. Maybe we were more than a little drunk. As I recall, anything less than staggering amounted to "a little drunk." I looked at Asheton. The gleam in his eye was incessant. The grin on his face was like a kid who was greeting Santa Claus. He had me. Reluctantly and carelessly I said, "I'll try it."

13

Delirious Alcoholic Megalosaurus

The year was 1977. I had just agreed to join the most dysfunctional group ever to set foot on a stage. You might challenge the notion that this band, Destroy All Monsters, takes the prize for dysfunction, but I assure you, we were the epitome.

The previous incarnation of the band had been an assortment of art students who satirized the playing of live music as a means to express themselves, using vacuum cleaners, tools, or any other type of noisemaking device, along with a few conventional musical instruments, to create a farcical "band." In the spirit of anti-establishment art, it worked and it served its purpose as spontaneous performance.

So far, they had only ever exposed "the act" to the public for free at private house parties. It was truly campus exhibitionism for its own sake. No one considered it as anything more than an art project and something fun to do on the weekend. So, when I say Destroy All Monsters was dysfunctional, I mean the later one that I was in. For all I know, the DAM that performed in people's living rooms to houses full of stoned student friends might have been a perfect manifestation of creative artiness. Without presumption or ambition, there were no limits on what they could attempt, and I'm sure their creative spirit was thrilling.

The guiding force behind DAM was a young man named Cary Loren, who claimed to be related to the famous Sophia. The troupe consisted of him and his muse/girlfriend Niagara, along with their art student buddies and a couple of local musicians. Loren had taken the name Destroy All Monsters from a '60s Japanese sci-fi film that pitted dinosaurs against a population of hysterical Japanese—a people stunned by the horrors of nuclear destruction and then saturated with Americulture. Add an obsession with Andy Warhol and a passionate worship of rock and roll and you have an idea what early DAM was about.

Loren saw the connection between the creations of Tanaka Tomoyuki, the cult of horror, the Pop Art of Warhol's Factory, the rock and roll world of the Rolling Stones, punk rock, and the unfulfilled destinies of local heroes the Stooges and the MC5. This swirling galaxy of images and ideas gave Loren the ingredients to realize his vision. The exuberance Cary and Ron displayed when they recruited me for their group was irresistible. For a moment, I thought I was really getting in to something.

I was, but not in the way I originally thought.

Ron had recently returned from an abortive attempt to form a band, New Order, in L.A. with Dennis Thompson and a few other Detroit characters. Apparently, that band had misfired at an all-important Roxy gig when the singer, Dave Gilbert, got stoned on angel dust, froze up on stage and forgot all the lyrics. That was all it took to put paid to the venture.

In DAM, Ron must have sensed another opportunity to have things his way in a band, because I don't believe Ron Asheton ever had any intention of becoming Cary Loren's guitar star. Then there was the intriguing little chanteuse, Niagara, whose vocal attempts barely qualified as singing, but who was nonetheless the focal point of the group.

Besides Cary, Ron, Niagara, and me, the band included the Miller brothers, a curious duo who'd been in a band called Sproton Layer. Larry played guitar left-handed and upside down, while Ben played the alto sax. (Their older brother Roger later played in Mission of Burma.) Both of them were musically educated multi-instrumentalists.

Personality-wise, however, they weren't a good fit with the artists and the fallen rock stars. Besides, having six people on stage sucked as far as I was concerned, and I often thought it might be better if the Millers left. I reckoned that if it were just Asheton and myself, Ron would settle down and the chemistry I had first envisioned would emerge.

The first rehearsal I attended was almost like a performance, with lots of people who weren't in the band hanging out. Cary described, demonstrated, and attempted to explain what each song was supposed to do. The drummer was only going to be around for one gig, and there was another bass player who was leaving for a stint in the Army. I felt like an intruder, but since I had been recruited play bass, I was there.

It was incredibly loud in that basement hole. The band's performance of Loren's "songs" staggered with guitar overload and irritating excess. Niagara's vocals were barely audible, while the assembled onlookers smiled and nodded their heads as if a rhythm were moving them.

When it was my turn to play, I fumbled through the mess almost like it was an MC5 performance. Amid the din, I strived to create the scripted dynamics Loren had set out. It sounded like hell. Asheton didn't seem too pleased with the results, but he put on a good face and appeared satisfied to all concerned. Ron wasn't about to be part of an orchestra, but time would take care of that.

The next week, the band played a gig somewhere; I didn't go. However, since they needed a drummer, now that the other guy had left, I suggested someone I had seen play at another friend's house, whom I had the impression was capable of playing a strong beat. We agreed to try him out at the next rehearsal. Meanwhile, Cary Loren informed me that I was certainly his choice to play bass and that all the slapping fives that had taken place at the gig I missed were ridiculous. What did that mean? Didn't Ron want me in the band? If not, why did he insist I join? I was confused.

We practiced with Rob King, the drummer I had suggested. We might have gone after Dennis Thompson, but if that had happened, all hell would have broken loose. Back in those days, Dennis would never have accepted the ragtag musical assemblage or a female lead singer. King was accepted as a suitable drummer. Now we were seven.

We got together for a little welcoming party at Cary's apartment. There was a manager named David Keeps, a friend from the University of Michigan who had a few business skills and a healthy bank account. Cary's small Ann Arbor apartment was crammed with people. Several cases of cheap beer were on hand. While drinking and talking, Cary assured me that this band would "make more than just the books." He meant that although the MC5 and the Stooges had been significant enough to be historically documented, this band would eclipse their achievement by being successful in the marketplace. So much for Art.

We started rehearsing at a house in Ann Arbor. I don't recall whose it was; I was borrowing a bass rig from one of the Miller brothers, so it might have been their parents' house.

One afternoon, we gathered for a rehearsal, with Cary conspicuously absent. We started playing through the material without him. After a spell of jamming and puttering around, sipping beer and gabbing, we took a break. I went upstairs to nose around the kitchen, and passing the open doorway to the living room, I noticed Ron and Niagara on the couch, making out. As far as I know, Ron had never had a girlfriend, nor had I ever even seen him with a girl other than his sister. I casually looked away, feeling that it was none of my business and not wanting to think about what the ramifications might be.

At some point I had figured that Niagara was available, but I hadn't thought of it as a pressing matter. Things had just gotten started, and it was too early to fuck things up by having affairs. Apparently Ron disagreed, but I didn't know whether it was a quickie or a coupling. It turned out to be the latter, and Cary reacted by leaving Ann Arbor for New York City. He and Niagara had been a couple since high school, and he'd been filming her and collaborating with her on wacky art projects for many years. The pain of having her stolen away by his rock hero was too much for Cary to bear.

During a "promo trip" to New York, he got out of a car on the

George Washington Bridge and wandered off for parts unknown.

By the time he resurfaced in Ann Arbor few weeks later, we had decided to proceed without him. According to the Millers and Ron, Cary was acting like a maniac, slobbering and talking incessant babble. We arranged a meeting at a tiny restaurant where Ron pushed for Cary's expulsion from the band. Everyone agreed that it would be ridiculous to try to work with him in his state of mental illness. He was summarily kicked out of his own band.

Now minus its founder, Destroy All Monsters struggled to find a direction. Ron and Niagara paired off, with David Keeps, known as "D.B.," acting as ballast. The Miller brothers kept a strangely low profile, while Rob King and I regarded the situation with skeptical pessimism.

Practice was shifted to the farmhouse. A spare upstairs bedroom became the practice room where Hiawatha's band the Cult Heroes and DAM held rehearsals. Anytime from late afternoon on, loud, unbridled rock and roll music could be heard thundering within the old walls. The police were never called because there wasn't anybody to call them. The Cult Heroes generally practiced early. A couple of them actually had jobs. But Destroy All Monsters was strictly a nighttime affair.

Ron and Niagara had made Ron's mother's house their permanent abode for the time being. They awoke around the dinner hour and, after taking their time showering and having chow, awaited D.B.'s arrival to take them to rehearsal, since neither of them could drive. At some point after dark, everyone would show up at Plymouth Road to begin drinking.

Each band member brought his own refreshment in a paper bag, except Ron and Niagara, who combined their lot. We usually started with beer, except for Niagara, who wasn't a beer drinker. Hers was a pint of Bacardi Light Rum taken straight, chased down with a can of Tab. She claimed that Tab had an extra big dose of caffeine, making it much more desirable. Soon, everyone's paper bag contained the same thing: a pint of Bacardi and a six pack of beer. Ron was also a connoisseur of imported beers. So, in addition to the Bacardi and a six-pack, a couple of imported bottles of beer became a staple on our menu.

As a rule, it took two to three hours of preparatory drinking before any guitars were brought out of their cases. D.B. called our practices "glorified cocktail parties." From the confines of the practice room, obnoxious blasts of electronic chaos sprang forth, punctuated by deafening cymbal crashes and relentless screeching. Every single person smoked cigarettes continuously, making the air barely breathable.

At a party one night, not long after Cary's dismissal, Ron's sister Kathy and I were standing in the living room when she told me point blank that Ron intended to take over the band and make himself and Niagara the main focus.

"My brother wants to take over this band," she said, "and if you let him get away with it, you don't have a hair on your balls."
I reeled at her words, because a girl had just challenged me like a dude, and because I knew she was right. I had sensed it already. Ron's attitude since Loren's departure had taken a turn for the worst. He carried himself as though he answered to no one. He and Niagara were untouchable, and I didn't feel any sort of connection with him musically. He was in his own space, and she wasn't in music.

While Niagara's vocal stylings might have added something to the arty abstraction of the previous version of Destroy All Monsters, with the rock and roll refugees of Detroit on board, she was an abomination. Her deadpan, flat, half-spoken vocals gave the music an air of laughable contrivance. Had Cary remained in the mix, it might have passed for satire, but her squawking away while the band attempted to be a tight combo just didn't cut it, at least not for me.

We started making records after six months or so. D.B. was footing the studio bill, and the records would appear on his label, IDBI. Ron had written a couple of songs with Niagara's lyrics. They weren't much in the way of musical invention—basically single-riff guitar parts with a plain vanilla chorus. One of the new songs was a riff they'd stolen from Cary. I didn't give a damn.

In those days, we still played whole band tracks live, recording all the instruments at once. Only the vocals and guitar solos were overdubbed. You could get a dynamite band track when all the players connected at once using this method. Building a song from isolated parts never can achieve that sort of energy.

I realized I had better get some writing done or I'd be nothing but the bass player, so I got my first song together for the next session. It was called "Meet The Creeper." It was a crude, off-tempo riff, but it was a start. After coming up with the title, I handed the lyric writing duties over to Niagara.

She totally got it. I was pleased when she gave me the lyrics to read. It was a clever, sardonic take on a Sherlock Holmes movie in which the Creeper, played by Rondo Hatton, appears as a cretin thug.

In the studio, I asked Larry Miller to create a dynamic guitar solo, using his unorthodox, upside-down technique. He nailed a totally original solo that could only have come from his hands. I was thrilled with it. Ben's sax solo also gave the tune a dramatic lift. I finally had my own song in the can. It would be on the B-side, with Ron and Niagara's Kennedy assassination song, "November 22, 1963" on the A-side.

When the time came for another single—because that's all D.B. could afford to pay for—I was ready with another composition that reflected a higher level of confidence. Although "Nobody Knows" was basically a simple four-chord riff, the song's dynamics were a bit more inventive, and my thoughts for the production were way more defined.

Again I gave the lyric writing chores to Niagara. This time she was on her own, and the existential musing she came up with was right on. In the session, Ron did everything I asked of him. In the end, the track fulfilled my objectives and exceeded my expectations. On the flip side, the Asheton/Niagara plaint "What Do I Get" completed the disc.

With an ex-MC5 member and a former Stooge in the lineup, DAM should have been a riot, a revelation, and the best of both of those now-defunct worlds. We definitely drew a crowd. We had the aura of impending drama. We had an inside track all the way. All we had to do was pick up the baton. True, Niagara's vocals were less than impressive, but that alone shouldn't have stopped us, and it didn't. Our Achilles heel was the lack of communication and confidence within the group.

Ron and Niagara were developing their own little cult of followers. The remnants of the former DAM band of art freaks still clung to the last vestiges of what had been—in this case, Niagara and her new guru, Ron.

Their clique sat at their feet, while Ron doled out sarcasm and wit. Their acolytes brought gifts of imported beer, imported cigarettes, pot, liquor, and occasionally cocaine. Ron liked having the reverential guests over to his mother's house in the evenings so he could light bonfires in the backyard, then sit and tell Stooges stories as long as there was anybody around.

Ron's brother Scott was playing with Fred Smith in Sonic's Rendezvous Band, our direct competition. We weren't nearly as popular as they were, and opening for them was the best we could manage. After a show in Detroit, Scott asked Ron if we were a joke band. I don't recall what prompted that remark, but any number of factors could have made an outsider wonder what we were trying to do.

Niagara's "act" was a strange display. Scantily clad in underwear or leotards, fishnets and high heels, she always smoked and drank liquor from a cup, at times throwing herself on the floor or lying down onstage. If she thought she was imitating Iggy, she wasn't even close, for her energy level was far lower than his. In general, she came off like a pathetic amateur who was trying way too hard.

Eventually the Miller brothers quit and it came down to the four of us. I thought that I would be happy at last, but the result was the exact opposite. Rob King and I were a bad influence on each other. We drank endless amounts of beer and talked sarcastically about Ron and Niagara. The divide between us was growing ever wider.

Instead of working together as a unit, we pitted ourselves against each other in a stalemate of egos. Ron acted as if he were annoyed to have to play songs that I had written and I couldn't stand being around his snobbish conceit. It was far from a good match. We had been good friends in the days of our former bands, but now we had no warm feelings for each other at all—a shame.

From the moment I joined the band, Ron turned from an ally to an adversary, for reasons I never could understand. Once he and

Niagara became intertwined, any chance for meaningful collaboration with him was over. I can only guess he had designs on her from the start, and once he made his conquest, he was content to turn the project into a super-hip couple show; at least it always seemed like that to me. He never confided in me on a personal level after I agreed to give the band a try, and things went from bad to worse.

The first couple of years, while we had the farmhouse, our practices remained drinking parties. As a group—meaning DAM, Pam, Hiawatha and the Cult Heroes, who were always around—we were comfortable and enjoyed each other's company. The effects of the alliance between Ron and Niagara, whom we started calling Boris and Natasha after the characters in *The Bullwinkle and Rocky Show,* weren't detrimental at first. It was more amusing than anything else.

When there's a couple within a band, it's hard for the rest of the group not to feel threatened by the union of two people against the rest. If the couple is a powerful creative force, the situation can be workable. But Ron and Niagara were producing mediocre material and had a work ethic that only served their personal whims and idiosyncrasies, such as sleeping until nightfall, appearing for band activities when it suited their habits, and presenting themselves as degenerate eccentrics. This only served to piss off everyone else and create a weird discomfort.

In 1979, D.B. managed to secure a licensing deal with the fledgling U.K. label, Cherry Red. We had three singles, a total of six songs recorded in a studio. He then took the perilous step of funding a U.K. tour in 1980. The tour was to last a month, comprising ten gigs. We would split our residence between London in the south and York in the north, staying at a hotel in each city.

We played twice at Dingwall's in London and in Hull, Exeter,

York, Newcastle, Leeds, Liverpool, and maybe one or two more. The British press was merciless. Our timing—arriving at the peak of a ska revival, between the demise of punk and the resurgence of metal—was impeccably wrong.

Ron and Niagara holed up in their room most of the time and would go out to do radio interviews unbeknownst to anyone except D.B. Once again, the group split into two factions: Ron, Niagara, and D.B. on one side, and Rob, myself, and George Christman—our roadie who bought his own ticket so he could come on tour with us—on the other. I don't remember any of the shows being outstanding.

At the end of the tour, we shuttled to Heathrow, where we learned that we were all holding standby tickets—except for D.B., who got on his plane and left us to fend for ourselves.

After two and a half days of sleeping on the floor at the airport, George and I took the tube back to London to camp out all night at the Pan Am office, so we'd be first in line for seats on a flight back to the U.S. A cold, sleepless night on a London sidewalk produced the five necessary reservations. With our last coins, we took the underground back to Heathrow and left the U.K. for home.

Returning to Ann Arbor presented its own dilemmas. The farmhouse had been sold out from under us the previous month, and the upstairs flat that Pam and I moved into was only a temporary fix.

I had decided before leaving for England that I wanted to split up. Pam and I had been together for three years, and she was getting on my nerves. So, before it went much further, I wanted to make my break. I knew it would be hard on her, and it was. Not only that: after leaving her, I had nowhere to live.

George, our roadie, was about to become our new manager. D.B., put off by Ron and Niagara's behavior, the failure of the tour, and the horrendous expense of bankrolling our month in the U.K., severed his ties with the band. By all accounts, a mutual hatred had arisen between the rock star recluses and the ever-affable D.B. Ron's constant ridicule had finally overcome his fascination with Niagara's vampish art mystique. He wasn't sinking any more of his time and money into this monster.

George had a good job in the University of Michigan computer lab. He had been somewhat connected to the Ann Arbor rock and roll scene, but was not a player. He was easily persuaded to rent a large house in town and purchase a vehicle for the band. He rented the upper two stories of an old house in town. The attic contained three small bedrooms in the gables of the house, with a big main room that had a stove, a sink, and a refrigerator. There was a minuscule bathroom with a shower stall, and a TV room with a second story entrance. I asked if I could move in with them for a while and, though I had to begin by sleeping on the couch downstairs, it was acceptable.

It was the beginning of a new phase of Destroy All Monsters. The past four years had been a journey through the punk era, even though were more of a non-classifiable anomaly than a punk band. At the end of the U.K. tour, I had every expectation that we were finished.

However, the legends of the Stooges and the MC5 were still powerful enough to secure us bookings in places like Chicago, Minneapolis, Cleveland, Pittsburgh, New York, Dayton, Cincinnati, Toronto, and of course, Detroit.

George bought a red Thunderbird for the band to travel in. It was a strange choice for group transport, but he was concerned that Ron and Niagara should have a stylish automobile to ride in. When we had a gig, George would rent a U-Haul trailer to tow behind the T-Bird, with the band's amps and guitars and drums inside. Ron and Niagara always rode in the back seat. I usually rode shotgun.

Pam was back, returning to Ann Arbor from her parents' place in Muskegon to confront me about getting back together. But I stood firm about wanting to break up and told her she had to go. I didn't like doing that, but what was I going to do? I had to break her heart and I hated myself for doing it.

I was alone, broke, and almost homeless. Then I remembered I had a bank account that might have had $25 in it. I walked down to the bank and withdrew all the funds. As I was coming out of the bank, I saw two girls whom I had met just before going to England. They were twins, blonde, probably 20 years old, if that. They raced across the street and threw their arms around me. To complete the homecoming welcome, they invited me to a party they were having at their place. That's what I wanted. I'd be there.

My life had become too predictable. I needed to spread out. At 36, I needed more, more of everything. I was about to get it.
I guess my freedom wasn't that important to me, because I started seeing one of the twins almost immediately. She was young and crafty. I'd been sexually frustrated for the past several years, and having a fulfilling encounter was refreshing; it reminded me how good it was to communicate passion to a partner.

I'd cheated on Pam, but it just wasn't what I wanted. Almost at once, the situation changed from budding relationship to living together in the Packard Street house with Ron, Niagara, and George.

Having money was important with a girlfriend on my hands,

and the band didn't supply enough work to pay rent and keep us in beer money, so I got a job. I worked at a construction site, cleaning the debris left by the drywallers and carpenters. Before long, I bought a $200 car, and for the first time since I was 18, I had some ambition to lead a normal life, without giving up any of my outsider mystique.

I started writing a lot just to make sure I had a voice in the direction of our music. I had written a song called "Life," sometimes called "Life Is the Place," sometimes called "Life Is Very Difficult," using my own lyrics. I discovered how to phrase choruses with verses so they flowed together without sounding disjointed. We were practicing in a friend's converted garage when I introduced three new songs. Niagara recoiled, shrieking to Ron, "Ronnie, he's taking over the band!"

For a while, we were matching each other song for song. Ron was starting to come up with much better grooves. I enjoyed the competitive spirit, although it wasn't like we were working together, which I would have preferred. True collaboration probably isn't possible: someone is responsible for the music, and someone else may write the lyrics, except in the case of the MC5, where we invented our parts on the fly.

Still, DAM started playing much better material. Most often Niagara was responsible for the titles and lyrics, and she did a good job of it. She was the lead vocalist, and it was her persona we were supporting musically.

We all felt more spirited as our music became less rudimentary. But unless all the members of a band feel unified, the sound they produce together is going to lack spirit. Only when everyone is on the same page does the music stand alone, without ties to an individual. It's a tough thing to fake, and for that reason, the bands that come by it naturally are the ones that sound the best. Playing music isn't a process of reciting tunes. It's a dedicated effort to express a passionate feeling. The truest music lacks ego, is not about an individual, but represents a universal human feeling.

I thought the right thing to do was to bring my MC5 balls-to-the-wall type of attack to the sound of DAM. Most of our songs had open-ended middle sections where prolonged jamming took place, and as inebriated as everyone was, things had a way of becoming terminally self-consumed.

We did a live two-track recording for a compilation of Detroit music called *Detroit On a Platter*. "These Boots Are Made For Walking," the Lee Hazelwood/Nancy Sinatra song and a natural for little Niagara, was our contribution. In keeping with our modus operandi, we extended the middle section and gave it a high energy run through.

Our band was often booked to open for bands like the Ramones, the Stranglers, and any number of touring punks of the day. When the Ramones partied at the farmhouse, Dee Dee Ramone confided to me that his heroin habit was so bad that he was burglarizing people's apartments and fencing TVs to feed the monkey.

Hugh Cornwall had also been a guest at the farmhouse when the Stranglers came to Ann Arbor, although I wasn't aware of it until Hiawatha told me the following day. Ours was the after hours place to go.

Although our band was clearly not a punk unit, we found ourselves lumped in with the punks. And my new girlfriend, Joanne, was a punk rocker. She had a certain defiance about her that drew me, and the combination of nurturing her psyche and reveling in the abrasive noise of punk rock set our relationship in motion.

Walking around town drunk with that rebel aura and exploring Main Street's caricature vignettes speeded our bonding. Her head was nearly shaved, and I groped for a look that clearly stated I was trouble. It was fun. It gave me a means to remain outside of society and eternally youthful.

Joanne was a college dropout who had recently returned to Michigan from Scarsdale, NY, where she had been briefly committed to an institution for attempting suicide after having her heart broken by her rich boyfriend. I was 15 years her elder, a minor celebrity and up to my ears in delusions, and neither one of us displayed any common sense. Within two months, she was pregnant. Of course, we sought to do the right thing; we decided to get married. We set a date for the Fourth of July, and a Salvation Army wedding as the acceptable punk ceremony.

On a hot and humid Saturday in July, I squirmed into a pair of super-tight leather pants, put on a white tuxedo jacket, and faced the sober captain of the Ypsilanti Post of the Salvation Army as he read the rites of matrimony to the nervous couple standing before him.

The trembling in Joanne's voice told the story. About 30 people, as well as our parents, had gathered to be present for the debacle, and after being made to promise all the abstract values of marriage, we adjourned to remove our costumes and relax before resuming the party with a reception in Detroit at a place called the Earth Center. From then on, my life took a different course. We took an apartment in a complex and awaited the upcoming birth. From what I remember of our everyday life, things seemed like adventures in a strange wonderland of marriage and party time.

I drank constantly, without any thoughts of the future. It was like a pretend game. Joanne was becoming agitated at being oversized and uncomfortable. Finally, in mid-January, we drove to the hospital to begin the excruciating task of labor. Night dragged on until, at 12:15 AM, I witnessed the Caesarian birth of a baby girl, whom we named Ursula Rane Davis. Ron commented that it didn't have a ring to it.

The activity and excitement surrounding the new birth was intense and satisfying. We were in love with our little bundle, affection flowing every moment, and endless visitors wished us all the best. For three months, the joys of parenthood were our daily routine. Each day a new sound or gurgle, signs of recognition and dramatic communication events unfolded, leaving us laughing and cooing and fawning over the precious little life we had received.

Then, out of the blue, an event that changed my life took place while Joanne and I were at a neighborhood park with little Ursula. I had drunk two or three beers and smoked a small joint. I went on a swing to show off for the baby. With the swing slowing down, I leaped from the seat to perform a "parachute" maneuver. For some reason, I thought a three-month-old baby was going to be amused at her daring dad performing tricks. Right after I released from the swing seat, I realized I was higher than I had thought.

When I hit the ground with both feet stiffened for the impact, an excruciating pain shot through my foot. I fell on the seat of my pants and immediately tried to stand up as though nothing had happened. The pain in my foot felt like I had driven my leg deep into the ground. I stood momentarily, then collapsed in pain back to the ground.

Hopping on one leg to where the car was parked, I started

the car and tried to drive with only my left foot all the way to the hospital emergency room. Joanne had never driven a car in her life. I got into a wheelchair and waited in agony to be seen. The pain was the greatest I had ever felt in my life, and when the X-rays revealed a crushed heel, I felt immediate panic, for there was nothing that could be done to repair the injury. For the rest of my life, I would be moderately handicapped by an ankle that was impossible to rotate.

The next three months were a hell of pain and frustration. I had prided myself on being free of injury and illness due to a delusion that God had selected me for some purpose. For the time being, I refused to believe drinking had anything to do with my mishap.

Maybe the small joint of marijuana had momentarily clouded my judgment; I'd admit to that possibility. I could sense Joanne's boredom at being strapped down with an invalid. I was as helpless as a baby, stuck in bed or on the couch, moaning and groaning, unable to act out my rock and roll persona. Not that we were in danger of losing our marriage—that would come later—but I knew she was exasperated, annoyed, and unhappy.

Eventually, I would heal, but some things would never be the same. The attachment I felt to my youth was severed. I wasn't able to play sports like baseball, or ice skate, or even run, for that matter. My misshapen foot would limit my activity, not to mention the pain and inflammation that occurs from weight-bearing stress. For the first couple of years, I would need cortisone shots directly in my ankle to alleviate the pain. I learned how to cope with my hobbled condition, but nothing could ever replace the delusion that I was invulnerable. Above all prior misadventures and traumas, I considered this my ultimate disaster.

DAM wasn't the MC5, we weren't the Stooges, we weren't

punk or metal or power pop or any of those things that might have helped us define an audience. Our singer was a bizarre character of dubious talent. The Frederick's of Hollywood corsets, leotards, fishnets, and heels were intended to be sexy and provocative, Niagara channeling Bridget Bardot or Barbarella.

I thought she did a decent job of rhythmic vocalizing. Her voice was atonal, but her phrasing was intriguing. It might have worked if someone had been able to give her some pointers on what to do and what not to do (as they did for Madonna a few years later). Unfortunately, we were on our own. People liked us, but there was no one savvy enough to organize our mayhem. After all, who can say what does or doesn't make it as performance art?

Ron maintained a stranglehold on the band by hibernating during daylight hours and accommodating his personal habits. He made it very obvious that he placed his idiosyncrasies before all other matters; interference would be unwelcome.

He and Niagara came across as eccentric as they were, immersed in TV sitcoms like *Gilligan's Island, The Adams Family, The Munsters, Flipper,* and every old movie that ever came on late night television. While the Stooges were dynamic and esoteric, the MC5 aggressive and challenging, this band was comical, but not in the "so-dumb-it's-smart" way of, say, the Ramones.

Rob King eventually quit, as I knew he would. He wasn't comfortable with anything as far as I could see, and his leaving was understandable. He had not a trace of personality, a completely defensive ego, and after not realizing any success in four years with the band, he thought it was time to forget about it. So, he left, and for the next couple of years we went through a revolving cast of drummers.

The rift between the celebrity couple and myself was permanent. Though we interacted, there was always that air of separateness. We drank unholy amounts of alcohol, but I always seemed to be a lot drunker than either of them. I remember a female rock journalist friend of mine once told me after a night of partying, "Michael, you really shouldn't let people see you in that condition."

It was a ritual Jekyll-and-Hyde activity. I couldn't wait to feel the effects of a beer, but after two or three, I was out of control and only just beginning. From then on, I was susceptible to ingesting anything and everything, with little regard for how I might appear or what the results of the debacle might be.

I told myself that I needed alcohol to overcome my inability to express myself freely, and that by being blind drunk, I was more in tune with my nature. In all my reckless mangling of personal affairs, not once did I ever admit to being wrong. I was content to either sleep off the hangover or resume drinking until, after several days of staggering, I passed out.

Any suggestion that I had a problem fell on deaf ears. After all, rogue behavior was part of my rock and roll mystique. The drive to be the last man standing wouldn't allow me to quit, even though without realizing it, I'd been the first to fall.

Through all my years, from high school and until my current age of 66, I never had the strength to admit the stupidity of it. The people who participated with me in these marathons of alcoholic abandon remained my friends, while those who didn't share my appetite for self-abasement slipped away unnoticed, until I found myself wondering why I was suddenly alone.

On the way back from one of our out of state trips for a gig that was even more inebriated than usual, I pushed Asheton over the edge when I put down the front passenger window in sub-freezing weather as we barreled along the interstate. At 70 or 80 mph, the rush of Arctic air must have been horrendous.

Ron was hollering at me to "Put the fucking window up, man," but I ignored him until he started beating on the back of the seat with his fists.

Farther up the road, we were pulled over by an Ohio state trooper, who looked inside the T-Bird and saw a pile of empty beer cans, with a half full case of beer sitting on the front seat floor. His initial comment was, "Whoa, that doesn't look good at all." Miraculously, he allowed us to continue on after we paid a substantial bond in lieu of a fine at the local Highway Patrol post. If things got any icier between Ron and me after that, I don't know, because I was already so tired of our relationship that I didn't care one way or the other what happened next.

Eventually we found a reliable drummer and the new material was sounding great. We were opening our show with an instrumental version of the James Bond theme, seguing into the song "Goldfinger" before Niagara's entrance. We were beginning to sound like a real band, but it was too late to turn things around. It was one of those situations where there is enough encouragement to keep you hanging in, but not enough success for you to evolve to the next level. The money was always a few hundred dollars, most of which was eaten up by expenses. Combined with our constant drinking and a new element, cocaine, things were going nowhere fast.

Anytime the band went anywhere, people showed up with coke. Ron and Niagara frequently disappeared into bathrooms with their admirers, re-emerging as though it was their right to be singled out for special treatment. While that tended to irritate those of us who were not included, it never occurred to them to decline the invitations.

I started a side project with my friend, David Davis. We recruited a former DAM drummer, who knew a guitarist that played cello in the Toledo Symphony, and that was the beginning of the Rite. I was signaling Ron and Niagara that I was ready to leave the fold. I'm sure they weren't concerned at all.

Things were deteriorating on every front. My life with Joanne was also drawing to a close, due to my drinking and womanizing. Even with a beautiful new baby to care for, I relished a life of dishonor. I thought cheating had no consequences, and pursued spontaneous extramarital affairs. I went to bars and parties. I paid visits to people that were drinking and getting high. My main goal was always to get laid. It was an obsession more powerful than being happily married.

In 1984, I decided I'd had enough of Ron and Niagara's pretentious celebrity posing and obnoxious trolling for cocaine. Ron had been doing his own drifting. He and Dennis Thompson had tried forming a supergroup called New Race with Radio Birdman's Ann Arbor expatriate guitarist Deniz Tek, traveling to Australia to record a live album during a one-off tour. Ron would have dropped DAM instantly had it succeeded, but it didn't. He returned to his mom's house, where he'd parked Niagara, and resumed the same old pattern.

I played my last gig with Destroy All Monsters at Joe's Star Lounge in Ann Arbor in June of 1984. When it was over, I packed my guitar and amp, loaded my car, and left without any farewell. As far as I know, it was the last-ever appearance of Destroy All Monsters in that format.

The three singles on IDBI/Cherry Red and the *Detroit On*

a Platter compilation comprise our entire recorded legacy (excluding live bootlegs and surreptitious tracks released posthumously by former band members)—not much to show for seven years' work. Decades later, I heard that a version of Cary Loren's original noise band, sans Niagara, had reunited to perform in Japan, home of its namesake. Full circle.

THE GRANDE FAMILY PRESENTS

13 & 14 FEB.

MC5
FLAMING GROOVIES

FRIDAY:
SHAKEY JAKE

SATURDAY:
VIRGIN DAWN

GRANDE BALLROOM

A DESIGN BY DARLEENE · PHOTO BY: LENI SINCLAIR

14

Play with Fire

I was pleased with myself for having departed from the court of the royal couple. Now I could return to life as myself, the former bass player of the MC5, without the stigma of being associated with Ron and his Raggedy Ann mistress, the quirky Niagara.

I had been silkscreening rock and roll T-shirts for my friend Kenny, who ran the local punk paraphernalia boutique. But Ken was selling the business to escape the Rust Belt and relocate to Arizona. I had the idea of going to community college and taking auto body repair classes. I found I was eligible to go to school virtually free with the various grants available, so I did.

When the new owner, Mark, came to take over the business, he shut down the silkscreen operation, leaving me unemployed. Mark was a decent fellow who owned stores in Chicago, that were similar to the boutique in Ann Arbor. As a final task, he asked me to fly to New York to meet his with brother, who would put me in a rental van loaded with bongs and smoking paraphernalia, which I would drive back to Chicago for $500.

While I was away on this errand, my wife Joanne was at the Iron Maiden concert back in Michigan with her new friends from the local high school hardcore scene. I also knew she was with a particular 16 year old, the bass player in one of the local bands. He was a short stump of a character with a mop of blond hair, usually poking out from under a black top hat. Things had been appearing abnormally friendly between Joanne and the young fellow when these people came by our house, making me aware that something was going on behind my back.

I wheeled the cargo van down the Long Island Expressway and into the Queens Midtown Tunnel, drove across Manhattan, through Times Square in the twilight with a full moon overhead, across the George Washington Bridge to New Jersey, and onto the Interstate bound for all points west.

I was drinking beer out of cans propped between my legs as I bounced along the highway. The song playing on the van's radio caught my ear: the new Sting single, "Fortress": "If I could build this fortress around your heart… I cannot fill the chasm." As the melody poured out of the little speakers in the truck, the ache in my gut started to swell until it filled my throat. My eyes welled with tears to the point of overflowing, and I burst into unrestrained crying. Rain had begun to fall on the roadway and windshield. I turned on the wipers with my eyes pouring.

I drove on. It was like the scene from Jules Dassin's 1962 movie *Phaedra*, where Tony Perkins is driving with the wipers on while crying and wailing, "Phaedra, Phaedra, Phaedra!" I pictured Joanne at the Iron Maiden concert, gyrating to the music and gripping her sweetheart in a passionate embrace. I cracked open another can of beer. It went on all the way to Pennsylvania. I drove through the night and arrived at Mark's midtown Chicago store around noon the next day, wrung out and exhausted.

I got settled in at Mark's swank apartment in a very nice mid-Chicago neighborhood. Over a fabulous meal of grilled swordfish steak and pints of beer, I told Mark about my domestic woes. He was very sympathetic as we discussed the ins and outs of what was happening and what I might do about it.

He offered me a job as a distributor of smoking paraphernalia in South Side Chicago. I really wasn't comfortable with that and politely declined the offer. We parted company the next day and I flew back home to Ann Arbor to what I surely knew was the end of everything.

About a week later, it came to a head. I had come back to the house to find Joanne gone and a note explaining where she had gone. Instead of accepting the lie, I hopped on my Yamaha motorcycle to do a little investigating. I knew right where to look, and there at a park, down a short ravine from the street, I saw Joanne and her high school boyfriend relaxing at a picnic table. From the hilltop where I stood, I fixed them with a stare until she happened to glance up and recognized me. I calmly turned, mounted the bike, and rode off.

When she came home, she actually had the gall to pretend nothing had taken place. I confronted her. In an instant, the emotions took over, and she was screaming with tears flowing down her face that she wasn't happy and wanted to leave.

My mind raced with possible options. Where would she live, where would I live? Our lease at the current house was up in a month. We would both need to find places. Then she hurled the unthinkable at me without remorse or hesitation. "I can't take Ursula. I'm incapable of taking care of her. I'll lose her!"

I could not imagine for one second being a single parent to a toddler. Ursula was four years old. She was bright, very pretty, the epitome of a beautiful child, and the product of radically anti-establishment parents. Her entire life had been spent in the company of rock and rollers, party people, and rogues of all sorts. What kind of menagerie would I surround her with as a solo dad?

Joanne insisted, "I can't be a mother. I can't do it!" It was plain; there was no way out, I knew I had to accept the fact that I was to be Ursula's provider and protector. I just had to; there was no other alternative.

Joanne packed her mounds of clothing, grabbed the few household items she wanted, and when I wasn't looking, rifled through my record collection and absconded with 20 or so of her favorite records to her new place, a room in a big boarding house in Ypsilanti. I was pissed. I had a couple of weeks left in our old house before I could get into a new place in Ann Arbor, so Ursula and I would have to camp in the barren old crib until we could move.

I had bought a rusty old '77 Camaro for a hundred dollars. It was my "project car" at the community college where I was taking auto body repair classes. I had to enroll Ursula in kindergarten for the new school year, and getting everything up and running was hard, but I did it without too much trouble. I rented a two-bedroom basement apartment in a building on a very nice street in town. We had a living room, a kitchenette, and a bathroom, plus our two sleeping rooms. A washer and dryer were just down the hallway.

The first weeks in the new apartment were fun. We were on our own, a little duo of brave pioneers. We shopped at the market with our food stamps and bought our favorite treats, as well as dinner items that I could put together without having to know anything about cooking.

I had explained to her that she and I were going to be on our own, and Mommy was going to be on her own. She acted as if she understood, but how could she possibly have? I tried to be as non-judgmental as I could in explaining. I didn't want her to feel responsible, but how could she not? How could she have thought anything but that Mommy didn't want her or me?

It didn't help when Joanne didn't contact us for over a month after we separated. I went from feeling crushed to being bitter and resentful. I hated Joanne. The harm she'd done to me paled in comparison to what she was doing to our child. She never came over to see where we lived. She never called to see how we were doing. What did I expect? I expected her to check in on us!

Ursula and I were doing all right. She'd be in her room, playing with her Barbie doll and her cassettes of sing-along children's stories. I'd be drinking my beers in the kitchen or watching TV. She went to kindergarten in the morning on the school bus, and I'd drive to my auto body repair classes during the day. Joanne was no longer a part of our lives.

There was a woman named Jody who lived in the building next door and had a little girl about Ursula's age. She made it very obvious that she intended to sleep with me, but she was married to a wiry little guy who looked like he was capable of violence, an ex-Marine type who was still working his way through the battlefield in his head. So, not only did I not want her, I also didn't want to be murdered because of her. She kept coming over to visit, and eventually she drove her husband away. Once he was gone, her visitations were incessant, a cigarette in one hand and a beer in the other.

One night I gave in. She was over at our apartment and after several cans of beer, she suggested, "Let's go in your bedroom." Feeling pangs of guilt over what her ego would suffer if I rejected her outright, I said okay like a passive victim. She made the conquest, but I was firmly opposed to our becoming a couple or moving in together, if that was her ultimate purpose. Soon after that, she announced that she and the little girl were moving back to Pennsylvania, and they disappeared.

In the spring of '86, I was at a house party with a crowd of high school-aged punksters and hardcore kids who'd latched onto the anti-establishment thrash music that mutated from the punk rock of the late 70's. I still had a group of friends from the farmhouse and DAM days, but I was also interested in the hardcore scene populated by those high school kids.

I spotted a young girl with medium-length blond hair, dark eyebrows, and the prettiest puffy lips I had ever seen. I gazed at her in the light, our eyes met, and she smiled at me like someone I knew intimately. Who was she? I had to find out. She approached and said, "Hi." In that moment, I thought I'd found someone I'd been looking for all my life. Although we were distant in age, I made it my mission to win her love.

I saw her again at another house party a couple of weeks later. We came together for conversation immediately. Her cheery disposition added to my already brimming interest. She gave me a brief summary of her life, which piqued my interest all the more. Now I was beginning to feel encouraged, but knowing it would take a long time to make something really happen, I relaxed and resigned myself to wait for other opportunities.

I had other female intrigues amid various crowds I was drifting through. All of them were younger than I, but that wasn't surprising, as I was older than anyone I saw socially. While sex was my goal, I was consumed by that teenage quest for the ideal partner.

I was in love. It seemed I had been searching for my ultimate since I first became aware of sex. That this one fit the frame meant everything to my warped sense of entitlement. The difference in our ages didn't matter. In fact, it added to the challenge.

One of my other encounters involved a young woman I'd recently met at a bar in Ann Arbor called the Blind Pig. I was out riding around on my motorcycle, hoping to chance upon my teenage heartthrob, when I decided to stop at the Pig for a beer. I sat down at a table where a couple friends were sitting and was introduced to their friend, a young woman who'd recently moved from Kalamazoo. We talked for a while, then I asked if she'd like to go for a ride with me on my bike. She said, "Sure," and off we went on my Yamaha 650. "You can take me back to my place if you'd like," she said. "I've got a couple of beers in the fridge."

It didn't take long before we were in her bedroom, having sex. I left thinking that if it were always that easy, I might be able to relax and have some self-confidence. A couple of weeks later, she called me at home, saying she was at the bus stop in town and asking if I'd come pick her up. She wanted to come over for awhile.
"Well, uh…yeah…um, I mean, yeah sure, I'll be right there," I sputtered, slightly startled by the request.

By "awhile," she meant overnight. I took her back to her apartment the next day wondering what she was planning. While I was always looking for someone to be with, once anyone shared that desire, I ran away, as far and as fast as I could. I was afraid this one wasn't going to go away quietly.

My little teenager appeared every so often during the summer. Each time, I tried to hold my desires in check by being casual, and above all, more poised than the rest of her hormonal crew. I could feel her admiration and fascination with me growing as our meetings, infrequent though they were, continued until one autumn afternoon, I ran into a couple of her friends at a house occupied by a local band. I asked about her and they confided to me that she was in the hospital recovering from a drug overdose.

I was shocked. "Overdose on what?" I asked.
When I heard the "H" word, I pretended to be appalled, but in my mind I saw the play that would bring me to the gate of my heart's desire. "What can I do to help her?" I asked the friend.

"Oh, do something extravagant," she replied. I certainly would.

I had the perfect idea of what to do. I had a friend who had a delivery job with a local florist. I called him and placed an order; a single red rose in a slender glass vase—extravagantly understated. I was now investing my ordinarily closely held money in the affair.

Her response was exactly as I'd hoped. The whole tone of our relationship changed. When we met again, she grasped my hand, locked her arms around me, and offered her mouth to be kissed. She sat on my knee while I lectured to her about those hard drugs. I implored her to not get sucked into the trap of heroin use, for she was much too beautiful a creature to let a stupid thing like dope take away her life.

After that, it became commonplace for me to hear a knock at my door after Ursula had gone to school around 9:30 in the morning. When I answered, my teenage dream would be waiting. Somehow, she was able to maintain straight A's while skipping school every other day to be with me in the subterranean apartment. In fact, she had several guys on the hook, and she made the rounds at her pleasure. Still, our time together was extremely intense.

Around this time, a friend who sang with local band called me with a strange request. He was going to take a month off from everything and do heroin. I couldn't believe what he was telling me, but he was sure about it.

He asked if I knew where he could score the drugs. As I knew that my sister and her boyfriend were currently using, it would be easy to obtain anything he wanted. He gave me $100 to get him a bag and keep whatever I wanted for myself. He said that he was going to do this for a month, then stop. It was risky, enough to make me think twice, but I opportunistically saw it as a way to get more intertwined with my new love and make a little cash at the same time.

My sister and her boyfriend had two children about Ursula's age, a boy and a girl—one older, one slightly younger. An endless parade of junkies passed through their house in Detroit. The boyfriend fenced stereos, watches, rings, guns; anything of value was bartered for dope. My first trip to their house was the end of my abstinence from heroin.

It had been ten years since the last time I'd played with fire. "Hey Mike, man, want a hit, man? It's on the house."

"Wow, I don't know. It's been a long time." I mulled it over a minute. I hadn't been thinking about it, but it was clear that I wasn't through with the idea of getting fucked up. I drank continuously and it had only been a matter of time until another opportunity to get strung out arose.

I drove home to Ann Arbor under the same hypnotic trance

that had once been my familiar space. The Camaro hummed and my gaze froze on the lines speeding by under the headlights. Was I awake or dreaming? I delivered the bag of skag to my customer in Ann Arbor and went home to the safety of my apartment.

It was December, crispy cold and sometimes snowing. Every other night, I went driving to Detroit, often with Ursula, who played with her cousins while the grownups cooked up their illegal potions and drank huge tumblers of vodka and Squirt. There were always enough funds for my own purchases, the free hospitality having exhausted itself.

The house was a disgusting mess, with unwashed dishes piled high in the sink, all manner of objects lying about the floor. Unmade beds and empty cups, glasses, darkened spoons, the television on at all times with no one watching, everyone nodding with their eyes closed, their mouths open.

In between shots of heroin, yellowed bits of crack cocaine were passed around in glass pipes. Going outside to the brisk city air had its appeal, just to get out of the den.

After my friend ended his sabbatical of debauchery, I toyed with the idea of not returning to the Detroit dope house. I may have stayed away for an entire week, but then, as always, I gave in to the temptation.

It's hard to say just how my return to heroin was connected to my relationship with the teenage girl. At first, we shared in the lowlife aspect of being social outcasts together. Then it became my thing entirely, in keeping with that other truism: that junkies are determined to lose everything but the dope.

The girl from Kalamazoo was coming around from time to time, eventually finding an apartment in town not far from mine.

We'd been together a couple of times since meeting, and one afternoon, she called me to come meet her at a bar downtown. She wanted to talk.

"Well, what is it?" I asked her. She looked me straight in the eye and announced, "I'm pregnant."

"What are you going to do?" I asked.

"I'm going to have it, it's a boy, I already know from a sonogram."

I took a sip from the beer I was drinking. "That's fucked, I'm not going to be there for you. You know that, don't you?"

She teared up and continued, "I know, but I thought you'd like to be a part of it somehow."

I was thinking how this interfered with my unrealistic relationship with the 16-year-old. "I'm not really interested, don't expect me to be around."

She sniffled and composed herself. "I just thought you should know."

It was the last thing I wanted to hear. My life was getting more complicated as time went on. I had managed to bag the beautiful teen, I was starting to get back into heroin, Ursula was getting more needful, and now a girl that I hardly knew, but knew she wanted to know me, was pregnant. Where would it all end?

The coming of spring intensified my love affair with the forbidden flower. Cherry blossoms, warm breezes, green grasses, and returning to the outdoors lifted the spirits of the winter-hardened folk. Off came the black leathers and knit beanies; life had returned to claim its vassals. I went back and forth from having a minor addiction to going cold turkey for a few days and leaving the effects of withdrawal behind.

I was still enrolled at the community college, and took a weightlifting class while nurturing my dope habit. Even I was puzzled by my behavior. The pregnant girl persisted in coming over to sit throughout the night while I went off to Detroit to take drugs and drink. It was remarkable how much abuse she would take.

My friend and former employer, Kenny Brown, reappeared in Michigan with Joanne's twin sister, with whom he was now living in Arizona. By now, it was obvious to an experienced observer—and Kenny was a very hip fellow—that I had unmistakably gone off the deep end with drugs.

Being the shrewd person he was, and inasmuch as he had the resources, he offered to take Ursula back to Arizona with him for the summer. In an amazing coincidence, my teenage sweetheart had informed me that her family was planning to move to California in August, taking her out of my love- and drug-obsessed life. Two drastic changes loomed in my not-too-distant future.

I thought hard about what I was going to do, and in a radical but intriguing vision, I entertained the notion of leaving Michigan as a way of hanging on to my love interest.

After all, California and Arizona are at least in the same time zone. It just might work, and it'd be a good way to start over with a clean slate. It meant leaving behind my local celebrity, saying goodbye to all my partying comrades—and saying goodbye, for the time being, to my parents. But it meant discovering a whole new environment and regional culture radically different from my Michigan home. I was sick of Detroit, sick of Ann Arbor, sick of myself, and tired of being the only lost and lonely surfer boy in town.

I told Kenny it sounded like a great idea. I would take a sublet over the summer, have a big garage sale in August, hitch a trailer to the back of the Camaro, and drive across the country in September to make a fresh start. But first, I'd have to survive the lifestyle I had acquired until my time of leaving, and I would need a couple thousand dollars to make the trip and get set up in Arizona: an unheard of amount for me in those days.

In July, the woman who had claimed me as her mate without consulting me had her baby, and it was…a boy. The night she delivered, I happened to be having a beer at a local tavern when a friend of hers implored me to go visit her in the hospital.

"It would mean so much to her," she said earnestly.

"I'm sure it would, but I told her from the start not to expect me to be around. I'm not into this. This is her decision."

She became clearer as the liquor kicked in. "I told her it wasn't going to work like she thought. She did it on purpose, you know. The first time she came over to be with you, it didn't work. So she came back again and the second time it worked, she got pregnant. She really loves you, you know."

"Are you kidding, she got pregnant on purpose so I'd be forced to be in a relationship with her?" I was astonished.

"Yeah, I told her it was uncool, but she had to go and do it." I was seething. "Yeah, I probably will go check her out, as a formality."

"Don't tell her I told you this shit. Please, Michael, don't let on I gave it away."

I assured her friend I wasn't going to bring up anything, and the next day I paid a visit to the young mother up in the maternity ward. I could never put it out of my mind that this girl had schemed her way into motherhood. It would be okay by me, as long as she wasn't trying to extort me into a bear trap of a relationship. I wasn't attracted to her in the first place, and the idea that it might interfere with my perverse love affair with my teenage queen was infuriating.

The summer sped by, with my flame leaving me behind in Michigan as August began. The next few weeks were perilous. I had about $500 when I decided to take a last trip to my sister and her boyfriend's place in Detroit to get high. I spent the next two weeks there, squandering all my money on drugs, getting my car stolen then miraculously returned, and sinking deeper into drug-induced disorientation than I'd ever done before. I was a wrecked and corrupted soul, in utter despair, with the prospect of being stranded in Michigan, homeless, broke, and unable to make the trip to be with my little girl, Ursula. At the very last second, I made my escape.

One of the characters who was hanging around that dope den when I was leaving said in passing, "So when we gon' see you again, Mike?"

"NEVER!" I thundered back, to his astonishment.

"Aw, come on, man…not never."

"Yeah man, never!"

I had a couple of things to do, besides getting sober. First and foremost, I had to get myself to a hospital to be tested for HIV. I'd been sharing outfits with any number of addicts, and been totally unconcerned for the consequences. Secondly, I had to gather my belongings and have a sale.

My friends from a band called the Laughing Hyenas had a house with a garage, which they agreed to let me use to set up my stuff for a sale. I crammed all my salable possessions in that old garage: oriental rugs, furniture, music gear, clothes, tools, and whatever else I didn't have to keep. I made $1,250 in two days. The biggest item, an immaculate '65 Stratocaster I'd paid $75 for a couple of years prior, I sold to a friend for $600; not a bad investment, considering those guitars go for $20,000 nowadays. The new mother and infant were there to help with the sale, even though it added to her woe.

I returned to the hospital to learn my fate. After several anxious minutes, a nurse came to the counter with some paperwork in her hands.

"Mr. Davis?" she asked, giving me a serious look. "Your test results are…negative."

I breathed a sigh of relief, exclaiming, "Thank you, thank you so much."

I flew down the stairs and out into the parking lot. Glancing skyward, I said aloud, "Thank you God, thank you for my life!"

I promised God and myself I would never use heroin again. It was the stupidest thing I had ever done. How could I be so unconcerned for my well being, or for the others who cared about me? What sort of imbecile was I? Every single thing I ever could want could be taken away forever by letting disaster be my shadow. I must repair this horrendous character trait, I thought.

But it was going to be all right. The night before leaving, I went to my parents' to bid them farewell. After I'd given my mom a goodbye hug, my father walked out with me to my car in the parking lot. A U-Haul trailer was attached to a hitch on the rear bumper. The moment was awkward. He told me that he understood I needed to seek something beyond the existence we had always known. He thought it was a good thing for me to be doing, even though he hated to see me go. He shook my and gave me a hug, not something that happened often.

"Take care of yourself," he told me, and with that, I slipped into the seat of the Camaro, fired it up, drove back up to Ann Arbor to spend the last night in Tree Town.

It took most of the next day to load up the trailer with a motorcycle, an SVT bass rig, a few guitars, leathers (for Arizona, ha), suitcases, small household items, furniture, and Ursula's items. By late afternoon, the car and trailer were crammed with my worldly possessions. I hugged the teary lady holding the two-month-old on her hip, feeling the shudder of her small body. It was almost impossible. I felt like the devil, delivering a bolt of sulfuric heartache. How could I condone my evil self? I had to shrug it off. What was I going to do, change my mind?

It was September 16, 1987. As I gassed up at the Shell station nearest the entrance to the freeway, it started to rain. "Well," I said to myself, "Here we go."

I fired up the old Chevy. I had repaired all the rusted areas in the car at auto body school. I'd built a whole new floor pan, replaced the quarter panels, patch the rusted doors and fenders, and painted it black. The motor rumbled with a mellow growl. I pulled the console shifter to "Drive," pulled out of the gas station, and made an immediate right-turn to the freeway entrance, I-94 to Chicago. I wouldn't even have to look at a map. I had it all in my head, from a song I'd first heard the Rolling Stones sing in 1964.

Well if you ever plan to motor west.
Just take my way, that's the highway that's the best.
Get your kicks on Route 66.

Ten years had passed since I was released from prison. Twenty years had passed since I'd joined the MC5. I was older, but less wise. I was a danger to myself. The possibility of permanent brain damage from constant inebriation was considerable.

I remember all of the MC5 members once inhaled Freon from a tank provided by one of our promoters. We didn't even know what it was until after we'd tried it. My marathons of intravenous heroin and cocaine use, endless alcohol bouts, cigarette smoking and lack of dietary discipline had taken a toll. My mind was full of ridiculous fantasy. How I avoided death or total destruction, I don't know. But in the moment, I was driven. More than simply abandoning a void, I had a goal.

The road stretched out endlessly in front of the Camaro's hood. Every state line was a victory. I sipped beer from a bottle or can held between my legs. After crossing the endless expanses of Missouri and Oklahoma, I began to get disoriented and paranoid. I drove through a small mountain range just outside Albuquerque, scared to death I was going to be swept off the road by high winds or big trucks. In the dark, I was completely terrified by the vague scenery along the highway. I held the steering wheel tightly while imagining deep chasms going over bridges.

Once I passed the Continental Divide, I felt like I was on the surface of Mars. I was scared shitless, but I driven by the golden glow of my infatuation with the girl of my dreams in California. Everything in my life narrowed to one goal; see her again. Ursula was stashed away with my friend Ken and her aunt. Though I wasn't thinking how my daughter might feel, she was at least in a safe place. My mind was consumed by the fantasy that held me as its prisoner.

I fell asleep at a rest stop just outside of Lordsburg, New Mexico. About 20 trucks, mostly with their diesel motors running, surrounded the little black Camaro with the U-Haul on its bumper. At about 4:00 in the morning, I woke up in a disoriented fog. A brisk

15

The Oven

We'd been here before, Ursula and I. The previous year, we'd flown to Tucson over Christmas break in January to visit. But that was in winter, when crystal blue sky and bright sunlight reminded us of how unique it was to be in this place, while people back at home struggled with snow and bitter cold. Back then, columns of Saguaro stood tall and serene, scattered randomly, monumentally still and silent, waiting for the time to spring their trap. But now it was mid-September, when the wall of late summer heat radiates from the ground in rippling waves of energy.

Tucson, Arizona: Nestled between brown rock mountains that rise into the cobalt sky, a layer of haze hanging just above the entire scene. Situated in the middle of the Santa Cruz Valley sits a grouping of a dozen or so buildings of four to ten stories, the downtown area of the "Old Pueblo."

Radiating out from there is a flat, ten-mile spread of mostly adobe neighborhood dwellings and businesses, lining a network of asphalt streets that comprise the city. The I-10 interstate slices diagonally past the downtown towers, separating the city from something called South Tucson and the surrounding desert.

On the way there, we had passed places with names like Cochise Stronghold, Fort Huachuca, Tombstone. My back-east imagination ran wild with cowboy and Indian visions, Apache verses U.S. Cavalry scenarios, TV westerns, gunfights at the OK Corral. On one long MC5 drive across the country, I had read a fascinating book called *The Truth About Geronimo*. How ironic to find myself heading for the place where that legend lived.

Kenny, once a fanatical rock and roll kid, grew up to be an entrepreneur boutique owner and Uber-hipster. He'd had a store in Ann Arbor called Make Waves that dealt in punk fashions, import records, joke sundries, and his personal fixation, paraphernalia for smoking herb.

He was one of those former hippies that drank very little, but couldn't get enough marijuana. He liked an occasional line of coke too, but weed was his main attraction. He had a keen mind for business and employee relations and was a very generous person, averse to wasting time. He also gave every artist in town a job. Ken liked me as a person and hoped to help me attain success and personal stability. He was also a quasi-family member, by virtue of taking my wife's twin as his companion.

For a long time, Kenny had been urging me to give up the endless dreary hopelessness of Lower Michigan and seek a new life in warm and sunny Tucson. On my previous visit, I'd been struck by the many examples of '50s and '60s Detroit iron on the streets.

I'd never seen so many unrusted, vintage automobiles—a particular obsession of mine—still on the road.

I think he'd sold his business in Ann Arbor for over $100,000 and retreated to Arizona to be close to the stash. Ken was also a man of voracious appetites. We were always dining out, with him footing the bill: Mexican, Italian, rich and spicy. After a joint of homegrown Tucson skunkweed, it was as close to paradise as he thought he could get. He was eager to initiate me to this lifestyle, and after several years, here I was, a newly migrated snowbird.

He was anxious for me to find local musicians to jam and form a band with. I guess he believed in me and had visions that I could one day emerge from my downward spiral of self-destruction. "There's this guy Rainer," he told me. "He plays guitar. I think you and him ought to get together. It'd be really good."

It turned out that Rainer Ptacek was an amazing bottleneck blues guitarist and singer, well known in Europe, particularly in Germany, where he had a legion of fans, as well as in Tucson. But it wasn't in my fortune to meet Rainer at that time. We only became acquainted later on, but by then, lots of things had changed.

After a week, I went out searching for an apartment. In the neighborhood near Kenny's house, I found a small apartment complex with about 20 units. Our two-bedroom apartment with a carport was right by the pool. If only all my cronies back in Michigan could see me now, I thought, lounging at poolside while Ursula played with her new friends.

Epic orange, pink, and purple sunsets every evening, followed by the softest warm afterglow in the darkness; who wouldn't be envious? The mysteries of the desert were all around. Spirits seemed to speak from the mountains. I was enchanted by it all. But I had a pressing rendezvous to keep.

"I'm in Arizona," I told her over the phone. San Diego was a 420-mile trip by car, but in my state of mind, a mere six-hour drive was nothing. It would be a simple matter of dropping Ursula off at Ken's for a couple of days while I consummated my craving for a reunion with my beloved. I was ever so close to success.

Sometime early in October, I set out west on the I-10 in the Camaro, bound for California. Connecting with westbound Interstate 8, on across Arizona to Yuma and into California, the Imperial Dunes and the Dome Valley, the Camaro was equal to the task.

Kenny had warned me about overheating going up the mountains, but I remained unafraid. I had built this car and maintained all its systems; it wasn't going to be a problem. I ascended the San Gabriels listening to Mozart, fascinated by the rock formations: piles and piles of enormous boulders. A solitary sign of civilization stood at the peak, a service station that signaled the start of the zigzagging 25-mile descent to the sprawling city of San Diego and the Pacific seacoast.

We met at a big shopping mall farther up the coast. It was unreal, like a movie. We spent two days playing in San Diego, going to resale shops and thrift stores, sitting in restaurants, going on carnival rides, and playing out the fantasy of our forbidden affair.

At times I became conscious of looking like what we were; a middle aged geezer with his Lolita. I wondered if she sensed it? When at last we parted, I was already planning my next trip back. As I climbed the heights that led back to the desert, I knew I could never satisfy the urge that I felt. My only goal was to make it last as long as possible. I tried to make believe it was possible to make her mine forever. I was setting myself up for a big fall.

Ursula and I settled in at La Terreza Apartments, which I soon began calling "La Cucaracha Apartments." I enrolled Ursula at the nearest elementary school and got a job delivering lunch for a local pub some friends of Kenny's owned, earning about $20 a day.

Stepping outdoors at noon was like walking straight into a furnace. Waves of heat radiated off the asphalt of Speedway Avenue, where cars waited in groups of ten to 20 for the red light to change. The immediate surge of 100-plus degree heat was enough to turn you into a sizzling cinder. I had known hot days in Michigan, but this was something else entirely.

I'd stuff myself into the Camaro with a few bags and Styrofoam boxes, cups of iced tea and sodas, and hurry to the businesses that had phoned in orders for lunch. It was good bar food and I got fed to boot, so I couldn't complain. However, the job ended after only a month, when the boss got busted in New York trying to make his own delivery: a vanload of coke and weed. The bar went down the tube, and his wife had to sell everything.

I got another job doing auto-body repair at a fast-paced production shop. Cars with dented fenders and crushed rocker panels would come into the bay. I'd straighten out the metal as best I could, Bondo up the panel, and sand it until it looked like it originally had. Every night, I'd come back to the apartment with a snoot full of Bondo dust and dried and caked Bondo under my fingernails, primer paint all over my arms and hands. To make things more challenging, I was also going to school. I'd enrolled at Pima Community College and registered for three classes: Sculpture, Airbrush Painting, and Photography. It didn't leave much time for Ursula, or anything else. I flew my teenage dream to Tucson to spend a few days with us. She and Ursula were very comfortable together. We were like a little pretend family. We cavorted around Tucson and I showed off all the local sights. It was a wonderful time, but then she left and everything was back to the way it always was. She was developing a new group of friends at her high school in California. It was only a matter of time before she would be seeing someone her own age. My personal disaster was approaching.

I was physically wrecked and mentally exhausted. I tried to keep my class schedules, but I was so tired from working all day, it was all I could do to stay awake. I had to drop out. In the meantime, I finally got the word I knew was coming. My heart's desire had been with someone else. All the delusions that motivated me came crashing down.

The separation wasn't quick, painless, or clean. It lasted several months, culminating in a pathetic trip to L.A., where we parted late at night, somewhere near the L.A. Coliseum. She was gone. I had to go home. That was all there was. I wondered how many years it would take to get over this one. I imagined it would be many. I'd always been a drinker. Now I hit the bottle hard.

The endless pain and self-pitying, self-obliterating drunkenness finally landed me in jail. Polluted beyond function, I went out driving for no particular reason. It was dark, and without looking, I made a lane change straight into the side of another car. When I attempted to escape, several other drivers who witnessed the event took chase. I was cornered in a cul-de-sac at the end of a residential street and held captive until the police arrived to take me into custody.

When I awoke in the morning, I was on a concrete slab, nursing a splitting headache. The cops said I could go home, handing me a fistful of citations: driving under the influence (DUI), blood alcohol misdemeanor (BAC), and leaving the scene of an accident. I had a court date. The police had parked my car at a distant location. I took a cab to my apartment and went to bed to sleep off the remaining intoxication.

By the next day, I was steady enough to go out, and I hopped on my bicycle, which I had stolen from the Salvation Army Thrift Store, and went out to find the car. I'd sold the Camaro after having it painted sky blue at the body shop where I worked. A young fellow graduating from high school bought it as a graduation gift.

The car I'd hit the other car with was a Monte Carlo. It had been parked at the farthest western outskirt of town, at a Circle K near the Indian reservation. After peddling for what seemed like hours, I spied the car at the end of a lonely street at the foot of a rocky hill. After stuffing the bike in the trunk, Humpty Dumpty made for home, feeling fortunate to have all of his pieces back together. I replaced the Monte Carlo's fender with one I found in a junkyard.

On New Year's Eve, I went up to Phoenix for a party one of Kenny's friends was throwing. I got pretty drunk and left the party, stopping at a convenience store to buy more beer. I kept driving aimlessly. After driving and making indiscriminate turns, I wound up in a big municipal yard, where I drove the Monte Carlo straight up a huge mound of gravel. The wheels started spinning, and I backed down to the bottom, where the vehicle got lodged in the dirt behind it. It was hopelessly stuck.

At dawn, I got out and started walking like a zombie. I was on an Indian reservation, but I didn't know it. Single-wide mobile homes dotted the flat barren mesa. I was delirious as I knocked at the closed trailer doors. Some people actually invited me to come in and asked if I wanted a beer. I rambled on about my broken heart and anything that came into my head. I was extremely lucky not to have gotten shot, or at least beaten up. I stayed for a while, then moved on. I was stumbling along a dirt road that led to a paved road when a police car pulled up in front of me and stopped.

One of the officers got out of the car and simply opened the rear door. "We'll give you a ride," he said politely but firmly. It was the reservation police. We pulled into a parking lot marked San Carlos Reservation Police Station.

"Okay, sir, we have a room for you. If you stay here for 18 hours, you will be released with no further complications. You are not under arrest. But if you choose to leave at any time before the 18 hours is up, you will be arrested and charged with public intoxication."

That sounded very agreeable. "Show me my room, please," I responded.

Several drunken Indians were invited to sleep it off during that day and later that night. They yelled and shouted, talked to themselves, and eventually slept. It was New Year's Day, 1988. It wasn't easy to stay the whole 18 hours. Once I sobered up, I was ready to leave, but the terms of the agreement had to be met.

Finally at 8 pm, I was told I could go. My car had been dislodged from the stone pile and parked outside the front door. I was most grateful for the compassionate treatment I'd received. I couldn't imagine the white man's police being quite so understanding.

It was a two-hour drive back to Tucson. While I was relieved to be free and unharmed, my mind was still dwelling on the shitty way my life was going. It had barely been a day, but I was ready for a beer.

I called Kenny to fill him in. He chuckled, "We weren't sure if you were still alive." I told him the story.

"You better come over and have something to eat." I slunk over to his house and tried to forget the ordeal.

Early in March, I got laid off from the body shop. They said they were downsizing, and someone had to go. Since I was the lowest man on the totem pole, it was me. Not that I minded; fixing cars was fun when it was my car, but cranking out other people's boring commuters was a drag, and the pay wasn't that good, since the shop took 60% of the ticket. It was back to welfare for us. I'm not sure what kind of toll all of this was taking on Ursula, but I'm sure it wasn't helping that her dad was depressed and alcoholic.

Eventually I found another gig, driving around Tucson and outlying areas, delivering garbage bags for a veterans' organization. The "vets" were a half dozen down-and-out characters, sitting in a storefront, working telephones, and calling themselves a VFW group. I made enough to keep a few dollars in my pocket from tips, and it was straight cash daily, so I didn't report it.

I was outside of town one evening with a backseat full of boxes of garbage bags. The sun was setting and the radio was on. The DJ was interviewing Wally Palmer from the Romantics, a Detroit band who were having some chart success.

"Oh, shit!" I froze. The Romantics were playing this night in Tucson, and here I was sitting out in the fucking desert with a car full of garbage bags. I leaned back and sighed. "What the fuck has become of me?"

The light of day was disappearing, darkness engulfing the desolate little arroyo where I was parked. My rock and roll life was now far in the past. I thought about going down to the show and trying to get in, but my pride wouldn't allow it. What would I say? What would they say? I lamented that I could have slipped so far.

It was coming up on 20 years since the recording of *Kick Out the Jams*. "Just let it go," I said to myself. That was behind me; nothing could bring it back or renew the glory. I was stuck out here in the middle of nowhere. The only things calling my name were those boxes in the back seat. I restarted the Monte Carlo. It was a good car.

Kenny had placed an ad in a community newspaper, *Tucson Weekly*, on my behalf. It said something like, "If you like the Stooges and the MC5, well known bass guitarist is auditioning guitar players for a possible music project." There were several responses. A few guys came over to demo their chops. Nobody could quite compare to my former mates, but one guy happened to mention, "Have you met Cameron?"

"Cameron?" I said.

"Yeah, he's from Detroit and he's some kind of a promoter."

The kid gave me Cameron's phone number, so I decided check him out. We met at a coffee house near the university. I recognized him right away. He had a "rock and roll" haircut, long in the back, but pulled back and falling over one side of his face. He was a guitar player who'd played in the Cadillac Kids, a Detroit band with a small following, but he did some promoting on the side. He really seemed like a shyster to me. He'd once booked DAM at a movie theater in Michigan. While we played live on stage, the film *Destroy All Monsters* played behind us on the theater screen.

One evening he called and asked if I wanted to go to the dog track with him. "Huh? Well, okay," I told him.

We went to a place called Tucson Greyhound Park. Cameron was a compulsive gambler, didn't drink, and was a member of Narcotics Anonymous. I would come to find out that he frequented the topless clubs around Tucson, knew many of the strippers, had regular after-hours secret gambling dens, and befriended a number of hookers. I didn't have a problem with any of that; I just thought it was an odd fixation. I guessed that before he went straight edge, he was probably dealing coke to the topless dancers and whores, and got so strung out himself, he'd lost it all, and then decided to get straight.

We talked about forming a band in Tucson. Cameron had some connections and although he was already in a band, he was interested. He was a decent guitar player and over the years, we formed a couple of different bands, recorded a set of songs, and played a gig or two before he succumbed to and lost his mind to drugs. I lost track of him after that.

A couple of friends from Michigan showed up after a year or so. We took a house in a different neighborhood, and soon, it was just like one of those Ann Arbor rentals, with a drinking bout every night.

Even my ex showed up for a while. She came to town, shacked up for about six months with a taxi driver who was also was a painter, then went back to Michigan. People would think they could find a cooler place than the old turf, but after they got a blast of the summer heat and found out life was even more disconnected in Arizona than in Michigan, they would skedaddle back to the Midwest.
I stayed because I knew the same redundant lifestyle was waiting for me back in Michigan. I stayed because I didn't want to return defeated. I stayed just to see what would happen.

I had the greatest old Marantz stereo from the '70s. I bought it with the very first royalty check I received in 1983, after 13 years of nothing. I had a good turntable and speakers, and every night we'd get a bottle of tequila, a gallon of orange juice, and pick lemons to squeeze from the lemon tree in the front yard. Then we'd listen to N.W.A. and Dwight Yoakam at pain threshold volume for hours. No one ever called the cops. In the daytime, I'd go to the public pool and swim laps to quell the heat. One day the temperature hit 116 degrees. Putting your arm out of the car window burned.

My good friend Tattoo Mike was a doorman at Mudbugs, the happening rock club in town. He was also a tattoo artist. All the bands that came to Tucson got tattooed before they went back on the road. Every so often he would call me up to say, "Hey man, GBH is here tonight and they all want to meet you. Get your ass down here." Or, "I'm doing a tatt on this chick from Girls School, they want to party with us."

I came to the club one night just as everyone was packing up. Tattoo Mike asked me if I'd ever heard of these guys from Australia, the Hard-Ons. I said, "No, man, but that's a good name."
"Well, they've heard of you," he said. In a moment, they all swarmed over to tell me how much the MC5 meant to them. It was slightly shocking, because I really had no idea to what extent the MC5 was known outside of Michigan.

Actually, when I first came to Tucson, I was driving down the street in the afternoon one day, when I heard a familiar song come on the radio. I perked up my ear. "What the hell is that tune?" I asked myself. "It sounds really familiar."

After several seconds, I realized it was "Kick Out the Jams!" It was the theme music for the afternoon hard rock program. "Fuckin-A, that's me!" Little by little, it was becoming obvious the old band had done something special. We might not have sold a zillion records, but what we had sold had been heard around the world.

My sex life had come to a halt once the teenage Lolita drama ended. I felt like an albatross amongst these Arizonans and for whatever reason, I just couldn't break through with the women. Drinking had replaced everything.

The woman in Ann Arbor who'd had the baby had contacted me via the State of Michigan, which wanted me to acknowledge paternity so they could recoup what they were paying her in welfare. I went ballistic. After that failed, she came to Tucson to visit. She imagined we were going to have intimate relations when she arrived. Had I been getting any satisfaction of late, nothing would have taken place, but I hadn't, and like the animal I am, I succumbed, which served to give her tenuous hope.

She prodded me to sell her my car. As fortune would have it, I had spied another Camaro that interested me, so I agreed to let her have the Monte Carlo for $1000—enough to buy the Camaro. The arrangement called for Ursula and me to drive back to Michigan with her and the baby, helping with the driving, and then fly back to Arizona. Six months later, she contacted me again, this time to tell me she had saved enough money to hire a moving van and drive back to Arizona in the Monte Carlo, with the intent of moving there. I shuddered. She was getting closer to achieving what she had set out to do in the first place: to be my mate.

As if by design, things deteriorated at the rental so badly that after all the utilities were shut off, I had to call and ask her if Ursula and I could camp at her place until we found a new apartment. Finding myself in a situation where someone was cooking and cleaning, not to mention available for sex, overcame my resistance. We stayed. Ursula's little half brother was two. This wasn't the first time I'd jumped into a relationship of convenience. In fact, the two previous affairs had both ended awkwardly. Would this one play out the same? The outcome would turn out to be one I never expected.

It had been a rough three years. While sinking ever deeper into a pit of my own design, I never considered the possibility that I was alcoholic. The most common behavior trait among alcoholics is our steadfast ability to deny that our drinking is a problem. Just as the junkie thinks of himself as resourceful, the drunkard thinks of himself as in control. In another bizarre twist of fate, the DUI charges had been dropped when the cops admitted they couldn't remember if they had advised me of my right to have a blood test on the night of the arrest. It seemed like a victory, but was it? I hadn't ever completely fallen off the ledge, but I was drifting. Still, it felt nice to finally belong somewhere.

16

The Mind Shifts

I don't know why, but I've never bothered to worry over the direction of my life ever since, well, first departing my parents' protective haven. Drug addiction, alcoholism, and futile romantic pursuits all marked me as either an emotionally disturbed individual or a damned fool. I was determined to experience everything and refused to be constrained by society, the law, or my own better judgment.

When Ursula and I started living together with the woman from Ann Arbor and her little boy, my life became a lot easier, at least as far as the mundane details were concerned. She bought and cooked the food, cleaned the house, and took the clothes to the laundromat.

But my drinking got worse. I met a few cronies—wannabe musicians or guys that wanted to bask in the tarnished glory of my former rock stardom—and most every night, someone or other would be at our little cracker box barrio house, supplying and consuming vast quantities of beer.

Through no fault of my own, I managed to avert disaster. On a trip to Phoenix, I wore out my welcome where I was staying after I became abusively obnoxious, and attempted driving back to Tucson totally smashed. At a desolate point in the desert, about 25 miles outside of Phoenix, I heard a loud clunk and the engine died. I awoke at sunrise with a horrendous headache and tried the key again, but the car wouldn't start.

Alone, penniless, and miserable, I got out and started walking toward Tucson, 70 miles away. Trying to thumb a ride, I lucked out and caught a ride with an 18-wheeler. I was back at the Tucson house before noon.

One day she awoke me an hour after I'd passed out. The Tucson band Naked Prey had asked me to be their bass player, and I had accepted their offer. Van Christian, the lead singer and bandleader, was on the phone. There was a photo session and interview for the band at the *Tucson Citizen*, the one major newspaper in town.

"Tell him I'm not able to make it," I moaned.

"Here he is, he wants to talk to you."

Van was a bully, a heavy drinker himself, not one to take no for an answer. "Aw, come on man, it'll be easy, we'll come by to pick you up."

"No, no, I'm in bad shape, I can't do anything right now, let alone get my picture taken." I was trying to convey how out of it I was, but he wouldn't let me be.

"We'll be there in an hour. It's cake."

I went with Van and Al Perry, a Tucson guitarist and a legend in his own right. I'd played one pretty uproarious show with Naked

Prey at Club Congress, an historic hotel bar and the site of most major touring band shows in Tucson, but the photo session was a disaster that cooked my goose completely. In the photo that appeared on the cover of the Sunday entertainment section, I looked like a man stumbling forward into an abyss, open-mouthed, with a bewildered expression on my fave. Van never called me back after that day, and the band Naked Prey ceased to exist. I heard that he simply told people who asked about me that it didn't work out, which was kind.

It was a time of beer for breakfast. The poor girl who'd come all the way from Michigan to be with the man of her dreams found herself with a maniac, a self-indulgent beast with no regard for anything real. It didn't help that I was egged on by reading the Jim Morrison biography *No One Here Gets Out Alive*, a tale of drunken, life-threatening antics. This situation lasted several months, until we moved to a bigger and better house just up the street and I managed to shed my drinking buddies.

Soon it would be Christmas, and preparing for the holidays with a real family filled our house with joy. I found some old ornaments at a resale shop and bought strings of lights to put on a tree. The lights were blue, the bulbs were red; I put a garland of white around the tree, and lit up the spectacle. Blue striped candy canes dangled from the branches as we beheld the most beautiful Christmas tree I'd ever seen in my life. I was shocked by the splendor of the little scene in the old house's living room. It felt like home: a woman, a couple of kids, a tree, and me.

That New Year's Eve, I decided I'd had enough of smoking cigarettes. It was becoming increasingly difficult to find pleasure in the habit. My lungs and throat were raw from coughing, and it just wasn't worth what it cost or the effort it took to feed my nicotine jones. I had a half dozen cigs left in a pack, and for all the obvious reasons, I decided to not buy any more, or at least see if I could kick the habit for good. It was a good resolution, and I mark it as the milestone date that I quit smoking. I have gone back occasionally, but not for long and not permanently.

My new girl landed a job doing hair and maintaining a fledgling salon on the hip street in Tucson called Fourth Ave. She was developing a clientele and bringing in the bucks. Then, out of the blue, I received a substantial royalty check, which was most likely the result of a version of "Kick Out the Jams" by Henry Rollins and the Bad Brains having been featured in the movie, *Pump Up The Volume*. It wasn't much of a payday, but it was certainly more than I'd seen in a long while. I immediately went to the grocery store and bought a copy of *Car Collector*.

It took less than a week to find it: a 1968 Impala SS 396. I spent the whole check on it. I replaced the Cragar spokes with a set of Chevy Rally wheels and put fresh rubber on it. It was a big bad Impala. Putting your foot down to the floor at a 30 mph roll would make the thing stand up and roar, and in a few seconds you'd be pushing 90. It was *fast*. Sitting on the porch staring at the lines and curves of metal, the perfectly sculpted bumpers with three taillights on either side, I just couldn't believe it was mine. The woman made fun of me, "Oh George"—she called me King George—"you're out of your mind." Indeed, I was.

That was just the start of our car collecting. A few months later, I spotted a 1956 Chevy with a "for sale" sign in its window. It was slightly more money than the Impala had been and required a bit of borrowing but when it was done, we had two classics in our driveway.

The '56 was a hulking box of pure steel. Having only been driven in Arizona, it had no rust, and it was solid as a battleship. No power steering, no power brakes, no power anything. But it was bea-ut-iful: a Sport Sedan hardtop with a wrap-around windshield, a wrap-around rear window, the eagle on the hood, the bullet head front bumper, and the gas tank filler cap inside the taillight. I was pinching myself.

One day in September 1991, I came home from my veterans' delivery driving job. Ex-Rationals and Sonics Rendezvous Band singer Scott Morgan had called from Ann Arbor. Rob Tyner had passed away.

How could that be? Rob wasn't an old man. I was told he'd had a heart attack. Some people don't ever see it coming, especially if they aren't always checking things with a doctor. It meant I'd never have the opportunity to straighten things out with him, but that wouldn't have happened anyway; our time had come and gone, and the chance of us meeting again was remote. Still, it was a sad event. I thought how his wife and family must have been caught totally unprepared.

Morgan had something else on his mind: they were planning a benefit event to honor Rob by raising funds to give to his family and provide for his children's education. Would I come?

I was more than willing to participate, but I didn't have enough money to buy a plane ticket. A couple of days later, he called back to say Alice Cooper couldn't make the benefit and wanted to donate his ticket to me.

I landed at Detroit City Airport, met by Sonic's Rendezvous Band roadie "One Arm" Joe Hurley and my daughter, Michele, who was now a grown-up 20-year-old. We drove to a restaurant/bar in

Royal Oak that promoted itself as the "Michigan Rock and Roll Hall of Fame." It was crowded and noisy. Wayne Kramer was there, looking slightly different than I remembered him—stouter and balder, but still possessing that kindly smile.

Dennis Thompson grabbed hold of my arm. "Michael, how the hell are ya? You're looking good, old man." Dennis had changed. He was verging on portly, his eyes bulging out of his head, still talking a mile a minute. We exchanged a few pleasantries and hugs, lots of "good to see ya's" and back patting.

"Where's Fred?" I asked. Then I saw him, in the middle of a crowd on the other side of the island bar. I hurried around the oval of wood and people to a spot directly in front of him. I stood there looking straight in my old chum's face. Our eyes met for a second, another second passed, and finally, as if a light flared in the space between us, he reacted. His blank expression gave way to a look of pure serenity. "Michael!"

It was the most genuine feeling I'd ever seen on his face, a moment of pure happiness. It made me feel warm and welcome, happy I'd come. Then, just as quickly as it had appeared, it faded like a meteorite plunging through the atmosphere to a cold planet.

It was then that I noticed a different Fred Smith than I had ever seen. His demeanor had become dark and sunken. His face looked drawn as if by gravity to some spot on the floor. What was going on? I dared not ask. The people crowded around him, vying for his attention, distracted us from any further talking. He went back to what he had been doing, sipping his drink and being totally blasé. I left to find the others.

The room was filled with excited energy. In an upstairs section, the band Soundgarden waited for us to sit and have a drink with them. They were playing at the Fox Theater with the Cult on the same night we were to play the Rob Tyner benefit, a strange booking strategy by the benefit organizers.

I was still becoming aware of the MC5's legacy. Finding that current groundbreaking bands like Soundgarden revered the MC5 was pleasantly shocking. After signing a slew of guitars and posters, we were marched to the main floor to dip our hands in a cement square, destined for the front entrance of the restaurant. The homecoming was turning out to be a prodigal's return to a hero's welcome.

My father had passed away a couple of years earlier. My mom and my sister, along with her two children, were living together in a townhouse in a suburb near Detroit. Naturally we visited, but I opted to stay at the promoter's house on the other side of town, where Wayne and his new wife were also staying. The following day, we had our one and only rehearsal scheduled late in the afternoon at a small studio on the east side of Detroit.

We arrived promptly to start setting up the gear, which amounted to plugging in and tuning.

As in the old days of the MC5, we waited on Fred. An hour passed, and we waited. Two hours passed, and we waited some more. Three hours passed from the scheduled time, and we still waited. Finally, after three and a half hours, Fred pulled into the parking lot, entered the studio, sat down with a mumbled, "Sorry I'm late," and broke out two bottles of white wine. He lit a cigarette, opened the first bottle of wine, and sat in his chair looking annoyed and stubborn. He was dressed in a drab blazer and cowboy boots.

No one was sure what to do. It was all on him, that's the way he wanted it, and no one wanted to make it any more unpleasant than it already was. We slogged it out for the next couple of hours, with the results being far from anything close to acceptable. We even got into a brief argument about how long the breaks between Rob's vocals were on the verse of "Kick Out the Jams." Without Rob to set us straight, there was no resolution. I was making a point to Fred about it, since I was going to sing the song, when he shouted at me at the top of his voice, *"I don't care!"*

It startled me to be spoken to that way. No one had ever spoken to me like that, except my father when was angry. It froze the atmosphere in the room and shut down any communication between us. In the end, I felt very unsure about how the performance would be, but it was the MC5, after all, and anything was possible, even disaster.

After all these years, we were going to be on stage again, the culmination of two decades worth of dreaming about what might have been. The practice had been a confusing one, without any indication that we shared any common experience or purpose.

Rob's death had been a grim circumstance to bring us together, but reuniting with the Five minus Rob still offered an opportunity to mend fences. But who was that guy that walked into the studio three and a half hours late, got drunk for an hour before consenting to participate, and then refused to cooperate with anyone? It was one of the rudest exhibitions I've ever had the displeasure to witness, and a personal disappointment.

With Wayne, it was a different matter. We went out for dinner at a Chinese restaurant and talked about the difficulty at practice. Fred's attitude was an impenetrable wall that would have to be tolerated for at least one more day. Nevertheless, I ventured to Wayne the possibility of the four of us doing some gigs. All the signs were positive that something was favorable regarding the MC5. Why not cultivate the legacy?

Wayne's response was strangely opposed to any sort of continuation. "I don't think the tickets are there," he said matter-of-factly. "There's a small market, but on the whole, I don't think we would do very well at the box office."

"But how do we know? We haven't talked to anybody about doing anything." I was anxious to return to performing, and the signs all pointed to our shared history giving us an advantage for once.

"I just don't think the band would sell," he reiterated.

I dropped the subject, disappointed by Wayne's disinterest and lack of desire to recoup some of our losses. I had the feeling he was only concerned for his own benefit. He'd been bouncing around New York and had a band with ex–New York Doll Johnny Thunders that went down the tubes from drug addiction; escaped New York for the warm ocean breezes of Key West; and was currently living in Nashville while his wife went to school at Vanderbilt. It was clear he didn't believe in the MC5's legacy enough to pursue any business with it, and I suspect he didn't to deal with the personalities of any of its former members, either.

We drank and partied with our hosts, all the while getting the respect and consideration afforded guests of honor. Wayne and I, at least, had what resembled an enduring friendship despite the unpleasantness of the past. I looked forward to the next night, when we would reunite on the stage.

The benefit was at the State Theater in downtown Detroit, one block from the Fox Theater, where the Cult and Soundgarden would be performing. Both of these theaters were built back in the golden age of movie houses, very ornate and grand, large-capacity houses with balconies and carpeted staircases. Wayne and I walked down the block to the Fox to watch Soundgarden and part of the Cult's set before our gig up the street. Soundgarden had invited us and put us on their guest list. We were impressed with both bands, particularly Soundgarden, who reminded us of our own band's experimental energy.

Finally, it was time for the big show. I made the inelegant choice of wearing the evening's souvenir T-shirt and a pair of Levi's for my stage outfit, those being the days before I had a manager to tell me I was being maladroit. The dressing room was stocked with every form of alcoholic refreshment. A couple of beers would be a good way to prep for the approaching challenge. My former band mates from Destroy All Monsters, now going by the name Dark Carnival, were doing the warm-up chores. I saw them descending the staircase to the stage; no words were spoken, no eyes met.

When they finished their set, I figured we had 20 or 30 minutes before we should go out. Everyone busily tuned and flexed in anticipation of our entrance—all but Fred, who sat on a chair, smoking and drinking a bottle of wine. As the time approached, the promoter and stage manager poked his head in the door asking if we were almost ready.

I asked Fred if his wife Patti was there. He cleared his throat several times, as was his habit when asked a question, and finally blurted out, "No." Rob's widow, Becky, came into the dressing room to thank us all for doing this favor for her family. Another 20 minutes went by, and again the stage manager came in to ask us to take the stage. Fred sat immovable in the chair, defying the question. I was getting nervous. I could hear the crowd chanting in the distance: "MC5! MC5! MC5!"

Twenty minutes more went by. The promoter came in to

plead, "Guys, we're losing them. They're getting hostile."

Fred motioned with a slight rising of his hand. "We'll be out in a minute," he said after clearing his throat. But he didn't move from the chair. His guitar was still in its case.

I was beginning to feel desperate. There was nothing anyone could do to persuade Fred to move. Dennis went out to fiddle with his drums. The crowd cheered, at last seeing a member of the MC5 on stage for the first time in 20 years. Quiet returned to the hall, and soon shouts of "Kick out the jams, motherfucker!" could be heard from different corners of the hall.

Dennis returned to the dressing room. "What the fuck is going on? What are we waiting for? Fred, do you not want to play tonight? What the fuck!" Fred glanced up at Dennis like he was a total stranger asking a question in a foreign language. I, too, was frantic with this impasse.

The stage manager ducked in one last time. "It's now or never, everyone is leaving. You can play if you want to, but they're going home. I can't keep them any longer."

"I'm going," I said to no one in particular. I walked out onto the big stage all alone, and as I did, the audience gave out another cheer, but returned to murmuring when no one else emerged after me. I plugged in my bass, gave it a few little bonks to see what it sounded like, and stood facing my amplifier, a victim of my own initiative. Dennis returned to his kit. Maybe it was going to happen, but by now the thrill of the evening, the Moment, the 20-year reunion, the anticipated return of the prodigal band, had slipped over the edge into infinity, falling forever from our grasp.

Finally, Wayne and Fred emerged onto the stage. The remaining crowd pushed to the front. A lot of shouting ensued. Wayne started the intro to "Ramblin' Rose." It felt awkward and geeky. I played my part, waiting intently for the groove to kick in. Dennis was smacking his snare and grimacing. The moment seemed unreal, larger than life; I felt naked and self-conscious. Front row faces gave impassioned smiles and nodded their heads.

I had been selected to sing "Kick Out the Jams," but Wayne launched into an extended version of the spoken introduction, which threw off the timing for the opening declaration. Wayne has some definite ideas about how music should be played, almost none of which I agree with. However, under these circumstances, there was no point to arguing about arrangements, and eventually, the song started as planned. At that point, I started to loosen up. The show was beginning to feel energized.

It was then that everything started going downhill.

At the end of "Jams," Wayne strode to his microphone to begin a carefully planned monologue concerning the formation of the MC5 and his first meetings with its members. He described his encounters with each band member in picturesque vignettes.

Upon finishing the litany with Becky, Rob's widow, whom he referred to as "that person there, in the side wings," he went on to declare that his purpose for being there that night was to "reclaim his brothers."

By this time, the audience was looking around, wondering how long they'd have to listen to Wayne talk before the band would play. I suppose someone needed to address the importance of our being there, but somehow Wayne had managed to subvert the focus of the event to himself and his personal attainment.

Fred started the music to "Black to Comm." Dennis snapped into the drum intro, which seemed to drag a bit in comparison with any previous version of the song we'd played. The drone of guitar and drums went on for a couple of minutes. As the music descended to a quiet murmur, Fred stepped to his microphone, withdrawing a folded paper from his blazer pocket. He unfolded it, and studied it for a moment as the audience waited in silence. Lifting his hand and waving two fingers at the audience, he spoke. "Hey there, hello. I'm Fred 'Sonic' Smith, no relation to Sonic the Hedgehog."

The audience snickered a bit. After a painfully long interlude, he began his "speech." He read the note he had written to himself. It went on for a good five minutes. I glanced at Dennis. He wasn't amused, and neither was I. After Fred finished, he backed away from the microphone and resumed the riff to "Black to Comm." The musical denouement lasted another 10 minutes, and the song that had started with a bang ended with a whimper. The crowd cheered. Down in the basement of the theater after the performance, a gaggle of photographers posed us in varying groups for pictures. And that was it.

I walked alone to my mother's car that I had borrowed for the evening. With bass guitar in hand, I listened to my footsteps clicking on the concrete sidewalk. Suddenly without any remaining purpose, I asked myself, "Now what?"

I headed west on Michigan Avenue toward my mom's place. Wait, I said to myself, Niagara lives out this way, somewhere farther west of the city. I had my old telephone book in my coat.

In the waning days of Destroy All Monsters, a Bluto-ish looking fellow who was supplying Ron and Niagara with nose candy started showing up at all of our gigs, providing transportation as well as drugs. After a time, Niagara abandoned the Asheton residence to shack up with the drug dealer, eventually marrying him. He had a house in the western suburbs of Detroit that I had been to on a couple of occasions, and I knew they'd all be there.

I stopped at a pay phone and called the phone number I had in my book. My hunch was right. "Niagara, it's Mike Davis, what's happening?"

"Mike Davis!" she screeched. "I adore you! Come over here right now!" She gave me the directions to their house. I was on my way; to what, I didn't know.

It was just the three of them sitting at the table, the mirror with a pile of white powder resting on its surface. Ron was there, the three of them comfortable with the situation as it was. To me, it was plain that jealousy didn't factor into it, making it quite easy for them to maintain a lasting friendship.

Being there was strange. For a moment, it felt like going to the Tyners' house without an invitation, but since Niagara had encouraged me to come by, there I was, face to face with my old nemesis. I started off as tactfully as I could.

"First of all, I want to say that if ever in the past I offended or hurt or in any way abused our friendship, please accept my apology for being a drunken asshole. I am truly sorry for any wrongs I may have committed."

Ron sat opposite me at the table, nodding his head and looking at me rather slyly. I couldn't tell from his expression whether he was accepting my apology or brushing it off as a ploy to gain his favor. He didn't respond to my statement at all. Instead, he launched into a critique of the evening's performance by the MC5 minus Rob.

"You guys nearly blew it—Wayne with that sermon, Fred mumbling about death, the short set. Really, man, you saved it. If it weren't for your singing on 'Jams,' the whole thing would have bombed. You pulled it out of the fire. You saved the night."

While I agreed with him that the performance had been a stinker, I wasn't certain that I had saved it. Still, it felt good to hear him say it. It was my hope that we'd patched up our differences, healed a wound or two, and could be better friends, but I got nothing else from Ron.

The very last thing Wayne, Dennis, and I said to each other before we parted company was we'd see each other next at Fred's funeral, which wound up being what happened. Fred looked bad, there was no question, like a man being consumed by a fatal illness. Whatever it was, it was serious, that much was obvious. Unfortunately, he distanced himself in a way that discouraged anyone from asking what was going on. My suspicion was that he had a severe liver dysfunction, but I couldn't say for sure.

Back in Tucson, a world away from the dirty snow and cold of Detroit, I was not a rock star. Far from it, I was a delivery schmuck for a bunch of telephone con artists. The pressure of Detroit, with its "closed shop" music culture and its Habitrail of clubs gave me the creeps. No wonder Asheton stayed at his mother's house and never went anywhere. To me, Ron seemed like a lonely guy, wanting an easy life while playing at being a celebrity. I feel the same way. The rock and roll world is always watching and never minding. Even when no one is watching, you feel compelled to play the role.

Our house was on a busy street by a traffic light, across from Tucson High School. It was noisy and too exposed. We started looking for another rental and after a while, we found a better house, farther from downtown. After sunset, I used to be able to go out the front door and see the temperature on one of the tall downtown buildings: 102 degrees at 10 pm; ghastly!

The new house was in the '50s style adobe with add-ons, a tad more modern than the former '20s style wood and stucco, with the heat coming through a metal grate on the living room hardwood floor. It had a Mexican tile floor and a washing machine in the kitchen. Frankly, it was abominable, but felt it better than the older house. The two kids had to share a room once again. They were constantly squabbling. I still drank.

It seemed we had moved up a notch. I spotted another cool car on my delivery route. This one was a 1961 Chevy Impala "bubble top." Those cars have a wrap around rear window that gives the car a space-age/*Jetsons* appearance.

Built just before the advent of fins, these cars are hot collector's items, and this one was sitting on blocks in a carport, covered in dust. I knocked on the door, found out the owner's price, and set about raising the money to buy it. I had to do it in installments, but I did it, and there I was, driving home in the sun-baked old Chevy. Now, I had three killer cars in the yard with no rust. I might be a lot richer today if I'd not gotten rid of them.

The next item of material gain was a boat. Arizona has a few unbelievable lakes set in the Superstition Mountains, all of them created by the Roosevelt Dam at the top, a 25-mile long body of water. Downstream, alongside the Apache Trail that runs alongside the Salt River, is Apache Lake, a 14-mile long body of water, followed by Canyon Lake, the favorite of Phoenix boaters. I drew an advance on my publishing and got us a nice little runabout to get us out of the summer heat.

I was in touch with Wayne Kramer, having exchanged phone numbers with him at the Detroit gathering. It had occurred to me after these many years that I had never received a royalty statement from any records we made as the MC5. I was getting royalties through a company I hired to monitor my publishing, but I'd never been paid for record sales.

I asked Wayne what he had received, and he told me he was getting a small check every now and then. I pressed him for information, but he could only tell me he had gone up to Elektra after he got out of jail and tried to claim his royalties.

He was told facetiously that someone claiming to be Roger Daltrey had come up there the previous week. So, he was going to have to bring a file of documentation proving he was who he said he was. However, he did tell me that there was probably a big check waiting up there for me. After hearing that, it was an idea I couldn't let go.

Things moved swiftly the following year. We had a boat, cars, dogs, kids, and now we were paying more in rent than we would have if we'd owned a place. We started looking into owning a house. Neither one of us had ever had a speck of credit. I wasn't working a real job and she was self-employed. Nevertheless, she said she wanted to live out in the country, have horses and do the whole Arizona thing. The idea was intriguing.

We drove around with an agent. He had three properties to show us. The first one we saw was a five-acre piece of land with a big Fleetwood doublewide mobile and a greenhouse out back. The owner had moved back to Germany and the sale price was attractive. The next one was so far away that we turned back, and the third one was next to a landfill; awful.

We sat down and wrote up an offer. Was this all there was to it? My beer-soaked brain was trying to navigate its way through the process: if this happens, if that goes that way, if I can do this…maybe this can happen. The seller agreed to our terms, I raised a $6,000 down payment, and all we had to do was get approval for a loan of no more than $60,000 to own the spread. We sold the two Impalas, I bought a pickup truck, and that was how we wound up in the desert with our very own five acres of Saguaros, Mesquite, sand, caliche, and rattlesnakes. It was 1994.

Unfortunately, removing the children from the city had an adverse effect, particularly on Ursula. She was becoming a teenager, and the lack of social interaction made her feel like a lost soul. The young boy couldn't have cared less, but for her, it was like being marooned on another planet. Tensions were also rising between her and the woman, who was not her mother.

The '56 Chevy was sold to save it from being destroyed going up and down the rough gravel road that led to our property. We bought two horses, saddles, tack, and assumed the life of desert dwellers. Things were all right for a short time, until I had the misfortune of being bit on the toe by a baby rattlesnake.

The woman was getting tired of being the only breadwinner in the house, having to drive back and forth over the mountain every day, and coming home to a beer drinking layabout.

After getting snakebit, I started feeling quite guilty about it myself. I had survived, but my being in the hospital for a week worsened the tension at home. I had quit my job with the veterans, because the cost of driving back and forth to town exceeded what I could earn making their deliveries. I thought if I could find a job on our side of the mountains, our situation would improve.

I drove out to Old Tucson, a movie set located in the desert, where movie and TV westerns had been filmed since the '50s. I thought if I could get a job doing anything there, it would be agreeable. On a whim, I stopped at the Arizona Sonora Desert Museum, a place I had visited before that featured desert gardens and animals in their natural habitat. It's a world famous Tucson institution and a year-round attraction for thousands of visitors. I filled out an application and went home. A couple of days later, I got a call to report to work, if I was still interested.

I was hired as a temporary in the botany department for a whopping $8.00 an hour. Our crew was responsible for clearing a trail in the desert that would eventually be a hiking trail for visitors to the museum. All rock, plants, and any interesting natural features were to be removed with the utmost care. It was a salvage operation.

In the five years I spent working at the Desert Museum, I met many great and learned people, made friends with whom I am still in contact with today, learned how to work beyond my previous limits, received a tremendous education concerning desert plants, and obtained skills that I never would have considered important. Hell, things are still alive at the museum that I planted, things that will live for hundreds of years, just like the MC5.

I started working and things settled down for a while. We had our horses to take out on the trails, such as they were. Some trails were dusty roads that meandered endlessly. There were small herds of cattle under the shade of the mesquite trees. Once an enormous bull appeared out of the thicket and scared the shit out of me. I kicked my horse to get us out of there before he came at us. Jackrabbits hopped across the flats ahead of us, hawks soared overhead, and vultures constantly circled. It was the kind of thing my dad would have loved to do.

Ursula started middle school, but it didn't last long. At first, she got into trouble by getting caught with a box cutter in her bag. I had no idea what she needed a box cutter for. Then it was something else, and then it was truancy.

She had befriended a certain girl who lived with her grandfather and had no parents anywhere nearby. It was a powder keg. What she really wanted was to get out of the house, out of the desert, and out of Arizona.

When she told us that Joanne, her mother, was agreeable to her coming to Michigan to live with her and her new husband and attend school in Ann Arbor, it was a relief to think the emotional battles within our house would cease. Without a great deal of thought, I foolishly told her she could go. It was too easy, satisfying Ursula's wish and quieting the conflicts we were having at home. I should have suspected it would lead to trouble later on. But the real trouble began after Ursula left us. With the disturbing element out of the picture, attention could focus on a deeper, more perplexing problem: my drinking.

The next two years would take their toll on my relationship with the woman from Ann Arbor. I was bringing home $500 every other week, but hoarding it to keep my beer supply flowing and buy whatever struck my fancy for my truck or the boat. She sometimes made as much as $300 in a day of hair appointments. She had also put me together with a client of hers who had a blues band. They wanted me to be their bass player and I thought it would fun to get back into playing.

I had sold my SVT to a punk rocker the previous year, and that rig wouldn't have been appropriate for a blues group anyway. The next best thing was an Ampeg Port-o-flex like James Jamerson used in the Motown studios, which I found at the local music store in downtown Tucson for $250. Nowadays, they go for $1000-1500, if you're lucky enough to find one. For one year, I was a blues bass player. Finally, when it became irritating to drive over the mountain every weekend to play three sets of the same music, I gave my notice.

In 1996, my friend Bill Frank, one of the many drummers that played in Destroy All Monsters, called me with a proposal. He had a band, a small European tour lined up, and an L.A. gig. He wondered if I might be interested in coming to L.A. to learn a few MC5 and DAM songs with his band, go to Europe to tour with them as lead singer, and play the one off L.A. gig. I would be paid a flat fee, along with all my expenses. It was a simple task. After playing their set, they would bring me on as a special guest. It would sell tickets and be fun, and I could make some money. I agreed.

I asked my boss at the Desert Museum for time off to go to Europe, and what with my being a temporary, it was not too much of a problem. The tour was short, but covered a lot of territory. We drove across the entire landmass of Europe to do five gigs. While it was very tedious, it gave me an idea of the true extent of the MC5's legendary status. Often the audiences were ambivalent, while the promoters were flushed with honor.

Shortly after I returned home, I took a phone call from Jeff Economy, who said he was a producer working with a small group of people from Chicago who intended to make a documentary film about the MC5. He said they were working on the production arrangements, and he would be back in touch with me.

He wondered how I felt about being the subject of a documentary film, and I must admit, it thrilled me to think anyone cared that much about the old band. I was also skeptical. Disappointment was something that haunted everything surrounding the MC5; that hadn't changed. My woman was hardly impressed. In fact, I got the feeling she felt the whole matter didn't concern her.

Meanwhile, another client of hers was asking her if she thought I would be interested in recording a couple of songs with him for a German deal he had going. His name was Rich Hopkins. He had been in a band from Tucson that made a few records and been with a major label a few years earlier. That band was called the Sidewinders. They were forced to change their name to the Sand Rubies as the result of a lawsuit, and ultimately the band dissolved after a series of personality clashes. We met at a local pub and were immediately comfortable talking business and other things.

Rich liked his beer and in me, he found the perfect beer-drinking buddy. With my small measure of fame and credibility, his deals and resources, and an affinity for the same style of rock music, we would have a solid partnership and friendship as well. His band, Rich Hopkins and the Luminarios, was basically a solo project with a revolving cast of characters.

The style of music we shared was a cross between pop and garage, psychedelic '60s and energy driven rock and roll. All of my early musical influences figured in Rich's musical world: the Byrds, 13th Floor Elevators, Troggs, Kinks, Animals, and an endless array of past groups both famous and unsung. It was a broad spectrum to draw from and a departure from blues-and-R&B-based rock—very white and jangly. It was a relief.

The project involved writing and recording two songs for Phillip Morris of Germany. The songs would be re-mixed by a group of contest winners from Germany, and the project would culminate in a big party in Taos, New Mexico, where a number of different bands from Tucson, also contracted for the project, would perform. The project paid pretty well, and I said I would love to participate.

Everything got off on the right foot. We made a very good recording, I felt strongly about my contribution, and I had a new friend. Rich then asked if I would be interested in playing permanently in his band and going on tour for a month in Germany. I was definitely interested. I suspected I could take the time off from the museum, it being a novelty to have a member of the botany department playing in a rock and roll band and touring Europe. I was very excited to be in a band again, on a label, going on tour, and playing live rock and roll. I could get back to the business of being Michael Davis.

I didn't notice the shadow falling over the big picture: all of this was creating a wider division in my home situation. I had it in my head that since this woman had tracked me down cross-country, hung with me through my infatuation with a female indecently younger than me, and endured my insufferability, it meant that I was immune to rejection.

The fact she had shown resistance to being intimate with me only increased my demands. Frequent arguing with the same recurring compromises was becoming redundant. My presumptuous indifference while guzzling beer endlessly had pushed our relationship to the edge.

When I came home from the Luminarios' six week tour of Germany. I was glad to be back and exhausted from drinking heavily for over a month. Then she announced that my friend Kenny Brown had died as if she were talking about a change in the weather. I gasped, tears filled my eyes, and for one tender moment, she came over to comfort me with a brief hug. Kenny had been something of a father figure for me and the news of his death affected me deeply.

I had a piece of mail from the accounting firm that paid my

royalties. I had forgotten that they were due. It was a big check for several thousand dollars. I suppose it was from all the sales since the MC5 catalog went to CD format. I was thrilled, but once again, she showed conspicuous indifference. I was aware that we were falling apart, but my arrogance prevented me from being more considerate. I didn't realize that it was time to pay for my conceit.

It happened a few days later, at dusk on a warm spring evening. She had brought home Mexican food in Styrofoam boxes. I don't even remember what started it. She made a comment that aroused my bad temper. I retorted, she retorted, and then I kicked over the tray with the food on it. In a moment we were standing toe to toe, shouting. She insulted me, and then it happened: I hit her, knocking her to the floor. She stood back up and tried to strike back, but I held her arms. It was the end.

Hearing the ruckus, the boy ran into the room to see us standing there, his mother holding her shoulder where it had struck the side of the couch.

"See the great man, he just hit me!" she exclaimed hysterically.

My next thought: I needed more beer. The boy was terrified, confused, dumbfounded. I drove his young friend home and stopped at the Mini-Mart for another six-pack of Corona. Back at the house, sat down outside and opened a fresh beer. Eventually she came and sat down.

"I don't want to live with you anymore," she said calmly and tearfully. "I know I chased you down and all, but I'm not in love with you anymore. I'm sorry."

I could have taken it for truth, which it was, and been civil about it, but instead I tried playing emotional games with her. I got very angry, as if that would revive her feeling for me after all I'd done, both on this night and over the past six or seven years. But at last, I said "OK, let's break up," and we went back in the house to sleep as we had been for some time, separately.

After that, it took her five months to move out. I was at work when she left. Her friend down the road pulled his trailer up to the house in the morning, and when I returned from work in the afternoon, the house was empty, except for a few pieces of furniture she didn't want and my horse standing in his pen out back.

The emptiest feeling I had ever felt filled my worn-out being. I strolled through the quiet stillness of the house, trying to find any semblance of farewell. Not a thing was there. Every trace of the woman and the boy was gone. All that was left was the dirt and scraps of paper, a pen, an old greeting card, a photograph: derelict trash. I was alone with my dog, a horse, a rooster and a hen.

17

The Road With No Name

At least four men with the name Mike lived on the road with no name.

There was a curious single character at the far end of the road, who'd built a ramshackle recording studio out of corrugated sheet metal and plywood. He knew about the MC5 and tried to get me to come down to his parties on occasion, but I was never in the mood to leave my refrigerator and walk or drive the quarter mile to his place. I think he was into electronic new wave pop weirdness, but I'm not sure, as I never visited him.

A bit closer to me was another Mike, who had been on this nameless dirt pathway for 15 years. He told me how the DEA would sit on top of the hill behind his house with a telescope watching him for months, thinking he was a drug smuggler.

They were also watching biker Mike and his wife Lydia, because they continually hosted parties, with hordes of bikers converging on their place. The couple had discovered Christ and given over their lives and one third of all their income to the Baptist church. Perhaps they had been drug dealers and got scared into their conversion after some close calls.

I was the weird one on the road these days; an ex-rock and roll star, a loner, an apparent derelict who had abandoned or been abandoned by the normal life. Most people on the road without a name knew me a little bit, but I could never get too close without giving up my solitude. My horse and my dog and my beer were all I really needed. I had to maintain my hallowed space there on what could have been called the "Rue de Michel" or "Michael Mews," a lane of beaten down dirt and gravel, unnamed, a mere notch of a line on the map.

It was September of 1997—a very dark year in my history. Finding myself alone in the desert was a shock, but I took it in stride and consoled myself with alcohol and self-entertainment. Over the years, whenever I entered into partnerships in business or love, I inevitably became annoyed with my partners and sought to free myself of them. I liked being me, and whatever happened, either by my doing or by outside agency, I would continue to feed the juggernaut inside me. Now I had narrowed my path until everyone else was eliminated, leaving me free to wreak havoc unchecked.

When had this started? At home, where my father's isolated disposition had left me feeling out of touch? With my mother's timidity and reserve, not wanting to arouse my father's ill temper? Or maybe with my sister's late arrival, displacing me as the only child at age 11? My parents' lack of communication birthed a feeling of detachment in me, and my subsequent exploits had left me feeling strangely isolated.

By the time my most recent family disintegrated, I had not only accepted it as my fate, but come to cherish it. When I lost it, my world was destroyed once again. It felt insurmountable at first, but as time passed, I got busy trying to right the ship.

One day during my Robinson Crusoe existence in the empty house, my dog Rooster that I'd adopted from the animal shelter left the property and did not return as soon as he usually did. I didn't worry at first because he roamed as he pleased. He was extremely fit, intelligent, and loyal.

By the third day with no sign of him, though, I started to panic. I drove around the dirt roads and remote places along the main road, shouting his name in all directions, waiting for his little brown form to appear, galloping up the dirt driveway. But nothing moved in the creosote-filled landscape. Coyotes yelped in the distance, and as darkness descended and twilight gave way to stillness, I felt even more lost. My buddy was gone and probably eaten by wild beasts. My spirit sank.

One afternoon about a week later, my telephone rang. It was my friend Amy, who lived down the main road by herself with a couple of horses and seven dogs.

"Hey Mike, is Rooster missing? I was just wondering because I thought I saw him out back where the flats are, by the big dry wash. If it was him, he's running with a pack of wild dogs out there, and I wanted to check with you if he was home or not."

My heart jumped into my mouth. "YES! He's been gone for days. It's got to be him. Amy, oh thank you, I'm getting in the truck and coming down there right now!"

I drove like a maniac, up the side of the barren flats where the unscrupulous dump their dead refrigerators and old couches, and sometimes take target practice at the trash hulks. Amy met me in her truck, and we looked out over the area.

"There are some dogs over there," she said. I looked at the group of three or four dogs, gave a loud whistle, and called for him. Their ears perked up at the sound, then one broke away from the pack and ran toward me at full steam. It was him, my little buddy, my lost Rooster coming home as fast as he could run. He jumped up on my chest and cavorted in a dance of glee. He must have lost his way in the desert brush, and luckily Amy had spotted him when she rode her horse out back on the desolate property by the Indian reservation. I knew he hadn't run away purposely. Something in me was restored.

I wrote a song about the episode, changing Rooster's name to Raeanna and composing a couple of verses that compared losing my dog to losing my girl. Rich Hopkins and the Luminarios recorded my song, and it was released on *The Glorious Sounds of Rich Hopkins and The Luminarios* by the German label Blue Rose in 1998.

Last year, I used to do a cakewalk
Standing out on the porch making small talk
Now my life is wind and thunder
Gonna hold my breath cause I think I'm going under
All alone, alone

Raeanna come, Raeanna come, Raeanna come,
Raeanna come home

Got along on a road to the highway
Got to head her off before she gets too far away
In my life it's wind and thunder
Gonna hold my breath cause I know I'm going under
All alone, alone

Raeanna come, Raeanna come, Raeanna come,
Raeanna come home

I waited up all night and searched all day
For the peace of mind Raeanna took away
I scanned the sky and I roamed the ground
But I know in my heart Raeanna won't be found.

When I was a kid, I used to do the backstroke
I skated in the basement and I hung around with my folks
Now my life is wind and thunder
Gonna be my death cause I think I'm going under
All alone, alone

Raeanna come, Raeanna come, Raeanna come,
Raeanna come home

After ridding myself of the five-acre property and relocating to a small one-acre lot with a singlewide mobile a few miles closer to town, I resumed my existence as a lone wolf with a horse, a dog, a cat, a rooster, and a hen. My little place was snuggled at the foot of a mountain called Golden Gate. The property had several tall saguaros, a couple of small acacias, and a large mesquite. Everything I owned fit nicely and it was cheap, although I barely managed the finances. Then, with two days to spare, I left for Germany and another tour with Rich and the Luminarios.

In all the years of the MC5 and Destroy All Monsters, touring had been a relatively leisurely affair. We rarely played more than a few dates strung together, and leaving the country was more about down time than actual gigging.

It wasn't until the '80s that lower tier bands went out on the road, with everyone packed into a single vehicle and sleeping on the floors of other bands' houses for lack of money. Only headlining acts with label support and management were able to pull off lengthy tours.

Our timetable in the Luminarios was 23 dates in 27 days. The rolling hangover from non-stop drinking over that much time is enough to floor anyone, physically and emotionally. Although not unlike my normal beer consumption at home, the schedule of constant travel without a break sapped all my energy after a couple of weeks. Somewhere in that third week is where I would hit the wall. Then I would take a single day off from drinking to regain my strength for the final week of the tour.

Upon landing back in Tucson, Rich and I would exchange bleary-eyed glances before I watched him straggle off down the airport corridor with his wife. In the warm darkness of the Arizona night, I shuffled to my truck in the parking lot, hoping it would start and carry me back to my acre of desert. It was like waking from a dream: back to my regular life and routine at the museum; back to shovels and digging bars, plants and irrigation, while remaining a curiosity to my workmates; back to my animals, my TV, and my Coronas in the refrigerator.

I was hurting all right, and it was my own fault. I missed my family life. I would drive past the road where she lived, wondering if I'd catch a glimpse of her, imagining she would come visit to see how I was doing, but nothing ever happened. They never answered their phone, and leaving messages produced no return calls.

I sent things in the mail that came back unclaimed. There was nothing I could do. They had scratched me from their lives, and made it clear that trying to get in touch was a waste of time. I was going to have to put it in my pocket and own it, swallow it, bury it, try to forget it.

I wanted more than anything to replace her and restore my situation. Being alone was hard to get used to. Waking in the morning silence, fumbling with the coffee maker, hearing only the sounds I made myself, waiting for someone other than me to create an atmosphere, the struggle of being alone was ongoing. But I still took inspiration from the usual sources: music and nature.

I liked to take Sonny Boy out across the road, past the meager neighborhoods of mobile homes on single acre lots, where a vast open area of more or less undeveloped land, striped with trails, provided good riding. The process of picking his hooves, brushing him down, saddling him and mounting up was fun and helped me put some pieces back together.

He was a pretty horse, Arabian blooded, but very even tempered. He liked to be tended to, and boy, did he like to eat! He had a bad habit of biting off branches and leaves from plants along the trail as he coursed by. Stubborn and wayward, it was a challenge to keep him paying attention to what I wanted to do. We'd go out on Sundays when all was quiet on the roads. Buzzards soaring overhead, hawks, doves, jackrabbits—sometimes I was astonished that I was out riding a horse on a desert trail all by myself.

Rooster always wanted to go everywhere, but having him along, loping ahead, not knowing what he might take off chasing after, was too worrisome a proposition. I had to shut him up in the house until we got back, usually a couple of hours later.

Thirty years had passed since *Kick Out the Jams*. Punk rock had come and gone. Hardcore and thrash were beyond the horizon. Speed metal and every other form of groundbreaking pop music seemed laid to rest. There wasn't anything to get excited about, but at least I was in a band.

The Luminarios had two destinations besides Germany: Phoenix and El Paso. Rich Hopkins was a trust fund kid who ran a local record label and fancied himself a sort of music philanthropist. He had been in an aspiring Tucson band at the end of the '80s that got signed to a major label, suffered some unlucky breaks and bad management decisions, and ultimately split up at the apex of their ascent, not unlike the MC5.

He was a talented songwriter and a fairly good singer, but an over-indulger in alcohol. He wanted compliant people around him, and if it wasn't his way, it was no way. But he had charm and wit, and he didn't particularly care if he was successful in the music business, opting instead for the typical "indie" band's self-sufficiency and informality, with a revolving cast and small-but-devoted fan base. We got along extremely well and shared a great many similar musical tastes, as well as an affinity for beer drinking.

Trips to El Paso amounted to three-day out-of-town vacations, all the while consuming vast quantities of beer and Mexican food. Hopkins generally paid for the food in lieu of any payment to the band members after he recouped his expenses for gas and hotel rooms.

There were probably ten dedicated fans that came to those El Paso shows, the rest of the crowd consisting of bar regulars. The club owner liked Rich and his booking us amounted to a fan's charitable gesture. We went on the El Paso excursions every six weeks or so. Rich even talked of moving there, an absurd idea, considering he had a home and a wife and child in Tucson. But Rich imagined himself living a freewheeling young stud lifestyle, and when you are wealthy, the possibilities are greater.

Occasionally we traveled to Mexico, playing in the resort town of Puerto Penasco on the northernmost coast of the Sea of Cortez. Rich's drug dealer brother-in-law had high-level connections with the local drug cartel politico there, and whether we played a taco stand on a dirt street or a restaurant down on the beach, we were paid very well for showing up. On one excursion, we were lodged at a compound in the middle of town with armed guards and steel gates. I worried all night that we were going to be attacked by assassins from a rival gang, seeking retribution for some offense our host had committed.

I remember seeing Rich standing across the street, looking out at the setting sun over the sea, high on acid, a Corona in his hand, as I set up my amplifier on the floor of an outdoor seafood restaurant. I couldn't delude myself that this was somehow connected to anything in the real world.

We actually undertook a brief Midwest tour, which I suppose was motivated by a whim of Rich's. Having absolutely no record distribution in any part of the U.S., there would be no chance of anyone knowing who we were. But maybe Rich thought my presence was enough to create a draw. That would only be possible in Detroit.

Our drummer was in Minneapolis, so that was where we started off. After flying there and playing one decent show, we drove to Chicago for a sparsely attended club date, followed by a drive to Lansing, Michigan, for another sparsely attended but rowdy evening, and another drive down to Detroit.

Rich booked our rooms at a big downtown hotel, where it was reported that Neil Young was staying while playing at Joe Louis Arena. We never ran into Neil, but I did manage to take Rich to the famous Lafayette Coney Island downtown for a taste of old time Detroit, which he appreciated.

We were booked to play a small bar called the Gold Dollar close to downtown, and we drove up and down Cass Avenue for an hour before we realized that the storefront was covered with a corrugated steel door to keep out thieves when the bar was closed. Detroit at this point was like something out of the movie *Escape From New York*. Except for the posh downtown hotel, a post-Armageddon mood informed a cold and deserted old city.

Finally at 8 pm, someone arrived to open up and the Gold Dollar began to fill up with a leather-jacketed crowd, many of my old friends and acquaintances, and the curious band people who had learned of the MC5's legend second or third-hand. My daughter Michele, and two of my exes were there, as well as a contingent from Ann Arbor.

The Luminarios had been playing "Kick Out the Jams" for some time. We played it on our German tours to ecstatic receptions, with me doing the lead vocals. But here and now, at the beginning of Rich Hopkins and the Luminarios' set in my hometown, our musical pace completely befuddled the high energy Detroiters. Two verses into the first song, the eager crowd that had gathered at the edge of the stage started looking at each other with dumbfounded expressions. The anticipation that had built now dissipated like air being let out of a balloon. Soon, they began to wander off back to the bar or their tables.

My pals were smiling, but I knew they were all asking themselves the same question: What the fuck kind of lame shit was this? For the prodigal son, returning as a poster boy for a middle-aged singer-songwriter's alt-country band was quite an embarrassment. For well over an hour, we played Hopkins' mid-tempo four-chord schmaltz, until anti-climactically, I got to scream, "Kick out the jams, motherfucker!" At once everyone took to the dance floor gyrating.

"It was cool, Michael," they would say, sparing me any confrontation or critique, but they were just being kind.

Before leaving town, I steered us to the old Motown house, Hitsville U.S.A. on West Grand Boulevard, now a museum. We decided to pay the five-buck admission and go on the tour. We stood in the tiny Studio A, where countless hits had been hammered out by the great Motown session men and the talented singers and songwriters that made the place a glorious monument.

In the gift shop, we bought souvenir T-shirts for our friends and ourselves. On the counter was a *Detroit Almanac*. Rich and I were standing there waiting to be rung up when I opened the book to a random page. Plastered across the page was my picture with the other members of the MC5 over a picture of the city of Detroit. I was flabbergasted; the other guys were gaping in awe. A proud moment, and an ironic twist to a strange couple of days, but we weren't out of town yet.

Driving down Third Avenue headed south toward downtown, I kept my eyes peeled for a crumbling storefront location I remembered.

"Right there! Stop the car!" I blurted. "You see that burnt out storefront, the one with the sign painted on the facing of the building that says Straight 8?"

They nodded, and I told them the story of Fortune Records, where great '50s and '60s R&B artists like Nathaniel Mayer, Nolan Strong, the Diablos, Andre Williams, and John Lee Hooker cut classics like "Mind Over Matter," "The Village Of Love," and so many others. It had been a recording studio in the inner city since the 1940s, serving up hillbilly music as well as blues and early rock and roll, just the kind of thing to make any deviant music historian drool. Now it was burnt and in shambles.

We got out of the van and stood in front of the gaping ruin. An old bum came shuffling up the street. Rich called out to him. "Hey man, how about taking a picture?"

The bum startled and groggily took a couple steps sideways, saying "Uh uh, no pictures."

"No man, not of you, you take one of us." We all laughed. The bum laughed, smiled a toothless grin, and shot our picture. Rich gave him a fiver, and we got back in the van and left Detroit. For all its degradation, I was still immensely proud of my old hometown. It is a city with real soul. There's no place like Detroit.

Our next stop was just across the Ohio River from Cincinnati in Covington, Kentucky. The venue was a huge Victorian mansion called Southgate House, refurbished into a multi-performance-room-cum-showcase bar. On this particular Sunday night, we were headlining in the main room.

No one came. The only patrons to pay admission were a band called Big In Iowa that also happened to be on our German record label. They drove, not from Iowa, but from their nearby Kentucky home to show support. Three band members and one girlfriend constituted our entire audience in a very large room. It might have been my most ridiculous performing experience ever, rivaling the time we played in the rain at the Munich Olympic Stadium to a scant 20 or 30 people.

In the morning, we struggled to right ourselves after the previous night's *Twilight Zone* experience and settled into our van seats for a very long drive to Kansas City, with an overnight stop in Logansport, Indiana, to visit our rhythm guitar player's grandparents. From the sublime to the ridiculous to the mundane, this tour was taking on a surrealistic nightmare quality.

Kansas City wasn't all that bad. The club was good and surprisingly crowded, and the people liked us. The only problem was that we couldn't find a hotel with a vacancy. Finally, we found a little run-down inner city fleabag joint that had a large single room with three beds and a rollout cot. We took it. No one wanted to get back on the interstate at three in the morning.

The next drive was back to Minnesota and the snowbound north—a very long haul. And the next gig topped all the others for absurdity. It was a huge room, a showcase club with fancy dressing rooms and a big stage. It was packed. From the front row of tables to the doors in the rear of the room, absolutely packed. We were opening for a cover band that did all Neil Diamond material. (I had no idea that there were people who were totally infatuated with Mr. "Kentucky Woman.")

Our first number was met by stony silence from the big crowd. After several songs received a similarly catatonic response, we were disturbed enough to want to leave the stage. I thought the people were being condescendingly rude. But when I did "Kick Out the Jams" at the end of the set, two guys in the middle of the room shouted "Right on!" They were apparently the only two people in the place who had experienced anything other than MOR radio. It was appalling.

The Neil Diamond band took the stage and started their set, met by an avalanche of cheers. On our way out, a couple of people said "Nice set" as I passed through the mass of drinking boobs and jocks. What world had I landed in?

We trekked over to the little rock and roll bar we had played on the first night of the tour. They were having a "Styx and Stones" cover night. All these local band people were getting up on the stage and performing either a Styx or Rolling Stones cover. It was very entertaining and helped relieve the Neil Diamond invasion of my soul. Upon returning to Tucson, I began thinking seriously of leaving Rich Hopkins and the Luminarios.

Back in the desert heat of Tucson, the thought of going out to play gigs seemed more and more futile. A wedding, a New Year's Eve party, the floor of a bar in front of a window facing the street, support act for touring bands at the Club Congress, no-pay gigs, travel gigs to ill-fitted situations, all seemed farcical to me. I was restless again, anxious to change everything.

Outwardly I was calm, but inside, I loathed my entire existence, still searching for a woman, a band, a home, a new vehicle, anything to rekindle the fervor that I had known when I was a young and bewildered artist. My vision of that persona was fading to a tiny speck, barely perceptible on the horizon. Subdued and apathetic, I plodded through each day without passion until, after drinking several beers, I blurred my senses into even more apathy.

I remember driving back to my trailer on the desert acre, alone in my truck on Christmas Eve. Christmas lights blinking on people's homes, "Feliz Navidad" on the radio. There would be no one and nothing special about this night for me. It was just another evening in the desert of Arizona, sun disappearing, time passing, coyotes yapping, quiet and still. The choices that brought me there had been my own. I neither regretted nor applauded them. I had what I wanted until something better came along.

I thought I had things pretty much in control with alcohol. That is, I refrained from opening that first beer for between 30 minutes to four hours. I wasn't some kind of mad drunk, not anymore. The days of senseless inebriation were behind me, where love affairs with teenage girls go crashing, and seven-year family affairs are shredded into emotional wreckage.

These days, I was a conservative drinker, but one who drank until the intervention of sleep brought things to a halt. An evening could be stretched out over a six-hour period of television, music playing on the stereo, mindless fantasizing, or puttering through old photographs, before recognizing fatigue had taken over.

It was early Christmas Eve when I heard a knock at my back door. As I opened the door, I wondered who it could be. There in the half-light stood Lydia, my neighbor from down the road with no name, a woman with big tits who was married to a reformed biker named Mike.

For a second, we stood looking at each other, then without warning, she broke into singing "Joy To The World." In the most uncomfortable two minutes of that song I had ever experienced, I averted my eyes from her bosom while trying to reflect on the sanctity of the moment.

She was by herself, and I couldn't help imagining she might offer something besides a carol. "How sweet it is of you to come over and sing to me," I said. "Want to come in for a minute?"

I was mistaken; she was on a mission to save my soul from any suicidal feelings I might harbor from being alone on this holy night. "No, thanks, I just wanted to let you know I was thinking of you. Merry Christmas."

She turned and stepped off across the gravel toward her house. Damn, I didn't even get a chance to hug her, and feels those jumbos when we pressed together in the name of Christ. I closed the door feeling rather stupid and lonely once again.

A lot of people believe there is an afterlife, but I think if anything exists after death, it isn't life. I think this life is it, and when death takes us, we disperse into "Le Grande Energie." Do we return? I doubt it. Heaven and Hell are figments of the ancients' imaginations. We are rewarded and punished in life, not in death. Here, every day is Judgment Day.

Do I believe in a creator? I do, but I don't pretend to know what or who it is; I only know that I feel grateful to it. All is creation; you are in it, along with multitudes of other tiny beings like cells under a microscope, moving around and finding our way to an unseen, unknown destination. Like me when I was living on the road with no name, we don't where we are, but we know that we are, and that has to be enough.

MC5
FRI JAN 17 RATS
PLEASURE SEEKERS
SAT JAN 18 WORLD
VILLGE PUB

ON BROWNELL STREET EAST OF MAPLE STREET

Tickets $3.00   Members $2.00

18

My Time After Awhile

The only way to describe those last couple of years when I lived on the nameless road would be confused and content. On my own, without the reactions and opposing opinions of others, I functioned fairly well, if chaotically.

I had little money, but managed my bills, and to my great surprise, began to receive offers in the mail for credit cards, loan refinancing, insurance policies, investment opportunities, and memberships in honky capitalist organizations like the A.A.R.P, Diners Club and others.

Spurred onward by growing acceptance in conventional society and invitations to spend, I went out and bought my first computer, a good bicycle, more music gear, and changed vehicles—not all at once, but as funds permitted.

At first, having any balance on a credit card was reason for panic, but it wasn't long before my wallet contained several of those little plastic tickets to play easy, and I scrutinized every offer for customer friendly manners, only accepting those I deemed worthy.

My job at the museum finally evaporated after five years as a temporary, and I did what was necessary to keep afloat by getting another job with a small landscape company in Tucson. Every day for a year and a half, I awoke in pre-dawn to get to my boss's house in town by 6 am for a day of mowing, pruning, raking, picking up dog shit, and whatever else needed doing on his clients' properties. I worked with a funny character named Fred, a transplant from back east who had lodged himself permanently, working for his old high school chum, Bruce, in Tucson.

Wild West Landscape was name of Bruce's company, one of a multitude of little landscape companies that serviced the wealthier residents of Tucson and a variety of businesses around town. A revolving cast of flunkies and oddballs came and went as time passed, but Fred and I were permanent until I left at the end of 2000 to take a job delivering flowers.

I am completely confident and comfortable behind the wheel of a car, and can navigate my way around a city grid like a modern day Magellan. I sometimes think I was born molded in a driving position, ready to be slipped behind the wheel of a car or truck. I rarely get bored driving, and locating a destination is as rewarding as anything can be. The money is good in the flower deliver business too, relatively speaking, particularly on holidays.

I started this job during Thanksgiving, one of the lesser flower holidays, but between Christmas, Valentine's Day, and then Mother's Day, a veritable windfall of cash takes place. I no longer needed to worry about making my modest ends meet for mortgage, insurance, utilities, or charges to credit cards. I had cash in my pocket and a free rein in my home. I had gained a measure of relief from financial stress, and some sudden new self-respect.

I had always been afraid of being a bum and could easily have found myself transient and homeless, given my compulsion for drinking. The social penalties for offending your friends can be devastating, and especially since I had whittled myself down to a solitary life in the desert, the fear of destitution always lingered just below the surface. Being vagrant on the oceanfront in Santa Monica was at least a couple of steps away, but whether drunk, mentally ill, or just plain isolated, a person without a dependable companion can make incredibly disastrous decisions.

My current domestic companions—Rooster the dog and Sonny Boy the horse—kept me more or less functional on their behalf. I can imagine that without being responsible for the needs of my animals, I might have fallen all the way down, letting the tide of drink carry me out to the sea of oblivion like the countless other drunkards that have let their self-respect and those who loved them fall by the wayside. But I was not going to let that happen. I decided I would take care of things, and perhaps life would be kind to me at some point. Perhaps I would find someone to share things with eventually. After all, no one knows what's in store, and for the present it was a time to heal.

In December of 1999, a film crew from Chicago arrived in Arizona to film my segment of the documentary *MC5: A True Testimonial.* They were calling themselves Future Now Films, a title taken from an MC5 song, written by Rob Tyner for the last album we made as a band, *High Time.*

They had been getting the basics together for the documentary by collecting donated video and photo archives from fans, and interviewing integral characters from the MC5's story: band members, band members' spouses, former managers, entrepreneurs, producers, collaborators, and so on.

We decided to film my segment in Tucson, as opposed to flying me to Detroit for our location shooting. I took several days off from my landscaping job, to the utter disbelief of my fellow landscapers, dumbfounded that one their co-workers was going to be in a movie.

Fred didn't believe me; he thought I was putting him on, trying to make a fool of him. He just shook his head, grinning away, "Yeah sure, have a nice time at the beach." Bruce, the boss, knew I had played in a band, although he hadn't heard of us, but after I brought him a CD to listen to, he came away with a good deal of respect, and was even trying to play some of the songs on his acoustic guitar. He was accommodating, saying, "All right, do what you have to do. See you next week."

Future Now Films had become an arch MC5 fan organization in the few years since they first contacted me through Jeff Economy, an early producer. I had met with them in Detroit on one of my frequent trips back there to hang out with my old crew of beer drinkers, and search in vain for woman I'd known in what felt like a previous life.

They were extremely exhilarated by the project, and documenting the entirety of the MC5's legacy was a passionate quest for them. Everything about "The Film" was highly energized and bore the mark of religious zeal. I was as excited about it as they were, although much of my excitement was steeped in anxiety.

I met them at the Congress Hotel in downtown Tucson, an historic old hotel, site of the arrest of John Dillinger, Public Enemy Number One in the 1930s, and home of Club Congress, the most important music venue in Tucson. The lobby and even the rooms retain the feeling of the old days when Tucson was mostly a dirt-street Western town that attracted refugees from distant cities, and was inhabited by generations of Hispanic families, Native Americans, and white folks that had ranches.

The night the film crew arrived, the band called Clovenhoof—an all-girl outfit managed by Angela McCormick, who used to work for Rich Hopkins' record label and do freelance publicity—was playing the opening set.

As I greeted Angela at the merch table and told her about the upcoming filming, Clovenhoof appeared in their stage outfits for the night: assless tight white pants, white go-go boots, and white cowboy hats. It was momentous, but soon the atmosphere distracted for me from eyeballing Clovenhoof's bared asses as the film crew, all six of them, converged upon me for the first time. We set a schedule for shooting the initial interview for the next morning, and said goodnight. I didn't stay for Clovenhoof's performance.

The following morning, the crew pulled into my gravel driveway, emerging from their van with their camera rolling. Laurel, the film's producer, embraced me in what might have seemed like the reunion of two lovers after years of separation. She spotted the fresh tattoo under my shirt like a serpent focusing on prey, and immediately started unbuttoning the garment, exposing me for the camera.

Slightly embarrassed, but aware of the performance, I complied for the shot. Laurel, a cameraman, a soundman, one assistant, the director, and a person who only came along for the purpose of meeting me filled my small yard, eagerly discovering the place of my solitary existence.

After taking pictures and video of my horses—I had acquired a second one—in the corral, the cactus garden, and the immediate surroundings, we went inside the caboose I called my house to get better acquainted.

I was shown the latest trailer for the film, which was now a five-minute long collage of video snapshots and footage with MC5 music and some talking by Wayne Kramer, who had already been filmed at Lincoln Park in Chicago, site of our performance during the 1968 Democratic Convention. I watched as the fleeting images of MC5 lore raced by. The high-energy two-second frames flashed hypnotically like rapid gunfire, gripping everyone in the room.

"Wow, I think you have something going here. It's more than interesting," I said, flattered and surprised. I had a few ideas for location shooting around Tucson: the Amtrak train depot, a rocky outcropping in the desert, and on top of "A" Mountain at the foot of the city.

We agreed on all of it and made our itinerary for the next few days. The excitement was mine as well as theirs; at last I was getting the opportunity to tell my side of the story. The world had been surmising the fate of the MC5 for 30 years.

Unlike other former band members who seemed to get interviewed constantly, I had done a total of two interviews that were broadly read in all the time since '72, and those only because of the newly burgeoning Internet. My story was waiting to be told, and I was very anxious to tell it.

That was how they found me, tucked away in a remote desert location, living alone, and scratching away my days as a landscape gardener. It would have remained that way had it not been for Angela.

We ran through the next few days, filming my fragmented comments about the happenings 30 years time ago. I spilled all that I could connect with in my memory, my attitudes, and my desire for redemption. Having suffered the slings and arrows of an era of bewildering circumstances, I wanted at least to be illuminating on some of the weirder nuances of our lost horizon.

But I feared I only was vague, and just as inarticulate as ever. Probably the best part of the whole sequence was that of being seen in the Arizona desert, and the unmatchable charm of Rooster, my precious boxer dog, whom I will miss forever.

We shared a personal closeness for those few days. I grew very fond of the filmmakers, David and Laurel, and Jim, and Tony the cameraman, and Ron the soundman. We had penetrated a bit of my soul whether we knew it or not, whether it was about the MC5 or not. We parted as friends; that we knew.

I later read that David, the director, had a major meltdown in the Hotel Congress one evening, being disturbed that there was "no story" here. At the time I felt that maybe I was responsible for that too. There was no escaping this sad state of affairs that always followed anything about the MC5, this unmitigated tale that seems to never end on a positive note, or that it just never ends completely, ever.

I don't think by any means, there is "no story" here. There is always a story, and I may not be that good at telling it, but there is certainly a story. The hard part is making a complicated story into a simple tale with a moral and a message, and above all, a lesson. In that, I have yet to find the key that makes plain, the magnanimous mess that is the MC5.

The film crew left Tucson, leaving me alone again on the gravel floor of the Sonora Desert that stretches all the way deep into Mexico, about an hour away should one have the desire to go there.

It had been a couple of years since the breakup with the woman from Ann Arbor, and it seemed I had finally escaped the misery of that defeat. Oh man, had I? How many of those wreckages did I still hold on to? Sandy, Joanne, and so on and so forth; how many more could I squeeze into one lifetime? Maybe it was time to give it up. I wasn't going to be happy, so why roll the dice again. I opened a fresh beer and watched as the sky grew dark violet.

The trouble is, I'm a lousy drinker. When other people drink a couple of beers, they seem to function without losing their perspective. I, on other the other hand, am on my way to becoming someone else, and after one or two more, I have entered alien territory.

It must be something in my metabolism. I can get shitfaced very easily. So easily in fact, that every time I start a drinking bout, the lifespan of my control is negligible. For me, using alcohol as an aid to social enhancement is like playing with a razor blade blindfolded.

Something in my character has always plagued me, even before I started abusing alcohol at age 16, something that began at an earlier age than I can remember.

I do want to understand and recognize just where the trouble started. I don't want to blame anyone, I want to identify the source of my unhappiness. It's a very strange thing to discover, because on the surface, I look and act happy, and I feel very happy as well. I've always thought of myself as a happy person, but something must underlie the self-destructive behavior that has been at the core of my life's drama. The face I show the world might only be the reflection of a distant memory.

Looking back, I can see a long trail of situations that were torpedoed in progress, going as far back as my early adolescence, possibly even earlier. The first time I ran afoul of the law, I was 12 or 13 years of age. My friend Roy and I had ridden our bikes up to the Federal department store, a couple of miles from our neighborhood. We were just messing around with nothing else to do, and going to the big department store relieved the boredom of the neighborhood.

I wandered by the record rack where the 7-inch singles were filed alphabetically in bins, and thumbed through the titles. My gaze fell on a record I'd heard on one of the radio stations my father had forbidden me to listen to: Clyde McPhatter's "Treasure Of Love." I looked around for a sales clerk or anyone who looked like a store employee. There was no one. I wanted the record and the thought of stealing it raced through my head, giving me an instant hot flash of anxiety.

I placed the disc in front of my chest, slipping it under my shirt, and gripped the sides so it wouldn't slip out. The counter was close to the store's front entrance, and I made straight for it. Roy was sitting on his bike next to mine several feet away as I went through the first set of doors. All at once his eyes grew very large and I felt a hand on my shoulder, halting me in mid-step. A middle aged, stocky woman was restraining me and telling me to come with her. I was caught! I remember turning back to see Roy pedaling off as fast as he could, while my bike sat unattended at the front of the store. I hoped it wouldn't get stolen.

After some pleading and crying to no avail, the store detective called my parents' number, and shortly thereafter, both my mother and father entered the office where I was being held. There was some discussion of the seriousness of my misdeed and what should be done about it. When it was decided that it was a minor mistake by a careless youth, I was released on the condition that I was not to not enter a Federal department store without an adult until age 18.

My parents' disgust pierced my heart in the car riding back to the house. I was as ashamed as they told me I should be. "What the hell's the matter with ya!" My mom was weeping slightly. My dad was cursing, not so slightly. He was calling me ridiculous names that had probably carried some weight in his day; "piss willie" or "panty waist," something along those lines. I sat, remorseful and silent while they carried out their assault. Uncomfortable as it was, at least I was the center of attention.

A couple of years later, a similar event occurred when my teenage friends and I cruised by the State Fair, where hundreds of cars were parked on the residential streets around the fairgrounds. Our idea of teenage entertainment for the evening was to steal hubcaps off them. Unfortunately for us, the Detroit city police were also cruising in the neighborhood, and I found myself in the back seat of a squad car, bound for the nearest precinct. I was 16.

Mom and Dad were summoned once again, and my father launched into the same tirade as we rode back to their house. By now, I might have been getting accustomed to being a culprit. Feeling shame was no longer an alien emotion; it was beginning to feel natural. There was a discussion of getting psychiatric help for my "problem." For that, I felt no urgency, because for one thing, it was costly, and for another, I knew they would just as soon forget about it.

I had been an only child until age 11, a situation I felt very comfortable in, when all at once my place at the center of the universe was usurped by a new arrival: a baby sister. And though I viewed the event with eagerness, I can't help but wonder if inwardly, I wasn't devastated by it.

I was certainly disturbed by it. I cared for Marilyn as though she were a new puppy: feeding and changing her; watching with amazement as she learned to walk and talk; leading her through the simplest acts and entertainments; discovering TV shows like *The Mickey Mouse Club, Romper Room,* and *Captain Kangaroo*—all these things were part of a fascinating new experience and responsibility.

But now, at age 16, with Marilyn at the precious age of five, things were beginning to get out of hand. The Russians had launched Sputnik, rock and roll was taking over the world, and I had discovered masturbation…. and beer.

The quiet reserve at my parents' house was comfortable and isolating. We didn't talk about anything as a group. They had their world and their memories, their goals and preferences. We children, and my grandmother—the most isolated person in the house—stayed conveniently outside the current, which was barely discernible.

I had my room and my solitude. I played or sat and daydreamed, waiting for any chance to break away. When the evenings wound down to the late night news hour, I would steal out the back door and sneak through the neighborhood, going between the houses, looking in people's bedroom windows for a chance to glimpse a woman undressing. The anticipation of seeing a bare tit or of getting caught in the process was exhilarating and irresistible. I did it for a long time, once being so bold as to streak down the block stark naked like a primate or a caveman.

I finally got caught coming in from one of my forays. "Where in the hell've you been? What the hell were ya doin' out there?"

I stood about two feet in front of my father while he seethed. I knew it was coming, I expected it, I waited, and he finally delivered. BANG! A hard right came crashing into the side of my face. I fell to the floor in a heap.

"Get up. Get up you son of a bitch!" He was breathing hard, looking for a way to quell his fury. I stood motionless while he tried to redirect his energy. I was putting these poor people through something they never had thought could happen to them. Their son was a pervert, a sicko, a peeping tom. Once again, the question of sending me to a psychiatrist came up. And once again, it was shelved.

Instead, they, or he, attempted to explain the sexual dilemma, back then referred to as "the facts of life." He had postponed this informative talk up until now due to his own discomfort with the topic, but since I seemed headed in a misguided direction, he was all at once up to the task.

It was ridiculous. I made certain to show no disrespect while he made a clumsy explanation of something that obviously was unnerving for him. My mom sat patiently and painfully at the side, her face wrought with distress. She was fighting back tears, and she was frustrated for lack of a voice. I was very ashamed, but I would survive.

I only once ever saw something I shouldn't have and I once overheard some sexual talking, but that was enough to keep me in pursuit of another inappropriate experience indefinitely.

I watched the lady across the street get completely undressed on one of my first forays out, while I crouched by her bedroom window. She was not a pretty woman by any means, but she had a nice body and a great pair of tits. And the sexual conversation I overheard in a darkened bedroom was between two people talking about having sex, but mainly she was telling him to "stop playing with that thing." In any event, after the night I was caught coming in, my career as the neighborhood voyeur was over.

It never occurred to me that I was disturbed. Whatever I was doing seemed totally natural to me, and I really thought there was nothing wrong with my behavior except that it conflicted with what society deemed appropriate. My parents' reserve was clearly a wide-open playing field for my weird imaginings and further isolation, and after bearing the brunt of their outrage, I was left alone to ferment. They were trying to cope with my misbehavior, but as they lacked the skill to extract the truth from me, it was no more than a temporary setback.

I would never forget the episode of silence that was imposed on me when I lost my temper in an open-hand boxing match with my father. And another longer-than necessary-period of silence I received some time later, for telling a lie. Somehow in those exiles from his love, I learned that I was conspicuously alone in my family; that another agenda had displaced the one where I felt secure, and my future was an immense puzzlement that held the potential of greatness and tragedy.

I remember when it began. We sat in a parked car on a side street off the big street. We had two sixes of Pabst Blue Ribbon. I don't know who got it for us, but we had it. Three friends in a car, underage, ready to get a buzz on. Snap went the tab on the can of cold PBR. I raised it to my lips and took a swig. Cold and tingly going down, it had a weird taste to it, not sweet like Coke or Pepsi.

Within the next few seconds, I felt the change come over me. I withdrew slightly from the present, my head spinning a bit. We grinned at each other, very proud of doing the big-time thing, drinking in a parked car.

After the first beer was gone, I opened another, but halfway through it, I wasn't sure I wanted any more. I was feeling uncomfortable, and by now the effect of the alcohol was becoming overwhelming. I forced myself to drink the rest of it lest I be labeled a sissy.

I started feeling like I wanted to throw up, but I held on. We had cigarettes too. I lit one and tried to relax. The three of us were good friends. We had been since grade school. All of us were competitive swimmers, not stars, but decent athletes. Here we were drinking beer and smoking cigarettes, acting like hoodlums and taking risks.

Juvenile delinquency was a side effect of the new rock and roll culture that was sweeping the nation. *Blackboard Jungle,* a movie my parents had ironically taken me to see, had made a great impression on me, with the Bill Haley and the Comets' song "Rock Around The Clock" gripping me from its opening note.

Something about being a "hood" breathed life into a very dull middle class life in our very plain middle class neighborhood. This was probably as close as we were going to get to it. After three or four of those beers, I opened the car door and puked. My head was still spinning, but I felt better. That was my first drinking experience, but it was certainly not the last.

In the times that I have recounted in this book, it becomes more than obvious that a recurring cycle has taken place over the years. From the time that I left my parents' den, until I landed, a lost and lonely soul, in the desert, separated by miles and years from all that once had been important, a pattern of calamity and repair is what is consistent.

My light-hearted amiable nature helped me find friends, lovers, and contacts along the way, but I always found a way to destroy what were strong beginnings. Not only that, but I never saw even a glimmer of that truth until now, until I wrote it all down.

I hope now I have learned how to live with it.

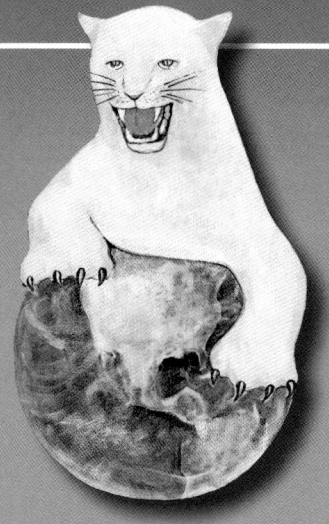

Epilogue

Although he continued to work on this book for some time after the story "finishes," there was much that Michael chose not to include: his 2003 reunion with Wayne Kramer and Dennis Thompson; his 2006 motorcycle accident; and, most importantly, his marriage to Angela, and the birth of the non-profit organization The Music Is Revolution Foundation.

He overlooked, too, the long-overdue recognition of his work as an artist, which went on to include everything from skateboard decks to MC5 merchandise, as well as the artwork for the '5's *The Very Best Of* album in 2009. All were unquestionably a part of his story, but perhaps he did not see them as a part of *this story*, the tale he tells here. Rather, they were the opening chapters of a whole new adventure.

Sadly, it is one that he would never write. Michael passed away on February 17, 2012.